The Deserted Village

The Diary of an Oxfordshire Rector JAMES NEWTON of Nuneham Courtenay 1736–86

Transcribed and edited with an introduction

by

Gavin Hannah

ALAN SUTTON

For Marcia, Marcus and Giles

First published in the United Kingdom in 1992 by
Alan Sutton Publishing Limited
Phoenix Mill · Far Thrupp · Stroud · Gloucestershire

First published in the United States of America in 1992 by
Alan Sutton Publishing Inc · 83 Washington Street · Dover NH 03820

British Library Cataloguing in Publication Data

Newton, James
Diary of an Oxfordshire Rector: James Newton of Nuneham Courtenay, 1736–86
I. Title II. Hannah, Gavin
941.07092

ISBN 0-7509-0205-1

Library of Congress Cataloging in Publication Data applied for

Jacket illustration: A view of Nuneham from the wood (from J. and J. Boydell, *An History of the River Thames*.)

Typeset in 10/11 Bembo
Typesetting and origination by
Alan Sutton Publishing Limited
Printed and bound in Great Britain by
Biddles Limited, Guildford and King's Lynn

Contents

Foreword

I am very grateful to Gavin Hannah for rediscovering these diaries in the Bodleian and for all his efforts with their transcription. I must admit that I found I learned an awful lot about history in general and about my ancestor (the 1st Earl Harcourt), in particular from reading James Newton's words which have been so admirably complemented by Mr Hannah's Notes and Introduction. I was amazed, too, when I saw the Biographical Index of some of the Rector's acquaintances. What a labour of love that must have been among those dusty old parish registers!

I was interested, as I hope all readers will be, to discover more about Nuneham Courtenay. It is a village that has obvious special connections for me as a direct descendant of the man who created it, and this book gives a unique insight into its formation. It is a village, too, that I know intrigues all those who pass through it, all too quickly these days, on their way from Oxford to Henley. Nuneham has a national interest as well, in being the model for Oliver Goldsmith's poem, *The Deserted Village*. So, these diaries, as Mr Hannah writes, are indeed 'lifted into the fabric of national history', while retaining all their local associations.

But, I suppose for me, one of the most thrilling features of the book was to find out more about the Reverend James Newton himself. What a character he was and how lucky was Lord Harcourt to have such a level-headed and practical person as a general ally! For it seems to me that the two men were close friends and got on very well, despite the occasional tiff.

As a farming person myself, I find that I can sympathize with the rector in many ways. I certainly realize just how busy he was. Indeed, these words are being written very much as my current activities with sheep and silage permit! To run a farm, maintain a family and look after business interests demands a great deal of effort and energy, as both I and James Newton know only too clearly. I was thus relieved to see that he ate well. His food may not follow the dietary precepts of today, but the dishes he enjoyed seem appropriate for this tough, eighteenth-century cleric. I think he certainly needed a good intake in order to fulfil all his own responsibilities, as well as sorting out other people's problems in the course of his pastoral duties.

This book has given me a great deal of pleasure and I sincerely hope that many others will enjoy it also.

Ann Gascoigne
The Manor House
Stanton Harcourt
Oxon
St John's Day 1992

Editorial Note

The text has been transcribed retaining James Newton's spelling, punctuation and capitalization in order to recreate the flavour of the original manuscript. An occasional comma has been included in the interests of clarity.

Editorial insertions are marked with square brackets [. . .]; parentheses (. . .) have been used for the diarist's own alterations.

JN sometimes wrote several days of his *Diary* at one sitting and occasionally confused the dates. Instances of this are explained in the relevant footnotes. The days of the week have been added to what are shown only as dates in the manuscript.

The folio numbers in square brackets are those of the original text, thus the numbering for each volume begins at 1.

Acknowledgements

Many people have had a hand in the production of this book and I am most grateful to them all. In particular, my thanks are due to the following: Mrs Mavis Batey for her initial encouragement; the Keeper of Western Manuscripts at the Bodleian Library, Oxford, for permission to publish the diary; the staff of the Bodleian Library, the library of The Society of Antiquaries of London, and of *Oxfordshire Archives* at County Hall, Oxford, for their unfailing help and patience with my constant queries; Mrs S. Bennett, Acting Library Administrator of the Royal Society of Arts; Jane Cunningham of the Courtauld Institute of Art, London; Dr Mark Curthoys, Archivist of Christ Church, Oxford; and Mrs Chris Butler, Assistant Archivist of Corpus Christi College, Oxford.

I am deeply indebted to The Hon. Mrs Gascoigne of Stanton Harcourt, a direct descendant of the 1st Earl Harcourt, for consenting to write the Foreword, and to Kenneth and Eileen Richardson, for so graciously showing me around their house, James Newton's former home, at The Old Rectory, Nuneham Courtenay. As a result of this visit their daughter, Lucy, was persuaded to paint the watercolour which graces the end of the Introduction. To Alan Sutton for agreeing to publish the material, and to the whole production team, I owe boundless gratitude. Any remaining errors are my own.

Finally, I need to thank my wife and family for their superhuman tolerance and forbearance while James Newton stayed with us and took over the whole household.

Gavin Hannah
Summer Fields
Oxford
June 1992

Introduction

The Bodleian Library at Oxford is the home of two small 8vo volumes, shelfmarks Bodl. MS. Eng. Misc. e. 251 and Bodl. MS. Top. Oxon. e. 670. They form, beyond all doubt, part of a diary written by the Reverend James Newton, Rector of Nuneham Courtenay from 1736 until his death some fifty years later.

The first volume covers the period from 1 January 1759 to 27 March 1760 and contains three blank sheets and 119 leaves. Two folios of the text are missing. The book measures 185 mm by 120 mm and has been rebound in calf.

Volume Two, measuring 195 mm by 120 mm, chronicles a single year, from 5 April 1761 to 4 April 1762. This has a vellum binding and consists of one blank sheet followed by 91 leaves. On the outer cover, the date '1761' suggests that it is part of a series.

The first volume was presented to the Bodleian in January 1986 and is inscribed 'to the memory of Richard Haydocke'. It has not received a great deal of public attention so far. The second volume was donated to the Library after the Second World War by a Mrs Kimber of Pangbourne and forms the subject of an article by Henry Minn in *Oxoniensia*, X (1945), pp. 79–92. Minn quotes randomly from the text and indeed interprets the Rector's material quite freely. Some passages are modernized, while others are not. Words and phrases are omitted or rearranged at will and several of the entries are presented on the wrong day. There is no attempt at a full and accurate transcription of the text.

Both volumes are written in a neat hand in brown or black ink. On occasions, several pages were composed at a time. The length of both the daily, and thus the monthly, material is remarkably uniform. There are, however, some very short comments in 1761, when the author was enjoying the delights of Bath, and some very long entries elsewhere, for example on the death of his mother. Very often, these were occasioned by the observation of some calamity or mishap to another person, or by a narrow escape from an accident to himself, leading the diarist to offer several pages of moral reflection. Such passages are usually along the lines of thanking God for his own good fortune, submitting himself entirely to God's purpose and trusting that spiritual benefits and advancement will come forth from any adversity.

Taken as a whole, both volumes of the *Diary* provide us with a detailed cameo of life in the eighteenth century. We are able to follow the daily fortunes of the inhabitants of Nuneham Courtenay, centred around all the goings-on at the rectory. Everything was particularly important at this point in the village's history, as great changes were afoot. Lord Harcourt was building himself a new country house and was about to move the entire community to make way for his projected park. All this, we may glimpse, as it were, from the inside. We thus have a unique insight into many of the attendant difficulties.

Mavis Batey, the garden historian, writing in *Oxoniensia* (XXXIII, [1968], pp. 108–124), has maintained that Lord Harcourt's activities at Nuneham are reflected in Oliver Goldsmith's poem, *The Deserted Village*, written in 1770. Nuneham Courtenay, she claims, is the model for 'Sweet Auburn, loveliest village of the plain.' Goldsmith saw the destruction of a village about fifty miles from London to make way for a rich man's park, and Nuneham fits this description. In Goldsmith's account, an old widow is left in her cottage after the removal of the rest of the inhabitants. This, too, happened at Nuneham. This is not recorded in the *Diary*, but Barbara Whyatt, the lady in question, appears regularly in the rector's narrative. Thus this *Diary*, with all its local associations, is lifted into the fabric of national history.

We are also able to journey to London to observe the life of a well-to-do cleric in the capital. The whole Newton account therefore provides a complement to works such as James Boswell's *London Journal* of 1762–3, and reveals yet more details of the city as King George III began his reign.

Then there are James's recollections of his diversions in Bath, as that place rose to social prominence during the eighteenth century, rapidly becoming a focus of polite society. Again, James's accounts of his activities add further material to our store of general historical knowledge, as we taste the sense of gaiety and excitement running through the Parades, the Pump Room and the Assembly Rooms. An excitement fuelled, according to the historian Mark Girouard, by the two powerful ingredients of 'sex and gambling'. Generally, James Newton was no more successful in the former than in the latter, but in each he had his moments.

Finally, there is a mass of incidental information revealed by the *Diary*, as we view the eighteenth-century world through contemporary eyes. We are privy to everything, down to the smallest, mundane details of daily life. We learn about travel between Oxford and London, a journey that could be rapidly undertaken in a coach or made in a more leisurely fashion with frequent wayside stops. We move within the city of London itself by water, on foot, by carriage or on horseback. We note the problems of hiring and maintaining servants, of collecting rents and arranging new tenants, of handling general family welfare amidst the vicissitudes of a harsh world. There are difficulties with repairing carriages, of trying to find hay for horses, of acquiring congenial accommodation or even a partner for life to adorn the tasteful rectory at Nuneham. There are clothes to be bought and the harvest to be gathered, as well as parochial duties to perform. Added to everything else is the need to cope with the greatest of all social upheavals, namely the destruction of one's home and village and the creation of an entirely new community structure.

National events intrude but little into the diary narrative, although there are some comments and observations on British fortunes during the Seven Years' War. James delights in the overall success of the nation and rings his church bells in celebration of victory, but he is not without pangs of guilt concerning the nature of war in general.

So much for the use and importance of the *Diary*, the time has now come to look more closely at its author.

The Reverend James Newton was born in 1714, the only son of James Newton MD of Clerkenwell, Middlesex. Dr Newton was 'keeper and physician to a private madhouse, near the Islington turnpike'. The Doctor was a keen botanist. He devoted a lifetime to the study of plants and laid out ground at the rear of his house as a Botanical Garden, where he cultivated many interesting specimens. In August 1730 a note in the *Daily Post* recorded a strange vegetable growing in Newton's garden: 'a white lily, having a cluster of roots from the uppermost end of the stalk, a rarity never before seen in this country'.

The botanical doctor probably derived his interest in natural history and madness from his own father, yet another Dr James Newton, who died in 1718. He had made a detailed study of plants and began writing a herbal in about 1680, a small portion of which was published during his lifetime and described as 'the work of his younger days'. The final version of this volume, 'containing the Prints and the English Names of several thousand trees, Plants, Shrubs, Flowers, Exotics, etc., All Curiously engraved on Copper Plates', appeared in print in 1752 and was assiduously marketed by the author's grandson, our diarist. The work comprised 176 plates and ten pages of letterpress printed by Mr Cove at St John's Gate. It also contained a dedication to Earl Harcourt by 'James Newton, Rector of Newnham in Oxfordshire'.

It was long believed that the author of the *Herbal* was the rector's father, but this does not seem to be the case. If the work indeed dates from around 1680, his father would have been only two years old at the time. Furthermore, James in the *Diary* specifically refers to his 'Grandfather's Manuscripts'.

It was James's grandfather, too, who first kept the lunatic asylum, which he did eventually pass on to his son. Throughout the 1680s and 1690s, the burial registers of St James's Clerkenwell contain references to 'Dr Newton's madhouse', a clear indication that the institution was flourishing well before the rector's father was old enough, or indeed sufficiently qualified, to manage it.

Very little is known about the early life of The Reverend Newton. He was probably born in Middlesex, but there is no baptism record in the family church at Clerkenwell.

We first meet James at Oxford in February 1733 when, at the age of nineteen, he went up to Christ Church as a Commoner. The college weekly battels books confirm that he was in residence soon after matriculation. In the following year he migrated to Corpus Christi College as a Gentleman Commoner, graduating with a BA in 1736. In the same year he was instituted to the living of Nuneham Courtenay, remaining there as rector until his death in January 1786.

James Newton served his parish faithfully until about 1777 before going into semi-retirement. Thomas Robinson and Andrew Price, both curates, then undertook the bulk of the parochial duties, before James was eventually succeeded by The Reverend Francis Haggett, who looked after Nuneham until 1825.

Jackson's Oxford Journal for Saturday 28 January 1786 noted Newton's death 'a few days ago', and also the fact that James had held his living for 'upwards of 50 years'. He was finally laid to rest in the family vault in the Old Ground at St James's Church, Clerkenwell, beside his parents and younger sister, Esther. A month later, Daniel Baily, an auctioneer, was commissioned to sell all the goods and household furniture from the parsonage.

Despite his natural inclinations, James had never married, so there were no close heirs. Nothing seems to have been passed on to his various nephews and nieces. His next of kin was his aged sister, Mary, living in London at Mortimer Street, Cavendish Square, and only two years away from her own death.

From the *Diary* we are able to learn a great deal about James's character. We find a man admirably suited to the life of a country parson. He was fond of animals, having at various intervals a pet monkey, a dog and a cat called 'Tyger'. He was a careful glebe farmer, taking a shrewd interest in all agricultural matters. He was an enthusiastic gardener and fruit-grower, no real surprise considering his family background. At his new rectory in 1761 he built a long, wavy wall offering maximum protection for his plants. He established trees, an orchard and a vine and took a pride in his kitchen garden which provided much fresh produce for his many visits to London.

James was a benevolent, yet strict, master to his servants. He helped them in times of adversity, but was ready to administer the whip when necessary. He was kind to the poor and needy of the parish, often providing gifts of money, food or drink to the sick and destitute. He seems to have been attentive to his parochial duties: he prepared his sermons and preached; he visited the sick and dying; he christened, married and buried as the occasion demanded; and he was always careful to appoint a locum when away in London or Bath.

The rector was a practical and realistic man. He had a keen eye for business and was not afraid to stand up for his rights, even to the extent of a mild quarrel with Lord Harcourt over the destruction of his church and churchyard and the rearrangement of his glebe. James was tolerant, bearing his lot with fortitude and patience at a time when his whole world was turned upside down in the space of five years, from 1759 to 1764. He was fond of the ladies, with several liaisons both within and without the periods covered by the *Diary*. He appeared keen to marry, but never found the perfect partner.

James was cultured and literate. We find him attending concerts in the Sheldonian Theatre during Commemoration Week at Oxford in 1759. He went to the opera in London, he read pamphlets on church building and the sermons of Archbishop Tillotson, and, of course, he wrote his diary. He even lent books to his servants.

Newton was a generous man who took an active interest in all local affairs. He made considerable subscriptions to the Radcliffe Infirmary and to the relief of the poor in 1772. But, in general, glimpses of his activities are rare outside the confines of the surviving *Diary* volumes.

In 1754 he was noted as 'clerk in Residence' in a poll of the Freeholders of Oxfordshire. Sometime after in 1766, we learn from his offer of a reward that he had some chickens stolen from his parsonage. A year later he offered another reward for information leading to the conviction of those who had started a fire at a house near the Golden Ball, which had caused considerable damage to a furze rick.

James Newton kept himself very active and, for the most part, seemed to enjoy the blessing of good health. The major ailments he records are a serious spell of toothache, nausea, a cold and a possible tendency to asthma. By 1762 he was aware of increasingly poor eyesight. We understand from the *Diary* that he had no physical deformities. He thus seems very lucky by the standards of the age. Perhaps this was something to do with his diet, for he certainly enjoyed his food. At various times his meals consisted of venison, turkey, geese, boiled fowl, mutton, pork, beefsteaks, rabbit, hogs' ears, chitterlings, soup and fish. Wine, port, gin, cider, ale, water and tea slaked his thirst, all of which appeared to keep him in good heart.

James divided his time between his parish duties at Nuneham and visits to Oxford, London and Bath. This appeared to be the normal routine for most of his life. In 1738 he wrote, 'Tis now upwards of a Year since I had the Cure [i.e. of Nuneham], part of which time I resided in the Parish, part of it in Oxon, sometime in Bath, & sometime with my Friends by London.' Robert Bradley or Richard Skinner acted for him in the parish during any absences. This is very much the pattern of life as revealed by the *Diary*.

Between January 1759 and March 1760, James made ten visits to London. The length of his stays varied from twenty-four hours, when seeing his bishop in 1759 regarding the territorial changes within his parish, to over a month, in January and February 1760. A most pressing and stressful time for him must have been during a three-week sojourn in April 1759 when his mother died and was buried, while the enclosure commissioners were meeting to finalize the arrangements back at home in Oxfordshire.

The purpose of his London visits varied between business and pleasure. We find him calling on his mother and moving his sister, Zenobia, into the family house in Cavendish Square, after the death of her husband in January 1759. James also visited his friends, the most prominent of whom was Admiral Long. He showed the sights to various ladies and arranged tenants for his properties, notably his shop in The Strand.

In Bath, too, which he saw twice during 1761, there was much to occupy him. He socialized in the Rooms and on the Parade, and engaged in some mild gambling and flirtations.

Oxford also was the scene of both duty and amusement. There were household materials to buy, coffee shops to frequent and concerts to attend, as well as college gardens to delight him. He made the most of all his opportunities and certainly led a busy, if privileged, life. Let us now turn from the man and examine the parish in which he felt himself called to serve.

One of the earliest descriptions of the present village of Nuneham Courtenay is provided by a German pastor, Charles Moritz. In 1782 he undertook a walking tour from London to Oxford via Henley and Dorchester. On arriving at Nuneham he speaks of 'two rows of low, neat houses, built close to each other, and as regular and uniform as a London street'. The houses still remain, together with an inn and a forge (now a garage). They constitute a Georgian version of ribbon development; nineteen pairs of chequer-brick cottages, each of one storey and an attic, on either side of the Oxford to Henley road.

But this was not always the case. The original medieval settlement lay just over one mile to the west on a spur of the Chilterns overlooking the Thames. All was well until Lord Harcourt built a new house and then decided to extend his park. The village was in the way, so it had to be moved. Enclosure took place in 1759 and land boundaries changed. Nevertheless, the inhabitants were fortunate that their lord provided them with new dwellings, 'happier mansions, warm and dry,' in most cases better than the original, old, 'tumble-down clay-built cottages'. But, in so doing, there was much upheaval and hundreds of years of history were swept away by the whim of a single aristocrat. The history of Nuneham is thus a perfect example of eighteenth-century patronage; it is a transplanted village. The early name of Newnham Courtenay became Nuneham Courtenay on the arrival of the Harcourts in 1759.

Robert Smith made a plan of the old village in 1707. Here we find farms, a corn mill, an ale house, a parsonage, a church, a manor house, cottages, a school, a pound and a common. Indeed, this was a nucleated settlement clustered around a duck pond and a village green. There were originally two fields, increasing to four by 1707: Windmill Field, Wheat Land Field, Lower Field and Long Furlong Field. The demesne arable lay in Hooke Hill, the Dewes, Payes Close, Palmers Leyes, Sheep House Piece, Stuble Ground, part of Gadberry's Leyes and White Lyons. The whole manor was valued at £13 in 1086 and at £40 by 1292.

The lordship of the village had changed hands several times since the Norman Conquest until, during the fourteenth century, it was acquired by the Courtenays, the Earls of Devon. Eventually in 1710, Sir Simon Harcourt, later the 1st Viscount Harcourt, acquired the estate from Sir John Robinson for the modest sum of £17,000, 'the cheapest pennyworth that ever was bought in Oxfordshire'.

It was then in 1756 that the 1st Earl decided to leave the ancestral home at Stanton Harcourt and to build himself a new country seat with fine views of the domes and spires of Oxford as befitted a man of taste. The Earl's new home, Nuneham Park, 'a spacious Mansion House', was to be a classical villa. As such, the most fashionable trends of landscape design were required to provide the appropriate setting. In this park there was no place for the old village; it was thus that it had to be removed.

William Whitehead (1715–85), the Poet Laureate, wrote a poem entitled *The Removal of the Village at Nuneham*. In this work he describes how Barbara Whyatt, an aging widow, was allowed to remain in her old cottage in the new 'enchanting scene' after the rest of the village had been demolished. At her death her house was pulled down and an inscription placed on the tree beside it, asking men of fashion to 'bow the knee' to 'her unlettered memory'. It is this Barbara Whyatt who finds a significant place in James Newton's *Diary* and who was noted by Goldsmith.

It was on 6 October 1759 that Robert Fettiplace, the Sheriff of Oxford, received a command to enquire by a jury on oath whether it would be beneficial for Lord Harcourt to enclose a significant part of the village. The area concerned included Windmill Field, Payes Close, Palmers Leyes, Black Wood, White Lyons and Gadberry's Leyes, all shown clearly on Robert Smith's map. An inquisition was duly held at Nuneham Park on Wednesday 17 October. As expected, the verdict was in Lord Harcourt's favour, provided that he undertook to construct new roads replacing an old footpath and a bridleway.

Territorial changes were imminent, too, regarding the rectorial glebe, and the *Diary* chronicles the arrangements James Newton made with his patron.

The old glebe consisted of about fifty acres, comprising twelve smaller parcels of land scattered about the estate. These included Bean Hill, Honey Furlong, Fisher's Green, Alder Hill, Rye Hill and the Hanging Furlong. The final agreement was signed at the end of April 1759, but the business had proceeded quickly. Lord Harcourt's initial petition dates only from 20 March. According to this document the glebe was so interspersed that the 'situation is a hindrance to the improvement that would otherwise be made there'. An exchange of glebe would benefit both the parishioners and the rectory. James appeared to have agreed in principle to the proposed changes, as indeed he recorded in the *Diary* for that day. Thus a week later on 27 March, the Bishop of Oxford gave his consent for matters to go ahead. A Commission was appointed 'to enquire into the truth of the facts'. Many of its members were James Newton's friends and neighbours, all of whom have a place in the *Diary*. They included Dr Bacon from Marsh Baldon, the Reverend John Pinnell from Ducklington, Mr Wastie and Jonathan Bush of Burcot.

The Commission made its report on 12 April and not surprisingly agreed that the exchange would be 'of great Benefit and advantage to ye Rector of Newnham and his Successors'. The new glebe consisted of just over fifty-four acres, a slightly larger area than that surrendered by James, and it was valuable property. In the tax assessments of 1786–9, the rectorial lands were rated at £28 3s. An interesting point to note is that James and his successors were entitled to a tithe of coal, should any ever be discovered within the confines of the estate.

The actual Deed document, together with a fine example of James's signature and his seal, is now preserved in the Oxfordshire Archives. An entry in the *Diary* confirms that it was signed in London on Friday 27 April 1759.

In common with many of the other inhabitants, the rector was to lose his house when the village was transplanted. Indeed, during the exchange of glebe negotiations, the Commissioners had respectfully pointed out that, while James was expected to give up his parsonage, with its kitchen, hall, parlour, bedchambers, stables and terrace, there was no provision for a new one under the terms of Lord Harcourt's first agreement. This difficulty was soon overcome, as shown by the fact that a comfortable, new, elegant rectory was built on high ground facing the river to the north-east of his old house. James appears to have disliked the site at first, but his enthusiasm grew as the building took shape throughout 1759 and 1760. The *Diary* gives some details. There was a yard with a pump and an assortment of outhouses, including a store for timber, a brewhouse, a barn and a lumber room. The principal building had a cellar, a bow room with a great ceiling picture, a 'first room' with a ceiling picture, a closet, a study, a marble hall, a kitchen and a staircase with a door (still to be seen in the present house in what must have been the servants' quarters). At least three bedrooms are mentioned, though there must have been many more judging by the overall size of the house. James's own bedroom he decorated with guns and pistols. Many of the rooms were adorned with pictures that he brought from London in 1761. It was a comfortable and cultured dwelling.

After 1790, the house was rented to Mrs Siddons, the actress, while Francis Hagget, the new rector, was at his stall in Durham. According to Hagget in 1824, the parsonage was damp and inconvenient. The following year thus saw many alterations and extensions to James's former home, at a cost of £3,000. The main body of the rectory, facing the Thames, was rebuilt, but the servants' wing at right angles to the main house remains largely unchanged.

The modern visitor to the village of Nuneham will find two churches, each dedicated to All Saints. But neither of them is the original place of worship. The 'third' church stands closest to the cottages and the main road. It dates from 1872–4 and was built in a neo-Gothic style by Edward Harcourt.

The 'second' All Saints, erected in 1764, is to be found on a hill in the park. It was designed by Lord Harcourt, assisted by James Stuart, and was the building that James Newton had to accept after the destruction of his Gothic church in which he worshipped during the period covered by the *Diary*.

Several fragments of the medieval church, including a fine thirteenth-century window with good moulded shafts, survive as a folly in the grounds of Baldon House at Marsh Baldon. Apart from this there are few traces of the old building. However, we are able to form an idea of its structure from suggestions for its restoration in 1758, advocated by Newton. These requests were, of course, never granted.

The 'first' All Saints comprised a chancel with two pews, a nave, a tower and a porch. There was a belfry containing 'a very pretty Sett of musical Bells consisting of Five'. Inside, the walls were whitewashed and hung with boards on which were written the Creed, the Lord's Prayer and the Ten Commandments. There was a chancel screen, a pulpit, a font, several monuments and a singing gallery at the west end. Hanging at the back of this gallery were the King's Arms and a table of benefactors. The old church was small as it could not 'contain the present number of inhabitants', which would have been about fifty households.

James's answers to episcopal visitation questionnaires, assuming he was being truthful, provide us with a glimpse of church life at Nuneham in 1738. Newton wrote that he had forty to fifty communicants in the parish. He held Communion services four times a year. Each Sunday there were two services, with prayers read daily in Passion Week and on the Monday and Tuesday of Easter Week. He catechized children in church and, for the most part, found them 'pretty expert in it'. There was a school containing seven boys and nine girls. The boys were taught to read and the girls, having a better deal, learned to sew as well as read! Such was the parish routine until Lord Harcourt decided to move the village. The church had to go as well, so the rector was in for a shock.

Lord Harcourt, as the lord of the manor, had considerable influence over Church affairs. By virtue of his social position he retained the 'advowson', or the right to present clergy to the living of Nuneham. For this he had to obtain the agreement of the Bishop of Oxford, but this was merely a formality. The bishop would always follow the lord of the manor's lead. This lordly power extended over a whole range of church matters and, in practice, Lord Harcourt's wishes were absolute.

We do not know exactly when James Newton learned of his Lordship's plans for a new church, nor do we know his immediate reaction. James was only too aware that there was nothing he could do other than to make the best of the situation and to accept it, perhaps, in his own terms, as the will of God. We do know though that the legal proceedings began on 15 July 1762.

On this date, Lord Harcourt, with others who contributed to the church rate, petitioned the bishop for permission to remove the medieval church and to erect a new one in its stead. Several reasons were put forward.

The church was 'very old and in a ruinous state'. It was too small for the current number of villagers to 'sit, kneel and hear divine Service and Sermons'. It was damp and generally unwholesome. None of these complaints had ever been voiced by James, who seemed quite content with what he had as long as some restoration work was carried out. Somewhat of an understatement then followed. To remove the church a small distance from its former position, 'will be convenient for the Earl and his family . . . and not in the least incommodious to the Rector and the Inhabitants of the . . . Parish.' This was indeed the case, but the intended church was to be about one-and-a-half miles from the 'New Town'. The real problem lay in moving the village, not the church.

The new building was to be placed twenty feet to the north of the old one. Lord Harcourt promised a sound construction in good stone with a copper roof. It was to be all fitted up inside in 'a decent manner' at his own expense. He even advocated selling the bells to defray the expected building costs of about £800.

John Hume, the Bishop of Oxford, agreed to Lord Harcourt's request as being 'highly reasonable and conducive to the Benefit of the Patron, Rector and Inhabitants of Newnham'. The bishop issued a proclamation on 31 July, which James read out at morning service on Sunday 1 August.

This proclamation described Lord Harcourt's scheme as 'a pious and generous design'. Anyone wishing to object was to appear at St Mary the Virgin, Oxford, on Saturday 7 August between 11.00 and 12.00 a.m. before the bishop's vicar-general. If there were no objections the plan was to go ahead. John Hume had seen a model of the proposed church and had approved it.

It would have taken a courageous person to voice dissent openly. Accordingly, on that fateful Saturday, the Reverend George Beaver, surrogate of the Reverend Dr Daniel Burton, the vicar-general, waited in vain throughout the appointed hour for any protest. By midday it was all over. The faculty, with permission to carry forward the proposals, was issued on the following Monday. Lord Harcourt had triumphed over both James and the villagers. A new church there was to be.

The church was of classical construction modelled on one of the temples of Palmyra. James Stuart, the architect, was a pioneer in the study of Greek antiquities. At the expense of the Dilettante Club, of which Lord Harcourt was a founder, Stuart had travelled widely in Greece studying its ancient architecture.

In spite of this, All Saints, James's new church, is more Roman than Greek in overall design. It is an austere, domed, heathen temple, conceived primarily as a landscape ornament rather than as a practical centre of religion. The convenience of the village worshippers, if any bothered to make the journey, was the last consideration. The focus of the building is a pedimented Ionic portico on the north side, which leads not to any doorway but to a blank wall. It serves in fact as an elaborate garden seat. The church acts mainly to assist the general picturesque effect of the landscape. It provides a focal point and was approved of by Horace Walpole as, 'a principal feature in one of the most beautiful landscapes in the World'.

But James Newton was not so enthusiastic. There were serious problems in trying to use it as a place of religious worship. There was no font nor any pews in the chancel. It was too far from the new village and attendance declined. James claimed that, with the old church, most villagers were 'well disposed . . . to attend pretty well'. By 1768, however, there were many 'who seldom come to church'. He did not catechize any more, but would have gladly done so if the children had attended. The peal of five bells was replaced by a solitary bell which was far too small to be heard throughout the parish. Lord Harcourt had been expected to provide a new set of bells but had failed to do so. Thus the parish clerk, or his deputy, was obliged to advertise the church services by going up and down the village with a hand bell, 'the like not to be met with in England'.

In the 1770s the congregation was still in decline. James struggled to hold regular services, but few came for instruction in the catechism and there was often no service at all for 'the Want of a proper Congregation'. In the rector's opinion, too many were absent, 'Some by way of excuses, the Want of better Cloaths, but I rather Fear, from the Want of better Hearts.'

The erection of the new church and extension of the park had also necessitated the destruction of the old graveyard and the removal of the gravestones, much to James's dismay. Many fine monuments, including some sixteenth and seventeenth-century memorials to earlier lords of the manor, were either 'secreted in a private place' or 'pil'd up one on another', instead of being 'fix't in their proper place'. The former churchyard was now a 'Pleasure Ground' for Lord Harcourt who, according to James, 'Mows and rolls it at his Pleasure'. James Newton appeared not to be at ease with what he saw around him. The later years of his incumbency were not entirely to his liking. Such is the local, social background to his *Diary*.

The Rectory, Nuneham Courtenay, from an original watercolour by Lucy Richardson

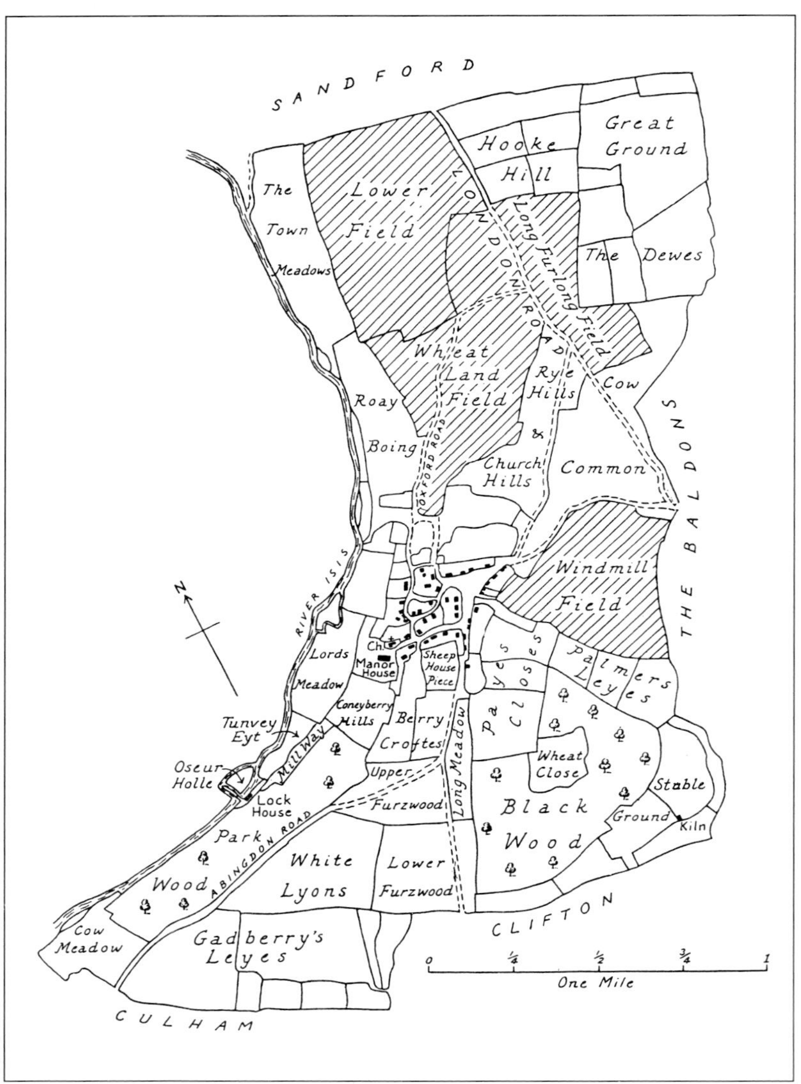

Plate 1 Sketch map of Nuneham Courtenay in 1707, based on an estate map by Robert Smith (reproduced from the VCH, *Oxfordshire*, V, p. 235; by kind permission of the General Editor)

Diary: Volume I

[f.1^{r}]

January 1759

Monday, the 1st A memorable Day, as being the very Day on which my dearest Bro[ther][1] Samuel Rock was buried in Newnham Chancel in the County of Oxford.[2] Self went there by Br[eakfast] in my Landau, but my Sister Rock, her Daughter & her Husband, with the sister of the deceas'd came thereabouts at 1 at Noon in a Mourning Coach.

Dr Beacon perform'd the funeral Rites & was much affected. My dearest Sister Rock forgot herself strangely & scream'd out & was so disfigur'd in [f.1^{V}] her Countenance that Self did not know her rightly just at first Sight. Alas she that had behav'd herself so decently, & well, did not now act her part in so becoming a Manner, but I trust God will not impute it unto Her as Sin. Her Grief was to big for her to contain, the Loss of so good & dear an Husband pearc'd her Heart so deeply that Panick, Grief & despairing Lamentations take Possession of Her Soul.

How different was her Behaviour when she was by Him at his last Breath, how patient & compos'd was her Mind at that solemn Hour, to what it was at his funeral Service. May I be moderate in my Grief, & not [f.2^{r}] lament my Brothers Death too much.[3] My Lamentations will avail Him nothing, but they may injure me much, & impair my Health & render me unable to perform the Function of my holy Order.

Guard me, O my God, I beseech against Excess in any of my Actions but may I direct them all under the Conduct of Reason & Religion. I have done my Duty by my Brother, while he was alive. I pray'd for the Restoration of his Health & assisted him with all my Might & now he is Dead, I have lamented much for Him, but I hope not too much, & that I shall soon enjoy my wanted Peace of Mind again.

My Sister Rock is the greatest Sufferer, her Loss is the most considerable, & her [f.2^{V}] Calamity the Greatest. Yet it will soon I hope wear away &

become tollerable Easy. She sh[a]ll continue to enjoy many Comforts of Life, & for these should be thankfull & not be too much dejected at the Death of her Husband. Give me Grace evermore, O my God, to be in readiness for my latter End, & no ways to be terrified at the Thoughts of my approaching Dissolution. A Conscience void of Offence toward God & Man is the best Preparation, and its my Study to acquire such a Conscience.

May my Brother's Death be useful to me, & remind me of my own Spectacle[4] of Mortality should [be] teaching the Living to prepare for Death & [f.3^{r}] Judgement. If we have got God for our Friend, what need we to fear, Nothing, but without his Friendship we may be looked on as ye most miserable of Men.

Tuesday, the 2nd Self sent from Caldecot [Caldecott] three Boxes full of Writing to Newnham & waited on my Lord Harcourt with them. Desir'd the Silversmith to wait on my Lord & Lady Harcourt for mourning Rings. Returned to Caldecot again. Mr Lawrence return'd his Gloves & Hatband.

Wednesday, the 3rd My Sister Rock's things wch should have been left at the Golden Ball[5] last Saturday were taken to Oxford & sent from thence to Abingdon and so they got at last safe to Caldecot. Thomas Hopkins was to have went [f.3^{v}] to morrow Morning to the Golden after them, but was counter order'd. A roast Turkey from Newnham for Din.

Thursday, the 4th Lord Harcourt's servant came to me about waiting on his Master. The Horses got to the Hay Ricks. A Wool Pack fell from a Horse & Thomas Silvester help't to get him up again, but it would not Do. Went to Newnham after Din & waited on my Lord Harcourt.

Friday, the 5th My Lord Harcourt came to my Home before Br & after Br Self set off for Caldecot with an Haunch of Venison a Present from my Lord Harcourt, & it was drest for Din. Two Letters from Polly, one for my Sister & the other for Me.

[f.4^{r}]

Saturday, the 6th Sent Thomas Silvester to Mr Pinnel with a Letter, & he retun'd with his own Hat. M[orning] P[rayers] Great Church,

Abingdon.[6] Went home with Mr Hawkins. Mrs Rock of Oxford not very well. N.P. [Afternoon Prayers] Abingdon & Sermon.

Sunday, the 7th Br at Newnham. A Goose for Din. Self, Thomas King, & Thomas Williams went to Longmead & Forewood.[7] The Gamekeeper came to me about my Lord Harcourts making a Draft on me for about £34. Went to Liddiar's & he was out of Order.[8]

Monday, the 8th Got to Caldecot before Br. Lent Mrs Rock of Oxford £4 4s 0d. Thomas Hopkins took her to Oxford in the Chariot, and my Neice was to have [f.4^{V}] return'd in it, but did not, as her little boy was not Well. Waited about the Wharf for my Neice.

Tuesday, the 9th Thomas King came from Newnham about a pair of Shoes, & Self sent Thomas Silvester with him to Bradly the Shoemaker. Gave a Guinea to Parson Portal's Wife on her Husband's Account, as he was from Home. N.P. Little Church Abingdon.[9]

Wednesday, the 10th Chaff & Straw from Newnham. Sent there six dozn & 1/2 of red Port Wine & two Boxes of Mrs Rock's. A Letter from Stewart, & One from Tom King's Father & a very good [one] from Polly in Relation to my Mother's better Health.

Thursday, the 11th Br. at Newnham. Visited several of the Poor sick People & order'd of them Victuals.[10] Packed up a Leg [f.5^{r}] of Lamb for Mortimer Street.[11] Stewart did not come according to his Notice.

Friday, the 12th Went to Oxford through Bagly Wood[12] & Saw a Man I suspected to be a Highwayman, but on Enquiry I had reason to think otherwise. Br with Mrs Rock. Bought a Chaff cutting Knife. Return'd with my Neice by Din. Rec^{d} a Letter from my Lord Harcourt.

Saturday, the 13th Br at Newnham. Paid Clarke on my Lord's Account £37 15s 3d. Went with my Horses in my Landau to Benson[13] & from thence took Post Horses, till I reach'd London. Din'd at Henly.[14] Drank Tea at Colnbroke.[15] Reach'd Mortimer Street about 11 o'Clock at Night & had the Comfort of finding my dearest Mother better than Expected. Sent my Sister [f.5^{V}] Rock a Letter. Part of a boil Fowl for Sup. Sent Tom King to his Uncle's. Brought with [me] a Ham, Goose & Apples.

Sunday, the 14th M.P. the Foundling Hospital[16] & there saw a Young Woman & follow'd her, as far, as her Home. N.P. St. Mary le Bone.[17] Met Major Bates in Mortimer Stret. William clean'd the Landau.

Monday, the 15th Call'd on Mr Noyse's. Went to Mr Cooper & he had no Money of Mr Rock's in Hand. Sent Writings to my Lord by two Chairmen. Drank Tea there & stay'd with him, till he had done looking over Them.[18] Sent my Sister Rock a comfortable Letter. Got my Lord to frank one about N[oon].

[f.6^{r}]

Tuesday, the 16th Paid Mr Bonus for cleaning & repairing Mr Rock's Pictures. Call'd on Mr Nickolls. Saw a beautifull Picture at Mr Bonus's. Look'd out for a House for my Sister Rock. Paid Admiral Long a Visit. N.P. St George's.[19]

Wednesday, the 17th Paid the Newsman 14s. 4d. My Lord Harcourt sent Home Scrutore[20] etc & Self sent to Him a Desk with Writings. Went to my Strand House & left Word for the Tenant to come to me at the Cofe [Coffee House.] Went to Westminster Abby. Enquir'd about Coach Houses & Stables. N.P. St George's & there saw One I had seen above a Year past. A Newnham Goose for Din.

[f.6^{v}]

Thursday, the 18th Bought a Leg of Mutton at Carnaby Market.[21] Rec'd £3 3s.0d. for Rent at my House in the Strand. Slaughter's Cofe.[22] N.P. St Georges Hanover Square. Tom King went off.

Friday, the 19th Went to Admiral Long about the Water in the Stable Yard. Order a dozn of Port Wine at Gilbert's.[23] Set the Bricklayer to work in the Stable Yard. Went to the old Baily.[24] Return'd Home to Dinner. N.P. St Georges. Drank Coffee at Lord Harcourt's.

Saturday, the 20th The Watchman call'd me & went with me to the White Horse Cellar, Piccadilly.[25] The man of the House knew I liv'd formerly at the Saracen's Head at Bath.[26] Br at Colebroke, & there exhibited a [f.7^{r}] Complaint against the Post Driver. Din'd at Henly. Went from Dorchester to Caldecot on the late Mr. Rock's Horse &

Thomas Silvester rode a Coach Horse. One of the Passengers belong'd to Christ Church, the other was going to Bath & the third spoke of dear Mr Rock's Death.

Sunday, the 21st Br at Newnham. Sent Liddiar & Whyat some Provision. After M[orning] Service, Self & Thomas Silvester went to Forewood. Return'd to Caldecot after N.P. by Tea time.

Monday, the 22nd Went in the Chariot to Oxford for my Neice & Br with Her. Call'd on Mrs Rock. Mr Glass not at Home. Return'd by Din. Sent Thomas Silvester to Newnham about killing a Calf & for Corn & Chaff.

[f.7^{v}]

Tuesday, the 23rd Thomas Williams brought Oats, Straw, & Chaff & return'd with Hay & strong Beer. A Newnham Goose for Din. N.P. the little Church.

Wednesday, the 24th Self & Neice went in the Chariot to Oxford. Thomas Silvester brought a roasting Pig from Newnham, & put a Puppy on him in a Basket, & the same Pig was drest at Mr Lannyans & turn'd out very bad. M.P. at St. Tabb's[27] & there saw Miss Umpheries. Paid Ward & Goodnough.

Thursday, the 25th Br & Din'd at Newnham. A small Congregation at Prayers. Sent Howse, Whyatt & Lydiard something to comfort them. Sent Thomas Silvester to Messrs Bush & Beacon. Returned to Caldecot.

[f.8^{r}]

Friday, the 26th M. & N.P. little Church Abingdon. Paid funeral Charges for my dear Brother Rock. Paid also the Farrier's Bill. Sent the Calves Skin to the Tanner's. Sister Rock receiv'd a comfortable Letter from Polly.

Saturday, the 27th Sister Rock sent the Chariot to Burcoat [Burcot] for Mrs Bush who din'd with Her & return'd Home again in it. Thomas Silvester brought the Mare & Six Assess from Newnham to Caldecot. Spoke to him for throwing the Dung into the Farmer's Yard.

Sunday, the 28th Rode to Newnham to Br & Thomas rode the Mare. Sent Bab Whyatt Meat & one Bottle of Wine & had Howse to Din. Pray'd by Richard Haisly. Went to Forewood [f.8^{v}] with my Bailiff before Din. Took a Leg of Veal with me to Caldecot in the Evening.

Monday, the 29th M.P. little Church. Took a Guinea to the Rev'd Mr. Nash according to her [*sic*] Desire. Rode to Newnham & Thomas went with both the Coach Horses. Gave Liddiar Cyder & Veal. The Taskers draw'd the Dung about the Long – Mead & Thomas Williams the Hurdles to Forewood. Pray'd by Haisly. A Letter from Lord Harcourt.

Tuesday, the 30th Sent Thomas Silvester to Bett Overton with a Twish.[28] M.P. great Ch. Abingdon. Gave Halloway 6d. & went toward Fuller's House, the Banker Before Din. N.P. Abingdon. Read the Papers at the Cofe.

Wednesday, the 31st Br at Newnham. Went to [f.9^{r}] Dr Beacons, & there heard of Dr Pitt's Death from Mr Glass. Sent Thomas to Oxford with a Letter for Lord Harcourt at London. A fat Hog Kill'd.

Notes

1 Samuel Rock was JN's brother-in-law.

2 Nuneham chancel was the chancel of the medieval church of All Saints, demolished and replaced by the classical structure of 1764 when the park was extended. For more details, see the Introduction. When the Harcourts moved to Newnham Courtenay in 1759, the name of the village was changed to Nuneham. JN always wrote Newnham.

3 Here begins the first of a series of moral reflections in the *Diary*. Anything was liable to trigger off one of these; usually JN had observed some unfort nate event or had had a narrow escape from disaster. He always sought ways of using adverse circumstances for spiritual improvement in order to be ready at all times for his own 'Latter End.' A death of course, gives him a marvelous opportunity for some philosophical thoughts in the true eighteenth-century rational mould.

4 By 'spectacle' JN meant appearance of; his own example in life.

5 The Golden Ball was a house on the Oxford to Henley road. It is now a roundabout, but is marked 'Golden Balls' on the current O.S. map.

6 The church referred to was St Helen's church, Abingdon. For full details see *Victoria County History, Berkshire*, (1924), IV, pp. 442–5.

7 Longmead and Forewood were parts of the estate.

8 By 'out of Order' JN meant not very well.

9 The church referred to was St Nicholas in the Market Place. For full details see *Victoria, Berkshire*, IV, pp. 445–6.

10 This is one of many examples of JN's kindness to others less fortunate than himself, suggesting a benevolent character.

11 Mortimer Street, Cavendish Square, London was where JN's mother and sister Polly lived. Another sister, Zenobia, joined them after her husband's death. When going up to town, JN often took a good supply of fresh country produce from Nuneham.

12 Bagley Wood was an area of about 390 acres of woodland on a sloping hill-side and, in earlier times, a notorious place for attacks on travellers. Around 1914 though, it was described as 'a pleasant place with an abundance of flowers'. See *Victoria, Berkshire*, IV, p. 393.

13 Benson in the eighteenth century was an important halt on the Oxford to Henley road. It was much used by JN on his travels. He would have broken his journeys at either The Castle inn or The Crown. See J. Sherwood and N. Pevsner, *Oxfordshire* (1974), p. 451. JN's journeys to London from Oxford usually took him a day. This was about the average time for the 1750s. See *The Encyclopaedia of Oxford*, p. 456.

14 Henley was another coaching stop between London and Oxford with a good number of inns. See Sherwood and Pevsner, *Oxfordshire*, pp. 635–45. JN regularly used the town as a staging post.

15 Colnbrook was then a wayside settlement on the Middlesex–Buckinghamshire border, just outside London. It was built on a major route, already a turnpike road by 1727 and an important crossing point of the river Coln. JN would have known the old wooden bridge, as the newer brick structure dates from 1777. Colnbrook was a large coaching centre with several inns dealing with travellers' requirements. To dine or drink tea, JN had a wide choice of establishments including The Catherine Wheel, The Cross Keys, The Star and Garter and The White Hart. See *Victoria, Middlesex* (1962), III, pp. 34–5.

16 The Foundling Hospital was established by Captain Coram in 1742 to care for destitute children. Handel was a great benefactor, donating an organ to the chapel in 1750 and giving performances of *Messiah* there. The chapel became a fashionable place to worship and JN was a frequent visitor. See *The London Encyclopaedia*, pp. 291–2.

17 This was St Marylebone parish church, rebuilt in 1740. The church was demoted to the status of a parish chapel after the construction of a new church (1813–1817) under the auspices of the Duke of Portland. Badly damaged in the Second World War, the old church was demolished in 1949. See *London Encycl.*, p. 741.

18 Lord Harcourt had a London home, Harcourt House in Cavendish Square, on the west side. This was built originally in 1722 by Lord Bingley and was thus known as Bingley House. The property was acquired by the first Earl

Harcourt and substantially altered by his son. The building was once referred to as 'one of the most singular pieces of architecture about town'. See *London Past and Present*, II, p. 190. The house was not far from JN's own home.

19 St George's, Hanover Square, was built for a fashionable growing part of London by John James in 1721–4. It has the earliest portico on any London church. See *London Encycl.*, pp. 707–8. Boswell made a visit in 1762 on Sunday 5 December. He heard a good sermon, yet was rather cold in his devotions as the twenty-four-year-old Anne Liddell, Duchess of Grafton 'attracted my eyes rather too much'. See, James Boswell, *London Journal*, F.A. Pottle (ed.) (1951), p. 142.

20 Scrutore is a variant of escritoire, i.e. a writing desk.

21 This market was between Carnaby Street and Marshal Street. It was also known as Marlborough Market.

22 Slaughter's Coffee House was at 77 St Martin's Lane close to Newport Street. It was established in 1692 by John or (more likely) Thomas Slaughter. It was a favourite meeting place for artists before the founding of the Royal Academy of Arts in 1768, and was frequented by the sculptor, Roubilliac, as well as James Boswell and Oliver Goldsmith. The coffee house was demolished in 1843–4. See B. Lillywhite, *London Coffee Houses* (1963), pp. 529–30.

23 Gilbert and Whipham was a wine merchants in Basinghall Street. See T. Mortimer, *Universal Director . . .* (1763), Part III, p. 32.

24 The Old Bailey was in regular use as a court since 1539. It was replaced by a new building in 1774. The present structure dates from 1907 and was extended in 1972. See *London Encycl.*, p. 133.

25 This was the White Horse Cellar coffee house, 157 Piccadilly. It was an important coaching inn, particularly for the routes to Oxford and Bath. The principal room of the establishment was situated in the basement, hence the term 'cellar'. Travellers could refresh themselves with wine or large beef-steaks. See Lillywhite, *Coffee Houses*, pp. 645–6; A.W. Groom, *Old London Coaching Inns* (1928), p. 39.

26 The Saracen's Head, Broad Street, was one of JN's regular haunts when staying in Bath. According to John Wood senior, the street in 1765 was thirty-five feet wide and contained fifty-six houses 'among which there are some that are handsome edifices'. J. Wood, *Description of Bath* (2nd edn, 1765), p. 332.

27 This is St Ebbe's Oxford, St Ebbe's Street. St Ebbe's was a medieval church given to Eynsham Abbey in 1141. It was rebuilt by Willam Fisher in 1814–17 and by G.E. Street in 1862–6. See Sherwood and Pevsner, *Oxfordshire*, p. 292; *Encycl. Oxford*, p. 387.

28 A Twish is an exclamation of vexation or annoyance. See *Oxford English Dictionary*, J.A.H. Murray et al., (eds) (Oxford 1888–1933).

February 1759

Thursday, the 1st M.P. Little Church. Edmond Baker came to Caldecot & went away again. Sister Rock sent her Maid Home in the Chariot. Turn'd Asses into the Island. Paid Farbrother's Bill.

Friday, the 2nd Br at Newnham. Sent Thomas to Dr Beacons with Compliments. Spoke to Dr Sipthorpe's Wife for her Husband to apply to be Dr Pitt's Successor.[1] Self & Neice din'd at Mrs Rock Lodging on the Turkey & Chine I brought there. Dr Pitt was agoing to be buried at St Jolls[2] [f.9^v] as Self was going Home.

Saturday, the 3rd Read the News at the Cofe before M.P. Took an Account of things my Sister Rock intends to have sent to London. Sent Thomas Silvester to Newnham for Oats. N.P. Great Church.

Sunday, the 4th Br at Newnham. Took Bab Whyatt Plumbs, Sugar Candy as a Present from Sister Rock. After M.P. Self & Thomas Williams went to Forewood. Met my Lord Harcourt near the Game keeper's, & receiv'd a Letter from Him the Same Day.

Monday, the 5th Mr Salmon begun measuring the Glebe Land,[3] & Self attended with Lord Harcourt etc but I got Home to Din between 2 & 3 & was much tird, but praised be God, did not [f.10^r] damage my health, & the rest did not return till about 6 at Night. Self sent Polly a Letter.

Tuesday, the 6th Mr Salmon went on with measuring the Glebe, but my Lord set out for London. Hooper brought me a Draught from my Lord for £30 but Self paid only £20 & at the same time paid him a Bill deliver'd in by Verney with a vast Abatement. Thomas Silvester sent Richard to my Lord's House instead of sending him down to the Field. Paid Betty Overton a Quarter's Wages.

Wednesday, the 7th A sick Fit before I was up. Rode to the Common after Mr Salmon & he was gone to Woodstock. Met Mr Wastie.

Employ'd Howse in the Garden. Self, Betty & Silvester [f.10^{v}] look about for a proper Place for my New House.[4] Cyder. And after Din. Got to Caldecot by Tea Time.

Thursday, the 8th Went with Messrs Salmon & Clarke about Measuring the Glebe. Sent Thomas Silvester to Oxford with the Chaff Box & the Harness. A Hogs Ear for Din. Betty sold a Calf for £1 7s 0d. Brought some Mustard Seed from the great House, & left a Tea Spoon there, & Deene's Daughter brought [it] up to my House.

Friday, the 9th While Mess[rs] Salmon & Clarke went away, Self & Nickolls look out for a proper Situation for my New House. A Shoulder of Mutton for Din.

[f.11^{r}]

Saturday, the 10th Self, Sister Rock, my Neice & Nephew set out for London & call'd at Mrs Bush's & She was very bad with the Gout, but he was not at Home. Din'd at Henly, & laid at The Sun at Maidenhead.[5] A Young man on a Mule who had been at Newnham about my Strand House[6] made himself known to me between Henly & Maidenhead. My Sister (etc) went to bed after drinking Coffee. Self had Beef Stake for Sup. The Soldiers sung & play'd on the German Flute,[7] & a Starling whistl'd.

Sunday, the 11th After Br. set out & din'd at Turnham Green. Reach'd Mortimer St about 6 o'Clock Night & found my dearest Mother tollerably [f.11^{v}] well. Sent the Horses to the Oxford Arms.[8] Admiral Long came, but my Sister did not come to Hand.

Monday, the 12th Rode with Admiral Long in Hyde Park & he try'd Poppit with One of his Horses in his Chariot & lik'd Him well, but was willing to make an Exchange, but I did not approve of it. Brought the Horses Home & sent my Sister Chariot to a Stable Yard, near the Chapple[9] at 2s. per Week. Waited on Lord Harcourt.

Tuesday, the 13th The Taylor brought Home my New Coat. Try'd the Coach Horses in my Landau. A Letter & Paprs from Lord Harcourt.

Wednesday, the 14th After Br set out in my Landau with my Neice, but the Horses did [f.12^{r}] not seem to go very well with Thomas

Silvester, & then Thomas Hopkins drove them. Din'd at Cranford Br[idge].[10] Laid at Maidenhead Br[idge][11] & had a boil Fowl for Supper.

Thursday, the 15th After Breakfast set. Sent my Lord Harcourt a very long Letter. Din'd at Benson. Put my Neice & her Son in the Stage for Oxford. Had my Landau repair'd. Had like to have been overturn'd in our Common[12] but got out, & praise be God, got Home safe before 8 o'Clock at Night.

Friday, the 16th This being a National Fast, Self fasted till Candle Light, & suffer none of my Family to Eat, till after N.P. were over.[13] My Neice sent a Letter about things she left at Benson.

[f.12^{v}]

Saturday, the 17th Went to Caldecot & brought the Plate away with me. Thomas Hopkins fill'd two Hampers with Liquer. Call'd for the Apothecary's Bill. Return'd Home to Din. Turn'd the Dung in Long Mead. Forgot the Barrel of Oysters.

Sunday, the 18th After M.P. Self & Thomas Silvester went to Forewood. Sent Dr Smith some Apple Pudding, & Bab Whyatt some Mutton.

Monday, the 19th Sent Thomas Silvester to Caldecot, Burcoat & Baldwin [Marsh Baldon]. Rec'^{d} a Letter from Lord Harcourt in answer to my last & he was not well pleas'd with the Contents of it. Self & Howse went about the Spot intended for my New House. Mr Bowly brought an Estimate of the Glebe. [f.13^{r}] Administer'd the Sacrament to Dr Smith.

Tuesday, the 20th Show'd Mr Bowly an Estimate of the Glebe according to my Account. Set out for London & took Howse with me over the Common. Din'd at Henly. Laid at Maidenhead.

Wednesday, the 21st Saw a vast number of fat Oxen on the Road. Br at Colnbrook, reach'd Mortimer St about 3 N. & found all Friends toller-able Well.

Thursday, the 22nd Sent a Letter by Mr Birch for Thomas Hopkins. Waited on Mr Cor. Din'd at Admiral Long's. N.P. St George's.

Friday, the 23rd Thomas Silvester trimm'd up his Horses. M.P. Conduit St[14] & N. Ditto. Went an House hunting. Two Hampers were brought here in a Cart. Lord Harcourt's man brought a Letter from Mrs Rock of Oxford.

[f.13^{V}]

Saturday, the 24th A Fellow begun working in the Garden & went away before Din. Lord Harcourt visited Sister Rock. M.P. St Anne's.[15] Met the Coachmaker at Mr Cor's. Slaughter's Cofe. Advertised for a House, & the Sale of the Chariot. N.P. Conduit St Chapple. Sent Thomas Hopkins a Letter.

Sunday, the 25th Took Polly in my Landau to the Foundling Hospital Chapple M.P. Call'd at the Admiral on our Return Home, & he had Company with Him. Went to St Mary le Bonne Church N.P. in my Landau & afterwards went to Hyde Park & then Home. Wrote part of a very long Letter to Lord Harcourt.

[f.14^{r}]

Monday, the 26th Sent Lord Harcourt a very long Letter, & he sent One in answer to it, rather longer. Mr Gambold came here. N.P. Conduit St Chapple. Cofe Bond Street.[16] Wrote part of a Sermon.

Tuesday, the 27th [Shrove Tuesday] Call'd on Mr Arnold. Foster had been at Dunning's, but was gone before I got there. M.P. St Andrew's.[17] Went in my Landau pretty near the Royal Exchange.[18] Bought Seeds at the Sun in Thame Street.[19] Paid Edwards for Oysters. Call'd on Constable in Abchurch Lane.[20] Din'd near the Royal Exchange. Went to the Punch House.[21] Heard a Sermon & Prayers near the same Place. Left my Landau to be repair'd [f.14^{V}] at Mr Berries in Leather Lane.[22]

Wednesday, the 28th Call'd at the Hawkers Office. M.P. St James's Clerkenwell.[23] Bought a pair of double Channel Pumps.[24] N.P. were over when I went to St George's.

Notes

1 Dr Sibthorpe did not get the job. Dr Pitt was succeeded by Dr John Kelly of Christ Church. See, *Jackson's Oxford Journal*, 30 January 1759.

2 This was St John's College.

3 All sorts of territorial changes were made in 1759 when Lord Harcourt extended his park and enclosed the village. JN exchanged his old glebe for new holdings of land. For details see Introduction.

4 JN's parsonage was due for demolition with the rest of the village, thus a new site had to be found.

5 The Sun at Maidenhead was an important inn at the corner of Castle Hill and the Marlow Road. It already existed in the 1660s. See *Victoria, Berkshire*, III, p. 99.

6 JN owned a house in the Strand which he let to various tenants. One of his major reasons for going up to London, apart from seeing his family and friends, was to check his property, arrange suitable tenants and collect rents.

7 A German flute was a transverse flute, perhaps made of wood. See Collins *Pocket Dictionary of Music* (1982), p. 174.

8 This was the Oxford Arms, Warwick Lane by St Paul's. It was a celebrated coaching inn, rebuilt after the Great Fire of 1666. Coaches and waggons departed for Oxford three times a week. The innkeeper also had 'a hearse with all things convenient to carry a corpse to any part of England'. It seems strange that JN sent his horses so far from home. There was another Oxford Arms at No. 6, Oxford Street, which was much more convenient. See Lillywhite, *Coffee Houses*, p. 721.

9 This was the Oxford chapel, Henrietta Street. It was dedicated to St Peter and built *c.*1724 from the designs of James Gibbs. See G.W. Thornbury, *Old and New London* (6 vols, 1879–95), IV, p. 442.

10 Cranford Bridge was a river crossing on the road from London to Bath. There was a bridge by 1274 which was repaired constantly until a new brick structure was erected in 1776. At Cranford, The White Hart inn was a centre for the stabling of post horses and it is likely that JN dined here. See *Victoria, Middlesex*, III, p. 178.

11 The first bridge over the Thames at Maidenhead existed sometime before 1297 when it was repaired. By 1451 the old bridge was again unsafe and it was renewed in 1750 at a cost of more than £764. This was the structure JN knew. It was replaced by a new stone bridge in 1772–7, built by Robert Taylor. See *Victoria, Berkshire*, III, p. 97–8; N. Pevsner, *Berkshire* (1966), p. 175.

12 See Sketch Map of Nuneham Courtenay, 1707, by Robert Smith.

13 This was recorded as a 'Day of Solemn Fast' in the press. See *Jackson's*, 16 February 1759.

14 This was the Trinity chapel in Conduit Street. JN refered to it as either Conduit Street Chapel or the Trinity Chapel. John Evelyn described it as 'new erected' in July 1691. It was built of brick and demolished in 1877. See *London Past and Present*, I, p. 449.

15 This was St Anne's church, Dean Street, Soho. It was built in 1677–86 by Talman and Wren. The tower was added in 1717 and rebuilt by S.P. Cockerell in 1803. For full details see *London Encycl.*, p. 691.

16 This coffee house in Bond Street was either Myatt's or Ben's [Benn's], New Bond Street. Both were convenient for JN after a service at the Conduit Street chapel. See, Lillywhite, *Coffee Houses*, pp. 121, 719.

17 This was St Andrew's church, Holborn, rebuilt by Wren in 1684–90. It was the largest of his parish churches. See *London Encycl.*, p. 689.

18 The Royal Exchange was a great centre of business and finance. It was built in 1566–7, destroyed in the Great Fire of 1666, rebuilt in 1669 and again destroyed by fire in 1838. The third building, by Sir William Tite, was opened in 1844. See *ibid.*, pp. 669–71.

19 The Sun in Thames Street was 'behind the Royal Exchange'. It was built in 1666 immediately after the Great Fire. See *London Past and Present*, III, p. 334.

20 Thomas Constable was a lawyer in Abchurch Lane. See Mortimer, *Universal Director*, Part III, p. 84.

21 This was the London Punch House, also called the London Coffee House or Ashley's, Ludgate Hill, Ludgate Street. It was set up in 1731 by James Ashley and was frequented by James Boswell. See Lillywhite, *Coffee Houses*, pp. 338–41, 671.

22 This was Berry and Barker the coachmakers, Leather Lane. See Mortimer, *Universal Director*, Part II, p. 22.

23 St James's Clerkenwell was in Clerkenwell Green. It was once part of a Benedictine Nunnery which was dissolved in 1539. The church was rebuilt in 1625. This was the structure JN knew before its alteration by James Carr in 1778–82. The steeple was rebuilt by W.P. Griffith in 1849, and further restoration took place under Sir Arthur Blomfield in 1882. See *London Encycl.*, p. 712. This was, of course, JN's family church. His family was buried there in their vault: his father, Dr James Newton, 12 November 1750, aged 72; his mother, Hester Newton, 19 April 1759, aged 84, memorial hatchment set up 21 April 1759; JN, 28 January 1786, aged 73; his sisters, Hester ('Tetty'), 2 May 1782, aged 60 and Mary ('Polly'), 15 September 1788. See *Burial Registers*, P76/JS1/65, P76/JS1/66 and the *Diary*, 19 & 21 April 1759. JN's other sister, Zenobia ('Sister Rock'), was buried by JN, 6 July 1779, at Nuneham.

24 These pumps were sewed shoes that had the seam uniting the sole and the upper sunk into a channel cut into the sole. As this process could not easily be carried out in thin, poor leather, it indicated a good quality shoe.

March 1759

Thursday, the 1st Self sow'd Seeds in the Garden. M.P. St George's Queen's Square.[1] Went to the Foundling Hospital. Went to the Coachman's & the Landau was clumsily mended. N.P. Trinity Chapple.

Friday, the 2nd Went with Sister Rock with Mr Cowden in my Lord Harcourt's Landau to Dr Commons[2] for he to prove Mr Rock's Will. Went to the old Baily & it was all over. Went to the Custom House[3] & din'd near the Royal Exchange & met [f.15^{r}] with a Jew who had travell'd with Sir Stephen Anderson.

Saturday, the 3rd Got my Landau Home from Berrie the Coachmaker. Sister Rock & Polly went in it to Islington Church Prayers.[4] Mr Cowden came here with an Estimate of the Glebe.

Sunday, the 4th Took my Sister Rock to St George's Church in my Landau & brought Her Home in it, on my return from the Foundling Hospital. N.P. Foundling Hospital. Went to Admiral Long's House & he was gone to Admiral Griffin's.

Monday, the 5th Call'd on Mr Prior in Lincoln's Inn, but he no Accounts of Mr Rock to pass. The Counsellor in Lincoln's Inn Fields not at Home.

[f.15^{v}]

Tuesday, the 6th Bought the Boy an old pair of Shoes. Bought Sage & Flowers in Covent Garden.[5] Sent the Boy Home with Tea etc. Saw the Counsellor in Lincoln's Inn Fields. Br at Slaughter's Cofe. Took a Turn in Westminster Abby.

Wednesday, the 7th Went to Islington Church in my Landau, & from thence to Stoke Newington.[6] Paid Dr Julius Casar. Tore Shoe in the Garden.

Thursday, the 8th Waited on Mrs Vernon. Paid for the standing of my Landau. Wrote to Mr Pinnel. Shoes repaired.

Friday, the 9th Paid Jordon, the Barber. Set out for Newnham. Call'd on Admiral Long. Din'd at Cranford Bridge. [f.16^{r}] Laid at Maidenhead. A Rabbit badly roasted for Supper. Mr Nash spent the Evening with me, & thought I overcharged him in the Reckoning. Laid in a sorry Chamber.

Saturday, the 10th Set out about 6 o'Clock M. & Br at Benson. Had Padbury to examine my Landau. Din'd at Newnham. Got out in the Crofts[7] & examin'd the Situation of the intended House, but was not pleas'd with it, & should have been glad, if I could.

Sunday, the 11th After M.P. went to Forewood with Thomas Williams. Sent Whyatt & Haisly part of a Cock. Pray'd by Him & Charles's Wife.[8] Burried Turner's Girl.[9]

[f.16^{v}]

Monday, the 12th Spoke to Crosse about the Coal. Call'd at Dr Beacon's but not at Home. Winnow'd Barly. Din'd with my Neice at Oxford. Gave Mrs Rock half a Pound of Dust Tea.[10] Paid Mr Glass. Boar Stag Killed.

Tuesday, the 13th Draw'd out Twelve Quarter of Barly. Took Howse from Forewood to the Golden Ball. Din'd at Dr Beacon's. Howse cut out the Boar Stag.

Wednesday, the 14th Draw'd Faggots Home from Forewood & begun plowing the Turnip Land. Employ'd Howse at Bab Whyatts Close, & took Him with me to the Crofts etc.

Thursday, the 15th Employ'd Howse before Br at Bab Whyatt's Close. Winnow'd Barly. [f.17^{r}] Boil'd Chitterlings for Din.[11]

Friday, the 16th On Examining the Gin & Rum found about four Gallons of the Gin taken out of the Bottles & two Bottles or more of Rum also. Remov'd the Wine & Strong Beer out of the Hall into the Cellar. Sent Barly & Wheat to Sandford Mill for grinding.[12]

Saturday, the 17th Br with my Neice at Oxford. Call'd on Mrs Rock. M.P. St John.[13] No Terrier to be found in the Bishop's Court.[14] Return'd Home to Dinner through Forewood. Took in half a Rick.

Sunday, the 18th Lord Harcourt sent Home my Sumpter Trunk.[15] Self & Thomas Williams went to Forewood. Waited on Lord Harcourt. Sent Whyatt & Haisly Provisions.

[f.17^{v}]

Monday, the 19th Self & Lord Harcourt examin'd the Crofts & a spot for the New H[ouse]. Lord Harcourt & Mr Bowly din'd with me.

Tuesday, the 20th Self & Lord Harcourt went about the new intended Glebe, & more Land was laid to it in Exchange for the Ayott & Fisher's Green Meadow. Before Dinner Self sign'd an Agreement for an Exchange of Glebe.[16] After Din Self & Betty went about the New intended Glebe.

Wednesday, the 21st Got up about 3 o'Clock M. & call'd Betty. Went to London in the Oxford Machine.[17] Waited on the Bishop of Oxford,[18] & he did not approve of my Business. Return'd to my Inn.

Thursday, the 22nd Return'd to Newnham in the [f.18^{r}] Machine & in good Health for wch Blessing I am thankfull to God.

Friday, the 23rd Br with Mrs Rock at Oxford & took her some Money. Call'd on my Neice. P.M. St John's. Call'd on Mr Ward the Uphosterer. Began packing up things at Caldecot. Din'd at Powell's.[19]

Saturday, the 24th Br at Caldecot. Cut Bushes for Long Mead. Kill'd a Hog. Self pack'd up China & Glass Ware.

Sunday, the 25th Self & Thomas Williams after M. Pr. went to Forewood & from thence to the Crofts. Sent Bab Whyatt & Haisly some Provisions. Went to Dr Beacon's about the Inclosure Affair.

[f.18^{v}]

Monday, the 26th Self Br at Mr Bush's, & spoke to Him about the Inclosures. Busy at Caldecot in packing up Things.

Tuesday, the 27th Mr Ward came to Caldecot to set a Value on the Goods, but Self alter'd his Mind, & it was agree'd he should come to Morrow & sell them Himself. While He & Self were examining a Bureau from Sarsden, he found in one private Draw £27 12s. 0d. & Self in another, several Letters wrote by Mr Rock by late Lord Harcourt's Orders, to the late Sir Robert Walter at Sarsden.[20]

Wednesday, the 28th This Day Mr Ward begun selling the Goods by Hand. Self din'd later.

[f.19^{r}]

Thursday, the 29th Bought a Leg of Mutton. Mr Ward went on with the Sale of Goods. Waited on Lord Harcourt & told Him of the Money found at Caldecot, & he thought my Sister ought to keep it.

Friday, the 30th Sent some fine Pork to London, & took some more to Caldecot. No[t] many Buyers to Day. Took to my Lord Harcourt an old Draught of part of one of his Estates.[21]

Saturday, the 31st Br with my Lord Harcourt & spoke to him about Money due to me & about allowing me a certain Sum for all my Tythes. As Mr Ward did not come to Caldecot Self sold some few odd Things. Hash'd Mutton & Dandelyon for Din.

[f.19^{v}]

Notes

1 This was the church of St George the Martyr, an early eighteenth-century building. See *London Encycl.*, p. 708.

2 This was the colloquial name for the College of Advocates and Doctors of Law near St Paul's Cathedral. See *ibid.*, p. 231.

3 The Custom House was in Lower Thames Street. The building JN knew was built by Thomas Ripley in 1717–25, to replace an earlier structure by Wren. See *ibid.*, p. 218.

4 The church referred to was St Mary's Church which was rebuilt in 1751–4. See *ibid.*, p. 737.

5 This is London's most famous fruit and vegetable market. It began in 1656 and was expanding rapidly when JN knew it. See *ibid.*, pp. 203–4.

6 This was an ancient village that was gradually swallowed up by London. In the eighteenth century it was a centre for non-conformists. See *ibid.*, pp. 827–8.
7 The Crofts were part of the Nuneham estate.
8 This was a Nuneham villager, Charles Scissell's wife, Ann.
9 This was Elizabeth, daughter of William and Mary Turner, who was baptized on 1 January 1758. See Nuneham, *Registers*.
10 Dust tea was powdered tea.
11 Chitterlings were the small intestines of a pig.
12 This was the water mill at Sandford on Thames, about two miles from Nuneham, by Sandford Lock. The mill was destroyed by fire in 1768, but by 1806 it was rebuilt. See *Victoria, Oxfordshire*, (1957), V, pp. 270–2.
13 This was St John's College, Oxford. JN was a frequent visitor there, often to look round the gardens.
14 Plans were afoot to move the village for Lord Harcourt to extend his park. JN thus wanted to ascertain the exact nature of his glebe holding which would have been specified in a document known as a terrier.
15 A sumpter trunk was a kind of saddlebag or a trunk used on a pack horse.
16 Obviously, much negotiation took place between Lord Harcourt and JN. This was the date of Lord Harcourt's petition to the Bishop of Oxford. For the final document with JN's signature and full details of the proposed exchange of glebe, see *Oxfordshire Archives*, MS. Oxf. Dioc. Pprs., c.2197., No. 8.
17 This was the name of one of the many coaches travelling from Oxford to London. It operated from the Bear Inn, High Street and Alfred Street. See *Encycl. Oxford*, pp. 35–6.
18 The Bishop of Oxford was Dr John Hume. He came from Bristol in June 1758 and was translated to Salisbury in September 1766. He married Lady Mary Hay in London on Saturday 5 August 1758. See *Handbook of British Chronology*, F.M. Powicke and E.B. Fryde (eds.) (1961), p. 245; *Jackson's*, 5 August 1758.
19 John Powell was a 'victualler & coffee house keeper'. See *Jackson's*, Saturday 10 April 1762. The location of this coffee house is uncertain. See N. Aubertin-Potter and A. Bennett, *Oxford Coffee Houses, 1651–1800* (Oxford, 1987), p. 41.
20 Sir Robert Walter, Bt., died on 20 November 1731. See *Gentleman's Magazine* (1731), I, p. 500. For Sarsden House see Sherwood and Pevsner, *Oxfordshire*, p. 752. The 'late Lord Harcourt' referred to is Simon, 1st Viscount Harcourt (1661–1727).
21 This may have been the Land Terrier dated 12 March 1651 among the Harcourt Papers in the Bodleian. See Bodl. MS. D.D., Harcourt c.286.

April 1759

Sunday, the 1st The plowboys Father came to see Him. After M.P. Self & Thomas Williams went to Forewood & then to the Crofts. Sent Bab Whyatt some Wine, Ale, & roast Pork. Rec'^{d} a Letter from Sister Rock. Had Bett Barns here. Roast Pork for Din.

Monday, the 2nd Thomas Williams was taken Ill very suddenly. Br at the Cofe House.[1] Call'd at my Neice's & She was Ill of the Measles. Order'd Thomas to follow me over Folly Bridge[2] & He like a fool waited for me there. Din'd at Caldecot & sent Things from there in my Waggon.

[f.20^{r}]

Tuesday, the 3rd Thomas Silvester planted things out of Caldecot Garden.[3] He & Treadwell got the Horses out of the Baldwin Pound. Self & Betty went about the New Glebe.

Wednesday, the 4th Br at Cofe. Went to the Sale of Goods at the late Dr Pitts.

Thursday, the 5th Rec'^{d} a Letter from Lord Harcourt. Busy at Caldecot in loading Hibbits Waggon for London.[4]

Friday, the 6th Self set out about 5 o'clock M. Br at Henly. Took a Place in the Cirencester Stage for London because it was very rainy & left my Horse at the Bell.[5] Reach'd Mortimer St about 6 N. in good Health.

Saturday, the 7th Hibbit draw'd my Sister Rock's Goods to Mortimer Street & there unloaded Them, but would not [f.20^{V}] let the Men carry some Boxes upstairs but was Saucy. Call'd on Mr. Birch & he seemn'd to take no Notice of me when I went in. A Lawyer made a false Demand on my Sister Rock for two Year's Rent of Land in Cambridgeshire.

Sunday, the 8th [Palm Sunday] M.P. the foundling Hospital & follow'd a Woman from thence to her House near Covent Garden. N.P. lazer Chap.[6] Drank Tea at Admiral Long's, & Mr Lally was there with some of his Scholars, & he desir'd me to search the Register at Watlington for the Death of a Woman.

Monday, the 9th Went to Queen's Square[7] & Dyott's Building before Br. [f.21r] Paid £4 16s 0d. for a Year's Land Tax[8] for my Strand House due last Ladyday & receiv'd a quarter's Rent of my Tenant. Din'd at the Widow Golding & a young Woman was there with her Child. Waited on Lord Harcourt & he wanted me to Victual the Commissioners,[9] but I did not think it right. Acquainted Admiral Long with the Erections at the Queen's Head, Ormond St. Found my dearest Mother very Bad.

Tuesday, the 10th Waited on my Lord Harcourt to acquaint him of my not going to Newnham on the Account of my Mother's Illness. M.P. King's St. Chapple, & met my Lord as I [f.21v] was (going Home) from it. Look out for a House for my Sister and found one empty near Oxford Chapple. Pray'd by my Dearest Mother. Wrote to my Housekeeper, Pinnel & Burdett. N.P. Conduit St Chap.

Wednesday, the 11th M.P. Berwick St Chapple.[10] Bought a pair of Stockings. My dearest Mother still dangerously Ill. George dig'd in the Garden. N.P. Conduit St Chappl. Bought Glasses in Bond Street.

Thursday, the 12th To Day the Commissioners were to meet at Newnham about settling the Exchange of the Glebe & the Enclosures. M.P. Berwick [f.22r] St Chap. My dearest Mother still vastly out of Order.

Friday, the 13th [Good Friday] M. & N.P. Berwick St Chap fasted All Day.

Saturday, the 14th [The whole of this entry is in a large, clear, neat hand] This Day at about one quarter of an Hour after five o'Clock in the Morning my dearest Mother breath'd out her last Breath in my Presence, Aged eighty four Years of Age.
[f.22v]
[Normal size hand again.]
Since it is the Will of my Heavenly Father to take my dearest & most pious Mother out of this sinfull & miserable World, may I with Patience

& resignation bear the Loss (of Her) & be thankfull for the long Enjoyment of Her. She dy'd full of Years & I trust full of Virtue, Goodness & every Grace & therefore through the Merits of her Saviour, She must be at Rest. What a Consolation must this needs be to me? how easy & resign'd should this teach me to be? what moderation should this give to my Grief – not suffer me to weep too much, or become troublesome to my Self [f.23^{r}] or Others!

When we see our Friends & Relations taken away from us by Death, its natural for us to Grieve & to be afflicted, for so much is due to them, & should we neglect so to do, we might justly lay ourselves open to much Censure, & our Humanity & good Nature might be call'd into Question. Therefore we must observe Moderation in our Lamentations for the Dead.

As my dearest Mother took a Delight in serving God & doing her Duty, I need have no uneasiness about her future State, no dismal apprehensions of her not being with God, but rather should rejoice & be glad, that [f.23^{v}] She hath spent her Days so well. Oh! May the Memory of Her be dear unto me, may I think on Her with the highest Degree of Filial Love, Reverence, & Duty & may I be thank[ful] for the Honourable old Age she arriv'd at & above all, for her ending her Days well.

I have surviv'd my Dearest Father, my Brother Samuel Rock & now, my Mother & am blest with a good Share of Health & above all, with a good Conscience & therefore let me not spend my time in a fruitless Sorrow for them, but beg of God to give me an easy [f.24^{r}] & contented Mind, & Grace to prepare myself for my latter End.

However some People may complain of the tediousness of time & that it lays on their Hands like an heavy Burthen & they know not how to get rid of it. I must confess for my Part that, I don't find it so, but that day after day, Week after Week, Month after Month & Year after Year seems to me to move on very swift & rapid & that if any thing gives me uneasiness, it is not the slow Motion of Time, but its Rapidity. The Distance from the Cradle to the Grave is Short, as soon as we [f.24^{v}] begin to dye & the Days of our Pilgrimage soon come to an End, & since this is the Case let me be the more careful & frugal in the Management of my Time, for it is that only that will intitle me to an happy Death. Long Life is not so much my Desire, as it is my Desire to spend & end, my Days, well. A virtuous Life only, let it be short or Long, will intitle us to Heaven. May I often meditate on Death & then I hope I shall ever be in readiness for Him. A sudden Death can do us no harm if we lead a life of strickt Virtue [f.25^{r}] & Holiness & may I ever do so. The best Remedy against the Fear of Death is a good Conscience. Death may appear very terrible to the Sinner, but not to the good man. The one has much Reason to rejoice at his near approach, but the Other, to tremble. If the Thought of Heaven or Hell can affect the Mind of Man, Surely the near Approach of these two Places must need create in Him the greatest Joy or the greatest Misery. When we are arrived at such a degree of Virtue, have so far surmounted all the Difficulties of our Christian Warfare as not to fear Death, then the Con-[f.25^{v}] sideration of our Heavenly Inheritance will give us Joy unspeakable & full of Glory. To live without the Fear of Death & to bear the Extreams of Prosperity & Adversity with true Fortitude & evenness of Temper is a most desirable Condition. As long as we live, we must expect to meet with something to trye our Patience, something to grieve us (some sort of) Trouble & Uneasiness, & not suffer us to enjoy a long uninterrupted Scense of true Peace & Content. It is my greatest Desire to serve God, my most ardent Wish to please him in all Things, & through ye [f.26^{r}] Merits of my Saviour, I hope, I do so.

To have every thing suitable to my own fallacious & erroneous Will & Pleasure, is not my Desire. I trust to Providence & into his Hands I most cheerfully commit all my Affairs & with Patience acquiesce in his wise management of them. We may lawfully pray for many Things, but let us not set our Hearts too much on them, & then if God Almighty shall most indulgently deny them to Us, we shall not grieve much for them. It is often seen that what we most ardently pray for would have prov'd a greater Curse then Blessing, had we been put into Possession of it. We dont know the event[11] of things [f.26^{v}] & this should teach us to bear with Patience our Present State & Condition in Life, for we are not certain that a Change may not be for the Worst.

While my dearest Mother laid Ill, I pray'd to God for the Restoration of her Health, but he judg'd most Proper to take Her out of this World, and as I trust she is a[t] Rest, I should (think) the Change is better not only for Her, but myself too. As she had lead a most holy & good Life, the sooner she was out of Danger of Relapsing & was rewarded for it, the better. And as for myself had she continu'd a few Years longer with Us, its possible I might have lov'd her too much, have taken too much Pleasure in attending on Her & then ye Loss of Her would have been ye more grievous to Me.[12]

[f.27^{r}]

Sunday, the 15th [Easter Day] Early M.P. & Sac^{rt} Hanover Square,[13] & there was a crowded number of Communicants, a glorious Sight. N.P. Berwick Street Chapple.

Monday, the 16th M.P. Berwick St Chapple & N. Conduit Street Chapple. A Letter from my (Lord Harcourt) Keeper Howse.

Tuesday, the 17th Ditto. Maddox St Cofe. Admiral had his Coach Horse duck'd out of his Life. Soak'd Bottles.

Wednesday, the 18th Compos'd part of a Sermon. Early M.P. St Annes. Bespoke a mourning Suit of Cloathes for George Brooks, & a full mourning Coat for myself. George hamper'd[14] his Thumb in the Table. Self & all my Sisters kiss'd my dearest [f.27^{v}] [This entry is in a large, clear hand.] Mother in her Coffin before it was nail'd Down.

Thursday, the 19th This Day my dearest Mother was buried in the Family Burial Vault at St James's Clerkenwell, & Self & my three Sister[s] attended her to her Grave.

[Normal size script again.] To attend a Mother to her Grave is a mournfull & solemn Transaction [f.28^{r}] & should fill the Mind with religious Reverence & Devotion & to weep on such Occasion is very commendable. May I always enjoy a tender, humane & Charitable Heart & not deny the Tribute of Sighs & Tears to proper Objects. May my Heart overflow with universal Love & Charity towards all Mankind; May I ever be ready & willing to assist the Wants & Necessities of the Poor & Indigent; May I weep with those that weep, as well as rejoyce with those that Rejoyce & in a Word, may I most religiously do my Duty toward, God & Man, & do as I would be done by.

[f.28^{v}]

That night my dearest Mother was buried, One or more was buried there too, & therefore I should not look on myself as the most unfortunate of men. For a Son to attend his Mother to her Grave is no uncommon thing for it daily happens. To follow a religious good Mother to her Grave is more eligable, than if she had dy'd without the Fear & Love of God. My Mothers Devotion was extraordinary great & my Lamentation for Her, should be the Less. Her Love of Virtue was sincere & ye delight she took in the Service of her great Creator, was her greatest Comfort [f.29^{r}] & Consolation, & therefore let me turn my mourning into rejoycing.

I saw my dearest Mother deposited in the Family Vault with the Remains of my dearest Father, & now she is no more as to this World, but through the Merits of her Saviour, she is at Rest & in the Regions of everlasting Happiness. The Days of my Pilgrimage will soon expire, & I shall be number'd among the Dead; my Continuance here cannot be very long, & the time of working out my Salvation will soon come to an End, & then adieu to this World & all his false & treacherous Enjoyments.
[f.29^{V}]
May the Memory of my dearest Mother be ever sacred & precious to me, may I meditate on her with religious Love & Devotion & may I endeavour to spend my Days as well as she has done. The Love of Virtue was her Delight & ye service of God her greatest Recreation, & I trust through the Merits of my Saviour to meet with Her in the Regions of everlasting Happiness.

Give me true Peace of Mind, O my God, & teach me to be contented in every State & Condition of Life; & when I come to dye, bless me with a good Conscience for Christ's his Sake. Amen.

[f.30^{r}]

Friday, the 20th Early M.P. St Anne's. Spoke to William Wells about my Housekeeper. N.P. Conduit St Chapple. The Taylor took back the Coat to Altar.

Saturday, the 21st E.M.P. St Anne's. Bought half a Pound of Tea at Twinings[15] for my Sister. Prowl'd about Covent Garden. Bought a pair of Stockings. N.P. Conduit St Chapple. My dearest MOTHER'S ATCHIEVEMENT WAS SET UP.

Sunday, the 22nd E.M.P. St George's Hanover. N.P. Berwick. Compos'd part of a Sermon.

Monday, the 23rd READ MY DEAREST MOTHER'S WILL. Sister Rock [f.30^{V}] behav'd extreamly Ill. George Brook's Mother came here. Saw a Boy damag'd by a great Beam in a Cart. Bought 3 Gallons of Wine.

Tuesday, the 24th E.M.P. St Anne's. Saw the Woman with her little Girl. Hunted about for a House bef[ore] Br. A Letter from Lord Harcourt. Had much serious Converstaion with Sister Rock. N.P. Conduit St Chap.

Wednesday, the 25th E.M.P. St Anne's. Went through St. James's Church[16] & saw a large Congregation, a fine Sight. Saw the Widow Airs at Admiral Longs & many More.

Thursday, the 26th E.M.P. St James's Church. [f.31^{r}] My Lord Harcourt sent my Gown by his Porter.

Friday, the 27th Self & Lord Harcourt waited on the Bishop of Oxford & there we executed a Tripartite Deed for the Exchange of the Glebe & the Enclosure.[17] Self went to Mr Casar. Met with Mr Parsons who wanted to dedicate a Book to his Lordship. Paid Mrs Vanham One Year's Rent.[18] Spoke to my Sister Rock about my Mother's Will. Took George Brooks with me to the White Horse Cellar Piccadilly, & Self set off in the Cirencester for Newnham.

[f.31^{v}]

Saturday, the 28th The Passengers breakfasted at Slow [Slough], but Self breakfasted at Henly.[19] One of the Passengers had been Curate of St Andrews[20] but now hath got a Son, Gentleman Commoner at Oxford. [One of] the Passengers was a dealer in Wool of Cirencester, & a young Woman who offer'd her Service to me. Reach'd Newnham between one or two N. & got out at Clifton [Clifton Hampden].

Sunday, the 29th After M[orning] Service, Self & Thomas Williams went to Forewood. Pork & Plumb Pudding for Din, & sent Bab Whyatt some of it. In the [afternoon] Self, Overton, & Bett Barns went to the Crofts. Sent S[ister] Rock a Letter. [f.32^{r}] Turn'd the Mare & Brown into the Vineyard. Got the Horses out of Clifton Pound. Thomas Silvester blooded the Coach Horses.

Monday, the 30th Din'd with my Neice Lawrance & her Aunt Rock.[21] Gave Mrs Rock my Sister Rock's Present of Coffee & one Guinea. Bought Cloath for Thomas Silvester's Mourning. Self deliver'd to Mr Beaver the Tripitarte [*sic*] Deed. Mr Ward not at Home. Bought for Thomas a Velvet Cap.

Notes

1 JN was a frequent visitor to Oxford coffee houses. Unfortunately, he does not always mention which ones he used. The first coffee house in Oxford was opened in 1651 at the Angel Inn. By 1740 there were thirteen such establishments. After April 1759, JN had to pay more for his refreshments: chocolate went up from 4d to 5d a dish and coffee from 4d to 5d a pot. See Aubertin Potter and Bennett, *Oxford Coffee Houses*; *Jackson's*, 14 April 1759.

2 Folly Bridge is the southern bridge into Oxford, taking the Abingdon road into St Aldates. This was JN's normal entry from Nuneham. For details of the bridge see *Encycl. Oxford*, p. 144.

3 JN was a keen gardener. It is thus quite in keeping with his general outlook to transplant items from his sister's garden when she moved.

4 Hibbit was one of the many eighteenth-century carriers operating in and around Oxford on local commissions or journeys to London. See *Encycl. Oxford*, pp. 455–6.

5 It is interesting to note that JN had to change from his own horse to the stage-coach on account of the weather. By 1759 there was a regular service from Cirencester to London via Oxford and Henley. See *Encycl. Oxford*, p. 456. In July 1759 the Bell was taken over by Thomas Hadley who had had a coffee house in New College Lane, Oxford. The previous proprietors, whom JN would have known, were Mr and Mrs Burdett. They retired, both being over seventy. See *Jackson's*, 28 July 1759.

6 This was St Giles-in-the-Fields, rebuilt by Henry Flitcroft in 1753. The site was originally a leper hospital (hence the term lazar), founded in 1101. The chapel was converted to parochial use after the Dissolution of the Monasteries. See *London Encycl.*, p. 710; *London Past and Present*, II, pp. 110–3.

7 Queen's Square was named after Queen Anne. It was built in 1708–20. For full details see *London Encycl.*, pp. 629–30.

8 Land Tax was one of the major taxes in the eighteenth century. Technically the rate was variable, but the tax was often levied at 4s in the pound.

9 The Commissioners were the men commissioned to carry out the enclosure at Nuneham in 1759.

10 This was Berwick Street chapel, St Luke's. See *London Past and Present*, III, p. 171.

11 By 'the event' JN meant the outcome.

12 His mother's death gave JN an ideal reason for one of his pieces of moral reflection. This one occupies nine folios of the *Diary* – nearly two hours' worth of writing!

13 This was presumably at St George's. This is only the second mention of the Sacrament in the Diary.

14 By 'hamper'd' JN meant caught.

15 This is R. Twining & Co. Ltd., 216 The Strand. Twinings have been on the same site since 1706 when Thomas Twining, supplier of tea to Queen Anne,

established his business. The firm claims to be the oldest ratepayer in the city of Westminster. See *London Encycl.*, p. 829; N. Grunfeld, *The Royal Shopping Guide* (1984), p. 166.

16 A glance at the map suggests that JN passed through St James's church, Piccadilly, on his way home to the admiral's. On the other hand, in view of the recent funeral, he may have visited the family church, St James's Clerkenwell.

17 A copy of the the Tripartite Deed, with full details of the territorial arrangements and JN's signature and seal, may be found in *Oxfordshire Archives*, MS. Oxf. dioc. Pprs., c.2197., No.8; *ibid.*, c.434, fos. 38–44.

18 The property is unidentifiable from diary evidence.

19 He presumably stopped at The Bell to collect his horse, which had been left there three weeks earlier.

20 If JN was referring to Oxford, this must be St Andrew's Church, Headington, a fine, early medieval church. For full details see *Encycl. Oxford*, p. 373; Sherwood and Pevsner, *Oxfordshire*, p. 336.

21 Aunt Rock presumably meant Samuel Rock's sister. She appears only once more in the *Diary*, attending her brother's funeral on New Year's Day, 1759.

May 1759

Tuesday, the 1st Sent Thomas Silvester, & two more men after Brown & the Mare. [f.32^{V}] Busy in writing out my Lord Harcourts Bills. Gave the Children Wine & Plumbs. A Pidgeon for Din.

Wednesday, the 2nd Sent Thomas Silvester with Jack Ewon & Howse return'd Home from look[ing] after the Mare & old Brown. Thomas Williams sold at Shillingford Market Beans & Barly. (Draw'd Furze to the New Kiln.)[1]

Thursday, the 3rd Thomas Williams kill'd the Calf. (Thomas Silvester & the other two return'd Home without the Mare & old Brown.)[2] Draw'd Furze cut in the Common on my Way to the New Kiln.

Friday, the 4th Sent two Legs of Veal to London. Furze draw'd to the New Kiln & Self went there. Sent Tom Chapman [f.33^{r}] Home to fill the Chaff House. ([Saturday 5] Paid Nutt late Brother Rock's Bill & allow'd for the Tythes of three Calves.)[3] Edmond Baker help'd to get the two Marble Statues into the Hall.

Saturday, the 5th[4] Draw'd out one Waggon Load of Beans & one of Barly. Self din'd at Watlington & had my Mare & Horse cry'd there. Enquir'd after Mrs Harris, the Taylor's Wife, & found she was Living & saw Her. Return'd Home to Tea.

(Monday 7)[5] Draw'd Things from Caldecot to Newnham. Din'd at Abingdon. A letter from Sister Rock. Spoke to the Woman about her Lame Sister. Thomas Williams sold Poppit, [f.33^{V}] & thirty Ews & Lambs, but not the Bull. Lord Harcourt came to Newnham. Sent Thomas Silvester with my Landau for Mortimer Street.

Sunday, the 6th Christen'd a Boy.[6] After M.P. Self & Thomas Silvester went to Forewood. Pitson gave Notice of the Asses being in Clifton Field, & I had them drove Home. Got Asparagrass for Mortimer Street.

Monday, the 7th Brought a Load of things from Caldecot. Din'd at Abingdon. Thomas Williams sold thirty Ews & Lambs & also Poppit.

Tuesday, the 8th Draw'd Furze from Sermon's to Forewood Kiln. Howse went from Home in the Morning & did not return till Night. Waited on my Lord Harcourt & Cummins came while I was [f.34r] with Him & told a long Story about his two Maidens.

Wednesday, the 9th Draw'd more Faggots to Forwood Kiln from Sermons. Master Thomas Williams went to Shillingford Market & struck up an Account of the Mare & Horse. Baptised Edmond Baker's Child.[7]

Thursday, the 10th Brought new Wine from Caldecot & several other Things & Howse drank too much. Spoke to the Cooper about my Asses. Return'd Home to Din.

Friday, the 11th William Clarke mark'd the Sheep & Ned Shephard & Horner help'd Him. A broil'd Chick for Dinner. Clanwill gave an Account of the Asses being in Clifton Pound. Draw'd 300 [f.34v] Furze Faggots from Nineveh to the Common Kiln.[8]

Saturday, the 12th Br at Cofe Oxon. M.P. Carfax.[9] Call'd on my Neice & Mrs Rock. Had the Mare & Gelding Cry'd. Bought Materials for a pair of Breeches. Call'd at The Taylor's, but not at Home.

Sunday, the 13th The Shoemaker had my Boots to Repair. Tom Chapman din'd here. Got the Asses out of Clifton Pound. Preach'd a new Sermon. Thomas Williams & Self went to Forewood.

Monday, the 14th Rec'd a Letter from Sister Rock. Draw'd Furze to Forewood Kiln out of Forewood. Din'd at Oxford. Sent Howse with Books from Caldecot [f.35r] to Mr Fletcher, & with other things to Mrs Rock. Sent my Neice, her eldest Boy & Aunt from Oxford to Newnham in an hir'd Post Chaise.

Tuesday, the 15th A roast Leg of Mutton for Din. Lyon & Ragman[10] got out of the Vineyard into the Lammas Close. Took my Neice, my Nephew, & Mrs Rock to the Crofts. Sent Thomas Williams to Thame Market with the old Bull, but he was not Sold. Begun brewing.

Wednesday, the 16th Ballanc'd Accounts with Mr Clarke in Relation to my Lord's Affairs, but no Money was forthcoming. Howse planted Potatoes in the Orchard. Thomas Williams began docktring four Horses for the Mange.

Thursday, the 17th Br at Oxford. Invited Mr Lawrence [f.35^{v}] to dine with me next Sunday with both his Sons. Sent my Sister Rock a Letter. Fish from the Locks for Din. The Taylor brought Home my Breeches & took them back to alter.

Friday, the 18th A Letter from Birch. Part of a Ham for Dinner & Mr Lawrence's Eldest Son din'd here. Had some serious Conversation with my Neice about the Loss of her Son & her Conduct towards her Children.

Saturday, the 19th Met Birch at Caldecot A Pig for Dinner. Howse brought from Abingdon a Leg of Veal. Settl'd two Years Tythes with Dame Andrews.

Sunday, the 20th Sent my Lord Harcourt a Letter. Mr Lawrence & his Son din'd here. Self & Thomas Willams went to [f.36^{r}] Forewood before Din. No Psalm at Evening Prayers.

Monday, the 21st Mr Lawrence took his Wife, Boy & Mrs Rock away with him to Dine at Dorchester. Self brought things away from Caldecot & had many Words with Birch whose Behaviour was very extraordinary. Sold the Bottles to the hardware Man. Return'd to Dinner. Thomas Williams sold the Bull at Abingdon. Bett Barns went Home not very well.

Tuesday, the 22nd Br with Mr Bush at Burcoat, & Mr Jennings call[ed] here in his way for London as I was agoing away. Din'd at Henly. Laid at the little House at Salt Hill, & had pickle Salmon for Sup.

Wednesday, the 23rd Set out about 4 o'Clock in the Mor[ning] & Br at Mortimer Street. Drank Tea with Lord Harcourt. Din'd with Admiral [f.36^{v}] Long. N.P. St George's Hanover Sq. Took an Evening Walk beyond Mary le Bonne Church, & went to view Whitefield's Tabernackle.[11]

Thursday, the 24th [Ascension Day] M.P. Berwick St Chapple. Bought Hay & Straw at the Hay Market.[12] Gave Admiral Long an offer of one or both my Horses by his Housekeeper.

Friday, the 25th Mr Cowden came here to let me know 2 o'Clock N. would be the Hour for me to wait on his Lordship. After Din Self waited on my Lord Harcourt, & Self made a great Mistake in my Account.

Saturday, the 26th Mr Cowden went with me to Mr Henton the Banker, & Self receiv'd of Him on my Sister Rock's [Account] [f.37^{r}] £191 12s. 6d. We also went to the South Sea & East India House.[13] Bought an Order for thirteen Tickets for £134 9s. 6d. including Brokerage. Call'd on Birch & he would not allow for the Plasterer's Bill & so I paid him no Rent. Settl'd Accounts with the Right Honourable the Earl Harcourt for my Sister Rock & Self.

Sunday, the 27th Self Br at Harrow on the Hill. M. & N.P. Harrow Church.[14] Din'd at the Ordinary.[15] Return'd Home to Tea. Found in the Road a Horse Card, & hid it in the Hedge.

Monday, the 28th M.P. St James's. Begun washing. Wrote out my Bill for my Lord [f.37^{v}] Harcourt to sign & also an Acknowledgement of having receiv'd £57 15s. 3d.

Tuesday, the 29th M.P. St James. Took the Landau side window to have a new Glass put in it. Din'd at Ilford & had much Wet. Paid Mr Noyes at Barking Money due to him from the late Mr Rock, but he could not sign'd the Receipt.

Self fell from my Horse & if my foot providentially had not slipt out of the Spring Stirrup, my Leg might have been broke, but thanks to God, Self receiv'd no Hurt. Alass I might have been greatly damag'd & hurt by the [f.38^{r}] Fall, but as I receiv'd no Harm on that Occassion, may [I] retain a due & gratefull Sense of the Mercy. To have been brought Home with a broken Bone might have given me & my Friends much Pain & Uneassiness, but to escape unhurt was a signal Blessing. May I never offend thee, O my God, by neglect[ing] to be truly thankfull to thee, for any of thy present & saving Mercies & Deliverances. When I have escaped any impendent Danger, let me not make slight of it, or impute it my own Ability, but to thy timely interposition. We live in the [f.38^{v}] Neighbourhood of strange & melancholy Evils & Disasters, & when they were just ready to seize on us, & yet by some unexpected Event, we have escap'd them, we have the greatest Reason to be thankfull to Providence, & to adore his indulgence towards us.

Its a pleasant thing to be blest with a gratefull Mind. When we pass over Mercies receiv'd from God & take no Notice of them, we not only offend Him & render ourselves unworth his further Protection, but we loose the Pleasure & Delight naturally arising in the Soul from the Practice of Praises & Thanksgiving.

[f.39^{r}]

To reflect on past Deliverances, if we have not been unthankfull for them, is a cheerfull & pleasant Employment. To recollect our many Escapes from great Dangers & Embarrissment (if we have not been wanting on our Part, to render our most devout & holy Praises to God for them) will exhilerate the Spirits, & suppress all gloomy & melancholy Thought to arise. In a Word, would we enjoy a cheerfull mind, let us practice the Duty of Thanksgiving for all God's Mercies & Deliverances bestow'd on Us, & then we may hope to be in Favour with Him, & at Rest in Ourselves.

[f.39^{v}]

Ingratitude is branded with the highest Degree of Infamy & ye worst Character any man can have, & renders ye Person guilty of it, odious in the Sight of God & man. May I never fall into this Sin, but practice the Duty of Gratitude with the greatest cheerfullness & delight.

Shall I receive favours from ye hands of God & not be thankfull for them, shall terrible Dangers threaten on every side & shall he deliver [me] out of them all & shall I neglect to be truly thankfull for them, I hope not?

Its my desire to please God, & while I retain a due & gratefull Sense of his manyfold Goodness, I trust, I shall be in favour [with] Him, & that's enough for Me.

[f.40^{r}]

Wednesday, the 30th M.P. Conduit St Chapple. Went to the Coachmaker in upper Mount St & paid him for Repairing the Landau.[16] Call'd at my Lord Harcourt's twice before Din but not at Home.

Thursday, the 31st Went with my Sister Rock in the Landeau to Miss Bush's Lodging Fleet Street, & show'd Thomas the Way to Mrs Lally's at St John's Chapple. Took a turn in the Park before Din. Sister paid Mrs Maw a Visit. Advertis'd Horses & the poor Woman of Drayton in the White Hall Evening Post. Rode to Mr Lally's at Paddington, but he was not at Home.

Notes

1 Material in parentheses was crossed out in the original.
2 Material in parentheses was crossed out in the original.
3 Material in parentheses was crossed out in the original.
4 JN corrected a slip here: six is crossed out and five is written thickly over it. On occasions he wrote his diary entries several days at a time, allowing him to forget!
5 Confusion continued with the dates. There are numerous alterations, but these events clearly refer to Monday 7 May.
6 The boy was John, son of James and Dinah. The child was buried 16 March 1767.
7 The child was also called Edmond.
8 Nineveh was one of the estate farms. It still exists.
9 This was St Martin's church. For full details see *Encycl. Oxford*, p. 409.
10 Lyon and Ragman were two of JN's horses.
11 The tabernacle was built in 1756 for George Whitefield, the Methodist preacher, so was new feature for JN to see. The building was extended in 1760 with a capacity for up to 8,000 people. For full details see *London Encycl.*, p. 958.
12 In the seventeenth and eighteenth centuries, a haymarket was literally an important market for hay and straw. For full details see *ibid.*, pp. 370–1.
13 South Sea House was in Threadneedle Street. It was once the headquarters of the South Sea Trading Company, the collapse of whose schemes ruined many investors in the South Sea Bubble of 1720. East India House was in Leadenhall Street and was the main office of the East India Company. JN made a prudent investment here as the Company flourished during the eighteenth century. The premises were built in 1726 and enlarged in 1799. For full details see *ibid.*, pp. 799–800, 250.
14 The church referred to was St Mary's on the Hill. For full details see *ibid.*, p. 737.
15 This may have been The King's Head inn which was rebuilt after a fire in 1750. See *ibid.*, p. 368.
16 This was Thorn & Co. Coachmakers, Upper Mount Street, Grosvenor Square. See Mortimer, *Universal Director*, Part II, p. 24.

[f.40^{v}]

June 1759

Friday, the 1st M.P. St James's. Went to Princes Street Cofe.[1] Went with my Sister Rock to the East India House & was most agreeably surpris'd. She was intitl'd to one hundred Pound Stock & have a Year's Interest more than She Expected. Bought at Ludgate Punch H[ouse][2] One Gallon of Rum. Tea at the Turk's Head Cofe.[3]

Saturday, the 2nd M.P. St James's. Bought Flowers at Covent Garden. Advertiz'd in the Gaserteer for A———.[4] Bought half a Load of Hay. Chang'd at the Bank a £10 Note. [f.41^{r}] Din'd at Admiral Long's. Took Sister Polly with me into Hyde Park.

Sunday, the 3rd [Whit Sunday] Sacr^{t} at Berwick St Chapple & went there with Surtut Coat[5] as it rain'd. N.P. Berwick St. went into Hyde Park. Walk't with Admiral Long & another Gentleman on the Pavement.

Monday, the 4th Went to Leicester Fields to see the fine Courtiers.[6] Din'd near the same Place & treated two more, & also a third at another Place & went with that Person to Lodging at Swallow St Meeting.[7]

Tuesday, the 5th Rec'd two Letters at Prince's St Coffe H. & found She was [f.41^{v}] gone into the Country. Wrote in Answer to them & deliver'd my Letter myself. Bought a Watch Ribbon. Lord Harcourt Family went out of Town. Bought a Bottle of Strawberries & the woman cheeted me out of 1d.

Wednesday, the 6th Br at Islington Wells.[8] Went to Newington Church[9] just as Pr[ayers] were done. Came home by Way of Hackney & met with much Whet.

Thursday, the 7th Advertising my Horses & the poor Drayton Woman. Enquir'd at Cornhill about Annuities for my [Sister] Rock & Mrs Rock of Oxford.[10]

Friday, the 5th Br at Islington Wells. Pr at Stoke Newington Church. [f.42^{r}] Went round by Hackney. Sent George to Mr Hardwicke for things. Self broke a Phial of Lavender water. In the Evening Self went to Chelsea.

Saturday, the 9th Self went with Sister Rock in my Landau to Miss Bush's Lodging, & Self footed it from thence to the Bank & took up my thirteen Tickets & then return'd for my Sister. Gave Polly a turn in Hyde Park. Got the handle of my Landau mended. Admiral Long & Mr——— drank Tea here.

Sunday, the 10th [Trinity Sunday] Br at Richmond Cofe. M.P. at Richmond[11] & then went to Kew & saw the new Bridge[12] & on my return went into the Garden. Din'd at the [f.42^{v}] Ordinary. N.P. & slept most part of the Sermon wch was not right. Tea at Cofe. The Oystler made Thomas pay 1s. for ye Hay of two Horses, return'd Home at Night.

Monday, the 11th M.P. St James's. A Person from the Bank came to see me desiring to have one of my Tickets for another Person, but Self did not gratifie Him. Admiral Long went out of Town.

Tuesday, the 12th Br at Islington Wells. Rode to Hampstead & Highgate & home to Din. M.P. St James. Went to the White Horse Cellar with a Letter for my Housekeeper. Saw a pretty Woman who lives at Hampton Oxfordshire. Spoke to Major Bates who was bound for Cockthropt.[13]

[f.43^{r}]

Wednesday, the 13th Heard a Sermon preach'd at St Lawrence's Church[14] in the City being the annual Feast of the Marine Society.[15] Din'd near the Royal Exchange. A Letter from Betty, but no Account of seeing the stray Horses. Rec'd the Collar from Newnham. Enquir'd into Mary Hall's Character & it was very good, but could not find Her out.

Thursday, the 14th Bought Coffee & Tea for my Self & one Pound of Coffee for my Self. Left an Account of my Stray Horses with the Painter.

Sister Rock went to see Ladyday Reed in my Landau. A Turbet for Dinner. George's Mother brought Him some things.

[f.43^{V}]

Friday, the 15th M.P. St Anne's. No Letters at Cofe. Took my Leave of Admiral Long & he complimented me with a Gazette Extraordinary. George not being very well rode with me in the Landau part of the Way. Din'd at Colnbrook. Laid at Maiden Head Bridge. Went to the Top of the Mount in the Church Yard[16] & near it stands a large old House.

Saturday, the 16th Set out before the Landau. Br at Benson. Talkt to Padbury about a Post Chariot. Reach'd Newnham between one & two N. Self, Betty & George went about the new Glebe.

[f.44^{r}]

Sunday, the 17th Sent Mr Bowley the Gazette Extraordinary. Self, Thomas Williams & George went to Forwood before Dinner. After Evening Service Self & Thomas rode almost to Oxford. Drank Tea at my Neice's & her Aunt & Mrs Lannyan was there. Samuel Lawrence was this day font breach'd[17] & look'd mighty well. Left Hat to be clean'd.

Monday, the 18th Lord Harcourt & Family came to Newnham. My Neice & her Eldest Son[18] set out for Bristol with her Maid.

Tuesday, the 19th Self Br at the great House & afterwards & went with my [f.44^{V}] Lord to the Crofts & there the Platform of my new intended House was laid out. Jackson mow'd down some of the Wheat & my Lord gave him something.

Wednesday, the 20th Draw'd Stones for ye Parsonage House from the late Mrs Costard's House. Met my Lord at the New Town[19] & he said nothing to me about not taking up the tythe Hay, but afterward told the Tything man that as I had been taking some of the Tythe, I might take All.

Thursday, the 21st Sent Thomas Silvester to Abingdon with one Letter for my Sister Rock & another for Mary Hall.

[f.45r]

Friday, the 22nd Calves Head for Din. Mr Nash of Sutton with three Gentlemen more came here & self shew'd them the Situation of my new House.

Saturday, the 23rd Br at Oxford. Call'd on Mrs Rock & Mr Lawrence. M.P. Carfax. Put up at the Wheat Sheaf[20] & had Lyon sho'd all round. Bought Materials for a Waistcoat. Spoke to a Baldwin Boy at Mr Austin's. The Housekeeper lash'd George Brookes for Breaking one of the Pig's Back.

Sunday, the 24th Self & Thomas Williams went to Forewood before Din. A Loin of Veal for Din & sent Bab [f.45v] Whyatt some of it.

Monday, the 25th Went to the Baldwin Taylor[21] before Br with Materials for a Waistcoat & Knucle of Veal for Din.

Tuesday, the 26th Met Mr Bush & his Son near his House. Put a Letter in the Post House at Dorchester for Mary Hall. Rode to Newington & call'd on Mrs Jones & found Lady Reed was with Her.

Wednesday, the 27th Elizabeth Overton having defrauded [me] of Wine, Strong Beer, Brand[y], Rum, Rack & Gin allow'd me £3 13s. 8½d. towards the aforesaid Damage.

[f.46r]

Thursday, the 28th Self, George, & Bett went to the Locks for a Jack. Draw'd from Caldecot to Newnham Coals & Bricks.

Friday, the 29th The Callar Maker did some Jobs & he was paid his Bill. Beacon, Chine & two Pidgeons for Din.

Saturday, the 30th Br at Oxford. Saw a Woman at Smith which I lik'd. Paid for cleaning Hat, bought George a pair of Stockings. Self & Howse farmn'd out the Tool House. Paid off Elizabeth Overton for Good & the same Day Mary Hall enter'd my Service in her Room.

Notes

1 This coffee house was in Soho and was a favourite haunt of James Boswell. For full details, Lillywhite, *Coffee Houses*, p. 459.

2 This was the London Punch House, Ludgate Hill. For full details see February 1759, note 21.

3 This is most likely the Turks's Head at 142 The Strand, opposite Catherine Street. Boswell gave details of it in his *London Journal*. However, the Turk's Head was a popular title for coffee houses and taverns. In London alone there were over fifty. Thus, without the name of the proprietor, we cannot be sure where JN had his tea. See Lillywhite, *Coffee Houses*, pp. 602–17.

4 This is mysterious. JN left a definite blank in the *Diary*. Was he doing something he shouldn't have been?

5 A surtout is a greatcoat or overcoat. See OED.

6 Leicester Fields was an area in Leicester Square, south of Leicester House. It was a fashionable place, yet popular also with the *demi-monde*. See *London Encycl.*, pp. 451–3.

7 A liaison with a lady may be involved here, but we cannot be certain of JN's activities.

8 This was Islington Spa or New Tunbridge Wells, a spa opposite Saddler's Wells. The healing properties of the water were famous from the late seventeenth century. By 1759 it was a well-known resort with lime walks, arbours, coffee rooms, dancing and lottery 'sheds', frequented by royalty and polite society. There were daily public breakfasts which JN often attended and as many as 1600 people took the waters in a day. For full details see *London Encycl.*, p. 414.

9 The church referred to was St Mary's in Stoke Newington, built in 1563. See *ibid.*, p. 748.

10 Presumably he made these enquiries at the Royal Exchange.

11 This was St Mary Magdalen church, largely rebuilt in 1750, thus new when JN worshipped there. See *London Encycl.*, pp. 647, 742.

12 The new bridge in Kew was an eleven-span wooden bridge, built in 1758–9 by John Barnard and so 'new' to JN. In 1782, Robert Tunstall obtained permission to build a stone bridge downstream of the old one. This was designed by James Paine and completed on 22 September 1789. It was opened with a procession led by George III. This structure was replaced in 1884–9. The present bridge dates from 1903. For full details see *ibid.*, p. 430; S. Croad, *London's Bridges* (1983).

13 This is Cockethorpe Park, Oxfordshire, which was begun in 1709 for Sir Simon Harcourt, grandson of the first earl. See Sherwood & Pevsner, *Oxfordshire*, pp. 633–4.

14 The church referred to was St Lawrence Jewry in Gresham Street. It was a twelfth-century church, burned in the great fire and rebuilt by Wren in 1671–7. It was rebuilt again in 1954–7 after bomb damage in 1940. See

London Encycl., p. 729.

15 The Marine Society was instituted in 1754 by Fowler Walker and others for the purpose of training poor boys to go to sea. For full details see *London Past and Present*, II, p. 470.

16 The churchyard belonged to the church of St Michael. The large old house JN refers to is an L-shaped half-timbered fifteenth-century gatehouse, probably a chantry house. See *Victoria, Berkshire*, III, pp. 107–9.

17 By 'font breached' JN meant christened.

18 The eldest son was Samuel Lawrence.

19 The construction of the new cottages on each side of the Oxford to Henley road was already under way. JN refers to these as the 'New Town'.

20 This was the Wheatsheaf in St Aldates, also known as The Wheatsheaf and Anchor. See *Jackson's*, 31 January 1759.

21 The Baldwin Taylor was the tailor at Marsh Baldon, a neighbouring village to Nuneham.

Plate 2 (top left) Simon, 1st Earl Harcourt, by Joshua Reynolds; by kind permission of The Hon. Mrs Gascoigne (photograph, Courtauld Institute of Art)

Plate 3 (top right) Lord Nuneham, later 2nd Earl Harcourt, by Joshua Reynolds; by kind permission of The Hon. Mrs Gascoigne (photograph, Courtauld Institute of Art)

Plate 4 (left) Lady Elizabeth 'Betty' Harcourt, by Paul Sandby; by kind permission of The Hon. Mrs Gascoigne (photograph, Courtauld Institute of Art)

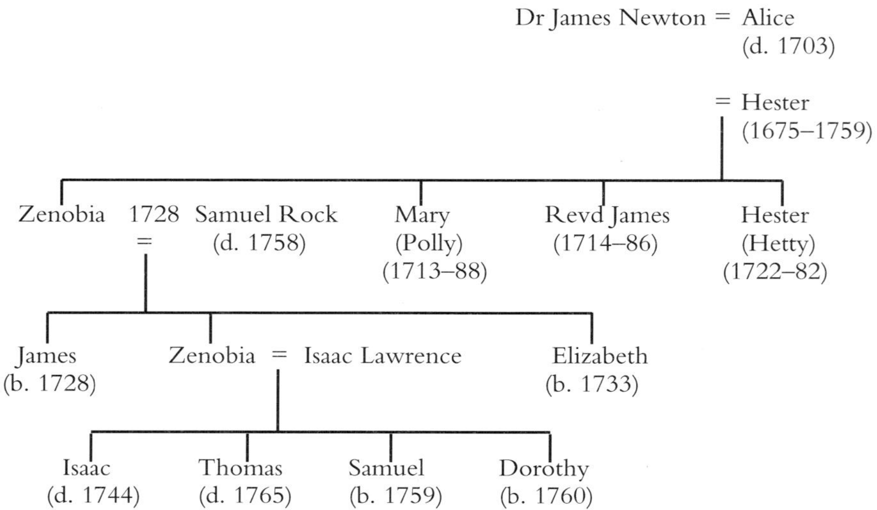

Plate 5 The Newton family tree

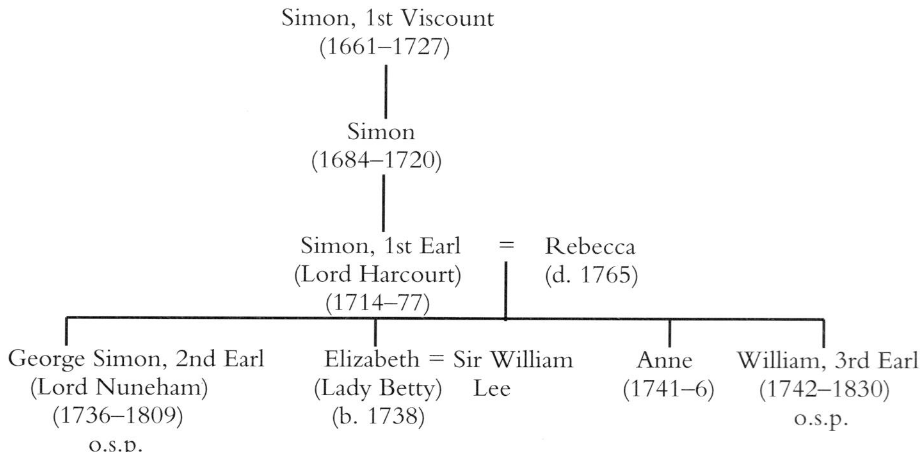

Plate 6 The Harcourt family tree

Plate 7 Nuneham Park from the south-west, by Paul Sandby; by kind permission of The Hon. Mrs Gascoigne (photograph, Courtauld Institute of Art)

Plate 8 A view of the north side of Nuneham church, by Paul Sandby; by kind permission of The Hon. Mrs Gascoigne (photograph, Courtauld Institute of Art)

Plate 9 Nuneham Park from Lock Cottages, by Paul Sandby; by kind permission of The Hon. Mrs Gascoigne (photograph, Courtauld Institute of Art)

Plate 10 The new church at Nuneham, by Paul Sandby; by kind permission of The Hon. Mrs Gascoigne (photograph, Courtauld Institute of Art)

[f.46v]

July 1759

Sunday, the 1st Pray'd by Dame Andrews. Thomas Williams took Elizabeth Overton's Baggage to Oxford. Thomas Silvester & Self went to Forewood. A Shoulder of Mutton for Din.

Monday, the 2nd Snub'd Thomas Silvester for not keeping George Brooks in Order & after he had been with me to Oxford, he was for going away. Rode to Oxford the Day, the Chancellor[1] made his publick Entrance, & bought some Hops of Mr Lawrence.

Tuesday, the 3rd Went to Oxford in my Landau [f.47r] & Br at the Coffee House. Din'd at the King's Head Ordinary.[2] Drank Tea at Mr Lawrence's & stay'd there till it was too late for the Oratorio. The Oystler over charg'd for the Horses & so Thomas came away with[out] any Payment.

Wednesday, the 4th Call'd at Mr Lawrence's for a Quart of Oyl. Set down at the Theatre.[3] Walkt about St John's & Wadham College Gardens. Saw Parson Griffith who cut his Throat, but did not speak to Him. Return'd Home to Din. Took to the Place House Rasberries & Cherries.

[f.47v]

Thursday, the 5th Din'd at Mr Lawrence's with Mrs Rock & Lannyan, & then we went to the Messiah[4] at the Theatre & Self treated Mrs Rock. Self accommodated Dr Patten with my Seat for the Sake of sitting next to the Widow. Gibson, George Brooks & Self saw a strange Light in the Sky in the Crofts.

Friday, the 6th Rec'd a Letter from Polly. Br at the great House. Draw'd Hay out of Lord's Mead. Cold Leg of Mutton for Din. Lord Hyde laid Here & two Servants.

Saturday, the 7th Br at Oxford. Had some Conversation [f.48r] with the Oxford Coachman about a new Post Chaise. Went to St John's Gardens. Spoke to Mr Webb, & invited Him to dine with me to morrow.

Cucumber & Bread & Butter for Din at the black Horse.[5] Heard the Italian Performers at the Theatre.[6] Advertised Mare & Horse.[7]

Sunday, the 8th Thomas Williams & Self went to Forewood before Din. A Calve's Head for Din & gave the Butcher a pint of Ale. Lord Harcourt & Family went away. Sent Thomas to Abingdon with a Letter for Sister Rock. Lent Master Field a Saddle.

[f.48v]

Monday, the 9th Wanted Edmund Baker to prop up my Rick, but he was in an hurry to go for Abingdon, but Howse did it very well with the Vessel Slider. Employed the Lame Man of Baldwin about the Hay. Leg of Veal boil'd for Din & Self had Scotch scollops,[8] & sent Bab Whyatt some of them.

Tuesday, the 10th Draw'd Hay to Anderson's Rick Yard. Sign'd at Anderson's the Briefs. Minc'd Veal for Din.

Wednesday, the 11th Br at Oxford. Saw the Gibson at the new Church, High Street.[9] Had a new Lash to my Whip & young Carpenter saw a fellow ride my [f.49r] Horse at Oxford. Enquir'd after a Man Servant. Begun digging the Foundation of my New Parsonage House.

Thursday, the 12th Went to Caldecot to pay Mr Birch but he had been paid by my Sister. Spoke to Elizabeth Wickes about send[ing] her Sister to the Hospital. Bought two Calves Bags.

Friday, the 13th Din'd at Watlington[10] & found Mr Harris's first Wife was living, for I search'd the Register. Rode with Dr Beacon part of the Way. Return'd Home to Tea.

Saturday, the 14th Br at Oxford. Paid Mr Pinnel for Officiating for me at Newnham. Bath'd in the River. Jackson finish'd mowing my Hyde.

[f.49v]

Sunday, the 15th Self & Thomas Silvester went to Forewood & turn'd my Lord's Bullocks out of Longmead. A roast Fowl for Din. Settl'd with Thomas about his Wages.

Monday, the 16th Heard violent Thundering before I was up.[11] Sent Thomas Williams to Abingdon for Bran. Sent Dame Fields Sister to make Hay. The great Trough remov'd into the Pig Yard.

Tuesday, the 17th Paid Thomas Silvester his Wages. Came late with a Load of Hay & made them Eat & Drink.

Wednesday, the 18th Backside sore & I could not ride. Baith'd in the River. [f.50r] Paid Ball's Bill, & he talk'd of raising Price of Shoing, & Self sold him a Lott of old Iron. Snub'd Jackson for coming after 6 o'Clock to work.

Thursday, the 19th Thomas Anderson came to me about a Field Keeper. Thomas Silvester got a Vessel of Water from the River. After Br Self set out in my Landau for London. Din'd at Nettlebed[12] & met there a Gentleman of Abingdon. Supt at Maiden Head Bridge.

Friday, the 20th Set out about 5 o'Clock M. & Br at Turnham Green[13] & the Landerdess[14] charg'd 1d. for Bason [f.50v] of Water & a Towel. Call'd at Mr Arnold's Lodging, but he was at London. Call'd at Prince's St Cofe but no Letters. Took to Newgate Street an Advertisement for———.[15] Got to Mortimer Street to Din. Admiral Long, Mr Arnold, Miss Tellure & another Lady drank Tea here.

Saturday, the 21st Settl'd some Accounts with my Sister Rock. Thomas got the Handles of the Landau mended. The Maid wash'd a Shirt for George. My foot better than it was yesterday. Kept at Home all Day.

[f.51r]

Sunday, the 22nd Br at Richmond Cofe & Din'd at my Inn. Heard two Charity Sermons & saw Mr Way & his Wife at Church.[16] After Morning Service rode to Kew & after Eve Service drank Tea at the Cofe & then set of for London.

Monday, the 23rd Br at Islington Wells. Spoke to Mrs Downing at Clerkenwell Church.[17] Sisters went to pay a Visit at Clerkenwell. Rec'^{d} a Letter from my Bailiff about pounding Asses at Clifton.

Tuesday, the 24th Call'd at the Cofe, but no Letters. Br at Islington Wells & when from thence to the Charter House to M.P.[18] Went to Mrs Pickerings. Made [f.51^{V}] enquiry about a Lodging for Tetty.

Wednesday, the 25th Br at Islington Wells. M.P. at Stoke Newington.[19] Convers'd with a Spaniard in Queen Elizabeth's Walk aged 102. Din'd at Admiral Long's with a Physcian & his Daughter.

Thursday, the 26th Br at Islington Wells. Sent the Bishop of Oxford a Letter. Went to Hackney Church,[20] but no Prayers there. Saw Mrs Ayres at Admiral Longs.

Friday, the 27th Br Islington Wells, & spoke to the Widow Pont for the first Time. M.P. Hackney. Admiral Long Came here & invited me to dine with him ye next Day.

Saturday, the 28th Br at Islington Wells. Rode [f.52^{r}] to Highgate, & then return'd back again for Drs Common & there search'd for Counsellor Pont's Will & found he died in Clarkenwell without a Will. Bought Hay & Straw. Din'd with Admiral Long & he talk't to [me] very roughly about my Sisters Affairs.

Sunday, the 29th M.P. at great Queen St Chapple[21] & came home in my Landau by the Way of Paddington. M.P. Mary le bone, & stay'd in the Church Yard before Service begun. Mrs Pickering din'd here. Poppit went lame his Shoe being bad.

[f.52^{V}]

Monday, the 30th Br at Islington Wells & had some small Conversation with the Widow Ponte, but seem'd not to like my Conversation. M.P. The Charterhouse. Rode to Highgate & Hampstead. Sister Tetty went to the D^{r}. N.P. Conduit St Chapple.

Tuesday, the 31st Made a short stay at the Well, as the Widow Ponte was not there, & return'd Home to Br. Admiral Long sent the Horse

Home & talkt to me about my Sisters Affairs. Went to Twynings for Tea. No Letters at the Cofe. Sister Tetty had a very bad Fit.

Notes

1 John Fane, Earl of Westmorland, Chancellor of 1759–62, was born in 1686 and educated at Eton College, Lincoln's Inn and Emmanuel College, Cambridge. He served as MP for Hythe from 1708 to 1711 and for Buckingham between 1727 and 1734. He became an Honorary D.C.L. of Oxford, as well as being High Steward. Horace Walpole writes of his 'coronation' at Oxford. The election was held on Thursday 4 January 1759, in which he defeated Richard Trevor, Bishop of Durham. The previous Chancellor, the Earl of Arran, had died on Saturday 16 December 1758. See *Jackson's*.

2 The King's Head was in Oxford High Street.

3 The theatre referred to is the Sheldonian Theatre, which was built in 1663–9. It was commissioned by Gilbert Sheldon, Archbishop of Canterbury, and designed by the young Christopher Wren, at that time Savilian Professor of Astronomy. See *Encycl. Oxford*, p. 430; Sherwood and Pevsner, *Oxfordshire*, pp. 255–6.

4 This performance was part of a week of Handelian music. Handel died in London on 4 April 1759, so there may have been a memorial element here. However, it seems more likely that the concerts were to honour the new Chancellor, the Earl of Westmorland. Tuesday 3 July saw a performance of *Samson*; on Wednesday 4 July, *Esther* was given, followed by *Messiah* the next day, 'by a numerous Band from London and other Places'. The principal vocal parts were taken by Signora Frasi, Miss Brent, Messrs Beard, Champness and Hudson, from London, supported by Master Norris of Salisbury. Tickets were obtainable from Mr Cross's Music Shop and at coffee houses, price 5s. See *Jackson's*, Saturday June 16 1759; Saturday June 23 1759.

5 This is the Black Horse in St Clement's. The seventeenth-century timbered building is still there. It became a hotel in 1937. See *Encycl. Oxford*, p. 43.

6 This performance involved an Italian Orchestra and singers. The opera *Ciro*, in three acts, was given by Signora Mattei, Signora Caloni, Signor Tenducci and Signor Quilici. The first violin was a Mr Pinto and the concert was conducted by Signor Cocchi, who had written much of the music. Between the opera's acts were numerous concertos and solo items. See *Jackson's*, Saturday 30 June 1759.

7 JN advertized for two missing horses last seen in Garsington Common and Stadhampton. One had belonged to the late Dr Durham, President of St John's College and was a present from Lord Lichfield. See *Jackson's*, 7 July 1759.

8 Scotch scollops were slices of meat cut up into small pieces.

9 The church referred to was All Saints church, built in 1706–8. It is now the library of Lincoln College. See *Encycl. Oxford*, pp. 10–11; Sherwood and Pevsner, *Oxfordshire*, pp. 287–9.
10 Watlington is an ancient market town. JN could have dined at the Georgian inn, now The Hare and Hounds. See *ibid.*, pp. 829–32.
11 This was obviously a bad storm. Fourteen sheep were killed by lightning at Woodstock. See *Jackson's*, 16 July 1759.
12 JN dined either at The Bull inn or at The Peacock. See *Jackson's*; Sherwood and Pevsner, *Oxfordshire*, p. 714.
13 For full details see *London Encycl.*, p. 895.
14 By 'Landerdess' JN meant landlady.
15 Another mysterious entry. See June 1759, note 4.
16 The church referred to was St Mary's church. See *London Encycl.*, p. 647.
17 This was St James's church Clerkenwell. For full details see February 1759, note 23.
18 The Charterhouse was a former Carthusian monastery founded in 1370. By the time JN used it, it was a school. See *London Encycl.*, pp. 141–2.
19 This was St Mary's church. See *ibid.*, p. 748.
20 The church referred to was St Augustine's church, now St John's. See *ibid.*, p. 723.
21 This chapel was built between 1693 and 1706 and occupied the greater portion of three houses – numbers 66–8 Great Queen Street. Its early history is 'shrouded in obscurity' and there are no references to services there in 1728–58. Hence JN's visit must be one of the earliest recorded. It was run by the Reverend Thomas Francklyn from June 1758 until his death in 1784. The chapel became a Wesleyan meeting house and flourished during the nineteenth century. It was destroyed in 1910. See *Survey of London*, L. Gomme and P. Norman (eds.) (1914), V, pp. 86–92.

August 1759

Wednesday, the 1st Set out after Br & din'd [f.53r] about 5 Miles short of Windsor on cold boil Beef. The Garden by the River is pretty enough. Got time enough to Windsor for Tea. Call'd at the Boat House after I had been at Eaton[1] & the Landerdess had got another Husband. Walk'd about the Terras. A Pidgeon for Supper.

Thursday, the 2nd M.P. Cathedral.[2] View'd the inside of the Castle[3] before Br & then set out for Henly & went a little out of the Way. Din'd at Nettlebed. Bailed the Horses at Benson & drank Tea there. Thomas drove pretty brisk from thence to Dorchester & crack'd [f.53v] the Foreglass it's likely at that Time. Got Home about 8 o'Clock Nt.

Friday, the 3rd Begun Harvest. A Robin perch't several times on my Head in the Parlour. Sent Bab Whyatt a roast Pidgeon for Dinner. Paid off Thomas Silvester.

Saturday, the 4th Br with my Neice. M.P. Carfax. Bought a Lobster. Enquir'd into a Fellow's Character at the Chequers in high Street.[4] Return'd Home to Dinner. Barr clean'd out. Pitson grub'd up two Cherry Trees in the Orchard. Brought up much bitter Stuff soon after I arose.

[f.54r]

Sunday, the 5th Sent Thomas Williams to Bray after the little Mare. Fish for Din, a present of the plowboys. Sent Bab Whyatt some Beacon. Poppit & Wantage got out of Longmead.

Monday, the 6th Thomas Williams return'd Home with the Mare. The Asses got into Clifton Pound.[5] A roast Cock for Din. Dr Beacon made me a short Visit. Made Praperation for brewing. Thomas Williams & his Boy went to Clifton for the Asses, but came without Them.

Tuesday, the 7th Brew'd four Bushel of Malt into Ale & Small Beer. The Remainder of the Cock drest for Din & Self sent part of it to Andrews.

[f.54^{v}]

Wednesday, the 8th A thine Congregation. Boil Pidgeons & Beacon for Din. Sent Pitson to the Asses in Clifton Pound with Grass.

Thursday, the 9th Br at Oxford. Buttons put to a Saddle. Went with Mr Trollope to Steward's & there he read the Extraordinary Gazette. M.P. St John's. Left an Advertisement for a Man at Jacksons.[6]

Friday, the 10th Bath'd twice in the River. Beans, Carrots, & Beacon for Din. None but Children at Prayers except Self & the Clarke.

Saturday, the 11th Br at Abingdon. M.P. D^{O} Went to Mr Yeateman about my Asses [f.55^{r}] in Clifton Pound. Went to Sutton [Sutton Courtenay] about the Apple Money, but found Emery, who bought them, had been Dead about half a Year. Rode home by the way of Long Whitenham [Long Wittenham]. Treated all my Labourers with plenty of Ale. Bath'd in the River.

Sunday, the 12th William Field & another made an Estimate of the Damage done by my Asses at Clifton. The Cows got out of Long Mead.

Monday, the 13th Begun making a Wheat Rick at Tom Anderson's. Us'd one of my Lord's Teams. The Cart Ladder could not be found. James Lawrence cut down a Tree in the rong Place. Nine Load of Wheat from Forewood. [f.55^{v}] And five from Nineveh.

Tuesday, the 14th Finish'd the first Wheat Rick & begun another. Lord Harcourt came here, & I believe, Sent Dame Andrews some Pudding.

Wednesday, the 15th Finish'd the second Wheat Rick & begun a little one in my lower Yard. Sent Winter & his Wife to reap Beans. William Clarke finish'd my last Land of Wheat.

Thursday, the 16th Bath'd twice in the River. A Carriage kill'd a small Hog by going over his Head. The old white Cock almost kill'd in fighting, & the Housekeeper kill'd him quick. Pounded a Sow & two Pigs out of Windmill Field.

[f.56^{r}]

Friday, the 17th Ball begun mowing Barly in Forewood, & in the Evening Self rode there by the way of the Ball.[7] Boil Pidgeon & Beacon for Din.

Saturday, the 18th Br at Oxford. M.P. Carfax. Call'd on my Neice. Paid one Year's Land & Window Tax being £29 6s. 4d. due at Lady day 1758. Mr Faquier spoke to me at my Parlour window. Had Breeches mended. Bought a Calves Head.

Sunday, the 19th Ladyday Harcourt at M.P. & sent Bab Whyatt, & Andrews some has'd Calves Head. After N.P. Self set out for London, & laid at Stoken Church.[8]

Monday, the 20th Br at the Crown at Uxbridge. [f.56^{V}] Din'd at Acton & the Cook seemn'd to be a breeding & Came from Witney. Reach'd Mortimer St by Tea time.

Tuesday, the 21st Went to Emery the Cyder Merchant, but gone into the Country. Took up a £10 Note at the Bank. Self Sister Rock, Polly, Mrs Whiteman & Dunning din'd with Hetty at her Lodging at Islington. Call'd at Dunning's.

Wednesday, the 22nd The Maid carried my Baggage to my Inn. After Br set out for Newnham & din'd at Gerard's Cross. Supt in the Kitchen at Highwickham. Took Notice of the handsome Parsonage House.

Thursday, the 23rd Br at Tetworth [Tetsworth][9] & there heard [f.57^{r}] a Confirmation of the good News of the Prussians beating the Russians.[10] The old Woman at the three Kings hath left her House. Reach'd Home in good Health about 1 Clock N. & am Thankfull to Providence for this Mercy.

Friday, the 24th Draw'd Oats from Sermons, & Furze out of the Common to lay at the Bottom of a Bean Rick. Field & Ball cocking Barly like two Rogues with two Rakes only. Boil Pork for Din. Order'd the Vetches to be cock'd.

Saturday, the 25th Begun a Bean Rick. Remov'd the Wheat in the Barn. Pretty Whet before I got out of the [f.57^{v}] Field. Sold Casey all the Cut Furze Faggots in Forewood at 14s. pr Hun[dred] in the Place. A Letter from Polly. My old Beldame drank some Wine out of the Bottle. Tap't a Vessel of Ale.

Sunday, the 26th Sent Thomas Williams to Abingdon with a Letter from Polly. Rec'^{d} One from Mr Goldwin about old Brown, my Horse. Went to Forewood before Din. Sent Whyatt some Fowl.

Monday, the 27th Br at Oxford. Took a Pound of Tea to Mrs Rock from my Sister. Call'd on my Neice. Mrs Tegg desired me to get her a Pound of Dust Tea. Show'd Mr Goldwin's Letter to the late Dr Durham's Man & the fellow who took Care of his Horses. [f.58^{r}] Finish'd a Bean Rick & then draw'd Beans into the Barn.

Tuesday, the 28th Finish'd reaping Beans. Draw'd Barly from Forewood. Pitson & Ball put the——— up. Sent George from the Hive to water the Horses. Thomas Williams & Casey took an Account of the Furze Faggots in Forewood.

Wednesday, the 29th Self & Bett Barns went to the Lock for a Jack & it was not very good. Order'd Bob Whyatt a Pint of Ale for his Trouble.

Thursday, the 30th Br at Cofe Oxford. M.P. St John's. Strol'd about Paradise[11] till I went to Din at my Neice's. Rec'^{d} a Letter from one at Whitchurch, Shropshire about a Mare, but its not mine, for I have got [f.58^{v}] her again. My Neice has had a Letter from her Mother & Tetty is better. Thomas Williams draw Beans from Nineveh & the Farmer behav'd like a Fool or Madman.

Friday, the 31st Employ'd some of the Labourers in rubbing Furze Roots in the New Glebe. After Pitson had set up two Hurdles in the Vineyard, he stole some Fuel.

Notes

1 This is Eton. For full details see N. Pevsner, *Buckinghamshire* (1960), pp. 116–32.

2 This was not a cathedral but St George's chapel, Windsor. See N. Pevsner, *Berkshire*, pp. 268–79.

3 See *ibid.*, pp. 279–98.

4 The Chequers was first referred to as an inn in 1605. During the eighteenth century it was often used for public exhibitions, such as the fourteen wild animals and a large fish shown there in 1762. For full details see *Encycl. Oxford*, p. 77.

5 This was at Clifton Hampden, a village with many 'tea cosy' cottages, about two miles from Nuneham. See Sherwood and Pevsner, *Oxfordshire*, pp. 549–50.

6 This was *Jackson's Oxford Journal*, which began as a newspaper by William Jackson in 1753 and survived until 1909. For full details see *Encycl. Oxford*, pp. 278–9. JN's advertisement read: 'Wanted, A Livery Servant who hath had the Small Pox, to drive a Post-Chaise, wait at Table and work in a Garden. No rough Rider from an Inn need offer his Service, but only such an one as can come extremely well recommended for his Honestry, Care, and Abilities as to the above Qualifications . . . '. *Jackson's*, Saturday 11 August 1759.

7 This was the Golden Ball. For full details see January 1759, note 5.

8 This was Stokenchurch. For full details see N. Pevsner, *Buckinghamshire*, pp. 244–5.

9 JN breakfasted either at The Swan or The Crown. If at the latter, JN would probably have met the tenant, John Hall. See Sherwood and Pevsner, *Oxfordshire*, p. 806; *Jackson's* Saturday 12 November 1763.

10 JN's news is not entirely accurate here. The Seven Years' War was in progress during 1759 and the Prussians, our allies, were hard-pressed by the Russians and Austrians. Indeed, at the battle of Kunersdorf on 13 August, Frederick II's Prussian Army was utterly routed. However, the Russians were suspicious of their Austrian allies and did not advance. Prussia escaped certain defeat when the Russians retired into Poland. See J.L. White, *The Origins of Modern Europe, 1660–1789* (1964), p. 236.

11 This was the market garden and nursery in the neighbourhood of Paradise Square. The garden was run by a Mr Tagg with whom JN had dealings. Many colleges bought their plants from this nursery, in particular Wadham and St John's. JN was a frequent visitor both to these college gardens and to the nursery. See M. Batey, *The Historic Gardens of Oxford and Cambridge* (1989), p. 123; Evelyn Brown-Grant, 'The Gardeners of Paradise', *Oxfordshire Family History*, Vol 3, No.7.

September 1759

Saturday, the 1st Draw'd all the Beans out of the Fields, & then begun drawing Barly into the Barn. Dame Howse went to Nineveh to tythe Barly. Four young Pidgeons took.

[f.59r]

Sunday, the 2nd Self & Thomas Williams went to Forewood, & afterwards to my new House. Sent Bab Whyatt part of a roast Fowl. The Plowboy caught some Fish, but Self would not accept One of them. Paid Betty Howse. Sold a Jack.

Monday, the 3rd Br at Oxford. Bought some Sellery Plants & brought them on my Mare. Sent two Letters about the Mare & Horse. Employ'd some of the Labourers about Mowing Hain. Sent Jack Howse to the Lock for Balm, but there was none.

Tuesday, the 4th Lyon trod the Barly Mow.[1] Howse finish'd planting the Sellery Roots. Rode to Nineveh & Betty Howse [f.59v] was tything Barly there. Spoke to Mr Brain about the Balm & I did not find that Jack Howse had been with Him for any.

Wednesday, the 5th Draw'd from Nineveh Beans. Draw'd to Tom Anderson's some Rye Hain & Self was pretty wet in coming from the Mowers. My Lord Harcourt spoke to me in my Backside.[2] Jackson caught a Fowl. Back'd & Brew'd. A Jack for Din. Sent Howse to Abingdon.

Thursday, the 6th Spoke to my Lord Harcourt in the Oat Ground, & the Horn'd Cattle had Damag'd the Tythes greatly. The Hair Thomas Williams found was drest for Din & Eat well, though it had like to have been flung away [f.60r] for Stinking.

Friday, the 7th Draw'd the Oats away from ——— towards Rome.[3] Draw'd two Load of Vetches out of Ray. Led Captain to the Team in the Field & a tall Gentleman on Horseback bow'd[4] to me.

Saturday, the 8th Yesterday or to day the little Oat Rick fell down. Begun a Barly Rick with three Teams. Employ'd Horner & Christiana Barns. Found there was to be no Bow Windows upstairs at the new Parsonage House according to the Plan.

Sunday, the 9th Cold Fowl & Beacon for Din. & sent Bab Whyatt some of them. Mr Bowly spoke to me in the Park about stocking the Hydes & spoke to me again about it [f.60^{V}] again in the back Court, but Self did not invite Him in. Spoke to Brain about the Harvest Home Supper.

Monday, the 10th Br at Oxford. Rid the Barly Field & Nineveh of Barly. Betty Howse staid at Home to wait on People from Abingdon.

Tuesday, the 11th Draw'd Hurdles from Forewood to the Hanging Land.[5] Pitson begun thatching Bean Rick. Went to the Pound where they were branding my Lord's Sheep. Bought Pitch & Ruddle[6] at Edmond's & there found some old Parish Accounts.

Wednesday, the 12th Took Surtut Coat to the Baldwin Taylor who mended it while I was with Him. His little boy [f.61^{r}] had bedaub'd Himself, & his Wife was much displeas'd at it. Call'd on the Collar Maker. The old Boar & some Pigs were Cut.

Thursday, the 13th Lord Harcourt & Family came to Newnham. Rode to the Locks for a Jack & Self sent Mr Brain some Cucumbers by his Son who brought it to my House. The Plowboy beat Christian Barns with a Whip. Lord & Lady Harcourt laid in their New House for the first Time.[7]

Friday, the 14th Br at my Lord's & Spoke to Him in the Crofts. Begun plowing there. Din'd with a Farmer at the Lamb at Wallingford.[8] Saw several french Prisoners.

[f.61^{V}]

Saturday, the 15th Sow'd Rye & Turnip on Church Hill for the Sheep in Spring. Went to the Baldwin Taylor for my Coat. Br at Oxford & left Leather Breeches to be wash'd. Neice was gone to Heddington. A Duck for Din. Lord & Lady Harcourt drank Tea with Me. Lady Harcourt was stung by a Whasp. Finish'd thatching Bean Ricks.

Sunday, the 16th After M.P. Self & Thomas Williams went to Forewood. A Leg of Mutton for Din. Mr Weston at Church at N.Prayers. Sent to the Clarke at Noon. Christian Barns & all her Children din'd here.

[f.62^{r}]

Monday, the 17th Hay from Nineveh. Lyon sho'd round. Horses turn'd into the Town Meadows. Sent Bab Whyatt some Hash'd Mutton & took to Her my Self a Quart of Mile Ale. Laid Cloath in Order in my bed Chamber.

Tuesday, the 18th Field begun mowing Ferne in Forewood. Took a Letter to Dorchester for Mr Goldwin at Sir Tho^{S} Reeves. Sent George with the black Jack[9] to the New Parsonage House full of Ale. Mr Ray came here but Self was not at Home.

Wednesday, the 19th Din'd at Abingdon Fair. William Clarke bought a Ram for me. Deliver'd a Letter to my Lord, Self brought from the Post House [f.62^{V}] A Letter from Mr Henry Goldwin about my Horse. Two Teams at plow in the Crofts. Repaired Plow. Gave Winter Ale who came about Furze Cutting.

Thursday, the 20th Lord Harcourt promis'd to call on me to go to the New House to consult about a Servants' Hall, but did not come. Went to Howse at Plow. Sent Dame Andrews something for Din. Order'd William Wells some Ale & Spent some time at the old House now pulling down. Deane did not care to take to the Letter for William Fish.

Friday, the 21st Howse & Jackson draw'd Furze faggots to Forewood Kiln. Self [f.63^{r}] set out for Wantage after M.P. Call'd on the Cyder Merchant's Widow at Sutton.[10] Din'd with the Landlord at Wantage & he seems to be almost at his latter End, strangely alter'd for the worst. May I think[11] on my latter End, & always be in readiness for it. As I indeavour to please God, I trust through the Merits of my Saviour, that I do so, & that I shall find Mercy from him at the Day of Judgement & be forever happy in the World to come. Return'd by Abingdon. Engag'd Moulder to help at Ferne Cart.

When I see any of my Friends or Acquaintance greatly alter'd for [f.63^{V}] for [*sic*] the worst & reduc'd to a bad State of Health, may I be sorry for them & pity their Condition but not forget to be thankfull to Providence for being more mercifull to me & for the Preservation of my Life to this Hour with the enjoyment of many Blessings, particularly a good Share of Health.

Health is the greatest good next to a good Conscience & may I ever enjoy the latter in the highest Degree & God's Will be done as to[12] the former. May I guard against Sin as ye greatest Evil, & never offer Violence to that awfull Faculty [f.64^{r}] my Conscience. Give Grace O my God, to spend my Days well & be evermore in readiness for my latter End & may I dye with the Hopes of a joyfull Resurrection to everlasting Life. Into thy Hands I commit my Soul & Body & through the Merits of my Saviour I trust I shall be eternally Happy. I am easy as to my Departure out of this World, I wait with Patience my appointed time, & when I find my Dissolution is near at Hand, may I triumph & Rejoyce & dye without Fear or Amasement.[13]

Saturday, the 22nd Set up the Ferne in Forewood & draw'd Furze Faggots there from [f.64^{V}] Messrs Palmer's & Sermon's Grounds. Intended to have draw'd out of the Wood Fuel for Whyatt but had not Time. Sent Bab Whyatt & Dame Andrews two Pidgeons. Carried Bet Barns in the Park as the Stubs hurt her Feet. Went about the old House while it was pulling down.

Sunday, the 23rd Boil Beef & Udder for Din. Sent Thomas Willams to Bray about the Stray Horse. Sent George & the Plowboy after the Mare but they did not find Her. Went to Forewood after M.P.

Monday, the 24th Howse plow'd in the Crofts & so did Field. Paid Him & Pitson. [f.65^{r}] Dame Baker paid Tythes. Thomas Willams retun'd Home with the stray Horse.

Tuesday, the 25th Br at Oxford. Call'd on my Neice. Saw Mrs Rock. Call'd for Leather Breeches. Bought Coffee & Tea. Beef boil'd too much for Din. Thomas Williams fir'd Hain in the Crofts. Sent Jackson after the Mare. Return'd Home through Cowly [Cowley]. Wisdom came to me ab[out] a Man.

Wednesday, the 26th Draw'd Furze Faggots to the Common Kiln. The Man from Sanford offer'd his Service. Thomas Williams went to Shillingford[14] with a sample of Barly, & a [f.65^{V}] written Description of the Mare. Went to the old House. Gave the Maid & the plowboy good Advice, & to the first some good Books. Spoke to Edmond Baker about my Cheese but he did not seem willing to buy it.

Thursday, the 27th Sent Jackson for old Brown. Din'd at Watlington & there had the Mare cry'd,[15] & a Domestic of one of the Dashwood's din'd with me. Return'd Home to Tea. William Clarke brought Home a dead Sheep.

Friday, the 28th Draw'd Manure from Long Mead to the Lammas Close. Walk't to the Golden Ball. Giblets for Din. [f.66^{r}] Sent Howse to tythe Ferne. Gave the Plowboy good Counsel. Thomas Williams & the two boys burn't Hain in the Crofts. Visited the old Place House after Tea.

Saturday, the 29th Draw'd the Remainder of the Manure from Longmead to the Lammas Close. Harrow'd with four Harrows. Hir'd Mary Giles at Wallingford Fair. John Gendenning din'd with Me, but did not care to tell his Name. Had Mare cry'd at Fair. Gave the Cryer a Pint of Ale & Nickolls of Baldwin, his Wife & Grandaughter a Quart. Return'd Home to Tea.

[f.66^{v}]

Sunday, the 30th Br with Lord & Lady Harcourt for the first time in their New Ho[use]. Sent Bab Whyatt a Leg of a Goose. Self & Thomas Williams went to Forewood before Din. A Letter from Sister Rock.

Notes

1 Lyon was one of JN's horses, used here to thresh barley. It is interesting to note the quickening pace of farming activity during this important time of the year.
2 By 'Backside' JN meant the back part of the rectory.
3 Another unexplained gap occurs in the text. Rome was the name of a house in the old village, supposedly an alehouse. There is no inn shown on the 1707 map, but there had been one in 1694 which was suppressed as disorderly. See *Victorian Oxfordshire*, V, p. 237.
4 'Spoke' is crossed out in the text and 'bowed' superscribed.
5 The Hanging Land was part of the estate.
6 Ruddle is a red variety of ochre used for marking sheep. See *OED*.

7 This was the first version of the house, designed by Stiff Leadbeater of Eton and begun in 1756. It was altered almost immediately on completion by the addition of rooms over the corridors linking the main block to the wings. Lancelot Brown converted the villa again in 1781–2. Further alterations were made by the addition of a new wing in 1832 and the remodelling of the entrance front in 1904. See M. Batey, *Nuneham Courtenay, Oxfordshire* (Oxford, 1979), pp. 9–15.

8 The Lamb was an early Georgian building in blue and red brick. It comprised two-and-a-half storeys with a middle archway. See Pevsner, *Berkshire*, p. 250.

9 A blackjack was a large leather beer jug coated with tar. See OED. By this date, work on the new rectory was well advanced and JN obviously wished to please his labourers.

10 This is Sutton Courtenay.

11 'daily think' is crossed out in the text.

12 'unto' is crossed out in the text.

13 This is another of JN's moral reflections triggered by the sight of the ailing landlord. Such passages serve to give us an inkling of his general attitude to life and of his theological stance. The style seems to contrast sharply with the practical entry of the following day's events!

14 'San' is crossed out in the text.

15 By 'cry'd' JN meant advertised as lost.

October 1759

Monday, the 1st Thomas Williams went to Abingdon with Cheese but sold None. Paid William Clarke & let him have sixty Pound of Cheese on trust. Br at Cofe Oxon. Din'd with Mr Austin. Return'd Home to Tea.

Tuesday, the 2nd After Br Self set out for Woodstock Hiring Fair & Din'd at [f.67^{r}] the Bear.[1] Great Plenty of Cheese. Went into the Park.[2] Bought Plumb Cake & Wallnutts. A man at the Inn told me of his Son for a Servant who lives with Mr Ives. Return'd Home in the Evening. Winnow'd new Beans.

Wednesday, the 3rd Sent Field to the Malster [*sic*] after Din. Howse began clearing a way things out of the Pond in broadmore Close. Snub'd Jackson in the Barn. Mr Thomas Williams draw'd Beans beyond Wallingford & came home very Wet. Wrote part of a Ser[mon]. Mr Baker set the Clock agoing.

[f.67^{V}]

Thursday, the 4th Howse & Field begun drawing the Mud out of the Pond, & Self went to them twice with Dick Barnes. Sparrow begun digging out the Foundation of the second Wing of my New House. The Asses got out of the hanging Close & Howse went after them. Sent George Brookes to Oxford for Hops & Granes.

Friday, the 5th Brew'd Small Beer & Ale. Went with Lord Harcourt to the New H[ouse] & consulted about the second Wing, & after that met Lord Newnham there. Sent the Work People Ale. Went to Howse & Field in Broadmore Close. Sent Dame Andrews [f.68^{r}] a Pidgeon. Lord Harcourt gave Dame Whyatt 2s. 6d. Went to Turners about Balm.

Saturday, the 6th Din'd at Watlington Fair. Mare cry'd. A footman bought a pair of Stocking of a Woman in the House. Joseph Clissle of Cuxham offer'd his Service. Call'd at Cuxham but his Master was not at

Home & there saw a very large He Goat. Bought Wallnutts of an old Woman & gave Her 1d. Gave a Boy 1d. for telling me of the Mare. Return'd Home to Tea, a Letter from Sister Rock.

Sunday, the 7th Paid Howse for his Boys. Leg [f.68^{v}] of Mutton for Din boil'd too much. No singing after Sermon. Self, Bett & Thomas Williams walk't to Forewood after Sermon. Joseph Clissle came here but Self did not hire Him. Sent black Jack to the Clarke's New House for a House Warming.[3] Mr Hall & Self went to the New House after Tea. Enquir'd of Field about the custom of the Common Meadows.

Monday, the 8th Turn'd all Cow Cattle into the Town Meads. George & the Plowboy set out very early to plow for the sake of going to Abingdon Fair.[4] Mr Williams sold 200 weight of Cheese. [f.69^{r}] Gave Mary Hall 6d. for a Fairing & George Brookes 2d. Sent the Carpenters the black Leather Bottle full of Ale. Jack bit me while I was getting him from———[5] Cold Mutton for Dinner.

Tuesday, the 9th Draw'd Dung on Broadmore Leys. Br at Cofe Oxon. M.P. St John's. Enquir'd the Character of William Morris at the Hynd's Head[6] & call'd for a Pint of Ale. Din'd with my Neice & drank there with young Weston's Wife. Dark before I got home. A boil'd Pidgeon for Din.[7] Mrs Rock sent three Guineas to my Neice's wch she had rec'd for ye Spinnet.

[f.69^{v}]

[Michaelmas October 10th 1759][8]

Wednesday, the 10th Begun to drag Harrow the Crofts. Thought the Turkey had been stolen but it prov'd not to be so. Br at Thame & din'd too. Gave Dame Allain's Girl a Plunb Cake. Cry'd the Mare. Return'd from the Fair time enough for Tea. Paid the Dairy Maid & the Plowboys their Year's Wages. Administer'd private Baptism to Well's Child[9] & was much puzzl'd to find my Way.

Thursday, the 11th Edmund Baker fitted the Cyder [f.70^{r}] Wheel to the Fan, & then they began winnowing Beams. Draw'd Dung into Fisher's Green. Bab Whyatt wanted to see me in a great hurry on Account of the vast demand made by Dame Pitson on Her. Put Isinglass[10] to the Wine. Look'd about Hawkin's Garden for Eggs.

Friday, the 12th Sent Beans to Benson House,[11] draw'd Dung to Fisher's Green. Great part of a Vessel of small [beer, ale?] run'd out, & another Vessel of Ale was drawn into another Vessel not having Hoops enough on. Howse dug'd up some Potatoes. The Plowboy & the Dairy Maid this day enter'd my Service.

[f.70^{v}]

Saturday, the 13th Br at Oxon & George came after me. Call'd on Beaver & then waited on the Archdeacon about James Lawrance's Affair.[12] M.P. St Mary's.[13] Din'd at the Visitation. Stewart tender'd me Marriage Fees for James Laurance. Went to Dr Hay at St John's College. Order'd things at Lawrance's[14] but did not bring them away.

Sunday, the 14th A Goose for Din & sent Bab Whyatt a Leg of it & gave her some Sugar Candy. Self & Thomas William went about the new Glebe.

Monday, the 15th Br at Abingdon after M. Pr Bought a Cheese & a Lot of Meat.[15] Rec'^{d} [f.71^{r}] Money of Full, for Coals. Spoke to Birch in the Butcher Row. Thomas Williams sold two Hogs & return'd with the Sow & Pigs. A Letter from North about a Debt due to Him from the late Samuel Rock.

Tuesday, the 16th Draw'd Mold[16] out of the lower Rick Yard into Comb bottom. The Abingdon Butcher sent the Meat Home & some of it was drest for Din. Two Pidgeons taken. Went to Lord Harcourt at my New House. Spoke to the young Shephard about throwing the Tiles down the Hill.

Wednesday, the 17th Howse & Field draw'd to Fore-[f.71^{v}] Forewood Kiln furze faggots out of Sermon's Grounds. Br at Wantage. Had some Conversation with a mighty pretty Girl at the Fair about having her for a Chamber Maid, but she did not choose to live with me. Took a view of Mr Price's House. M.P. at Church,[17] & there saw Miss Matthews. Spoke to a Farmer who knew Lord Harcourt. Saw a Fellow hold a boy up on his hand on his Head as high as his own Head. Another Man got money by making much Noise & saying he had been crucifyed.

[f.72^{r}]

Thursday, the 18th After Br set out for Home. Call'd at Ditcot [Didcot]. A Pidgeon for Din. Self & Howse went about my New Glebe.

Friday, the 19th Henry Brickal from Oxford offer'd his Service & to morrow I am to inquire his Character. Made the Carpenters & Bricklayers drink. Drag Harrow'd the Crofts. Winnow'd Barly, Beans & Rye. Edmond's man made a Hog Trough. Took some young Pidgeons. Roast Beef for Din & sent bab Whyatt & Dame Andrews some of it.

Saturday, the 20th Br at Cofe Oxford. Thomas Williams took nine Bushel [f.72^{v}] to Sandford, & Pots to Oxford to be tin'd & bought sevral things Home in the Cart from Mr Lawrance's. Treated the Ringers & my Servants & Labourers with two black Jacks of Ale for the good News of taking Quebec.[18] Bottl'd the Rum & Brandy.

Sunday, the 21st Mary's Father brought Her Things. The Perton [Pyrton] Hayward brought the Mare Home after she had been Absent about a Month. Self & Thomas Williams went about the New Glebe & saw in Combe Bottom a Sheep out of Order. Paid 6d. for the pounding of 6 Pigs.

[f.73^{r}]

Monday, the 22nd A Letter from Sister Rock. Henry Brickal enter'd my Service. Read News at the Golden Ball. A roast Fowl for Dinner.

Tuesday, the 23rd Henry Brickal clean'd the Landau & Harness. Displeas'd with Housekeeper about the Knives. Self help't to burn the Hain in the Crofts. The Door & Frame of the Stove prov'd to be old.

Wednesday, the 24th Found a Pain in the insteap of my left Foot when I got up but thanks be to God it went off about Dinner Time. The Monkey got Loose. Henry Brickal left a Candle burning in the Stable in a Candle Stick. Thomas [f.73^{v}] Hopkins paid Mr Bush for the Wine & left with Me £3 8s. 0d.

Thursday, the 25th After Br Self went to the Auction at Ditcot intending to have bought a speaking Trumpet, but it was sold before I got there & the old shabby Goods sold very well. Reach'd Wantage by Dinner time. Drank strong Beer at Mr Price's House, & Tea with the general Receiver of the Land Tax at Wantage. A Welsh Rabbit for Supper in the little Room near the Kitchen, & was pleasantly enough entertained with the People there, particularly Mr [f.74^{r}] Oldworth, an elderly Man & a drunken Millar.

Friday, the 26th Self Br with Mr Oldworth & invited him to my House, but he excus'd himself. M.P. Wantage & then set out. Overtook the Postman in the Meadows, & parted with him for Sutton [Sutton Courtenay]. Call'd on Mrs Emery & she speaks queerly of her Son in Law & his Partner. Got Home to Din. Howse kill'd an Hog. Went to Howse & Field who were spreading Dung.

Saturday, the 27th Henry Brickal drove me to Oxford in my Landau being the first time of his driving me, & it [f.74^{v}] was a very wet day. Br at the Cofe. Bought some things at Mr Lawrence's. Paid Mrs Rock £2 2s. 0d. on my Sister's Account.

Sunday, the 28th This being the Day of my Nativity,[19] I am thankfull to Providence for ye Preservation of my Life to this Time & for all the Comforts & Blessings[20] I have enjoy'd & am now in the Possession off, & also for my Preservation from many known, as well as, unknown Evils that have been just ready to have fallen on me, hadn't not thou, O my God,[21] in thy great Mercy timely kept them off.
[f.75^{r}]

However, some may complain of the tediousness of time & that it lays heavy on their Hands, methinks, it is not so with Me, & I hope never will be so. For on the Contrary, Time seems to flye & Months & Years to make very quick Revolutions & to hasten me on in the Journey of Life, w'^{ch} ere long I shall finish, God grant it may be Well, & then I may hope to dye in Peace.

May I be so carefull & diligent in the Management of my Time, that I may always be able to reflect on my past spent Days with Pleasure & delight, & think that way to spend [f.75^{v}] them again. I could not spend them or be able [to] reflect on them with greater Pleasure & Delight.

If I know my own Heart, (& in this important Article I hope my heart don't deceive me) I think it is [my] most ardent Wish & Desire to serve God in the best & most perfect manner I am able, & that is it my greatest Delight & Felicity so to Do. Let the World go how it will, rough or smooth, may I preserve an eveness of Temper & not be too much affected in either State. If Plenty & Abundance should fall to my Share, may I be humble & thankfull [f.76r] to Providence for it, & not despise my poor Bretheren, but rather study to render them Partakers with me in the most usefull & effectuel Manner. And on the Contrary, If Want or Poverty should be my future Lot, may [I] acquesce in it with Patience & spend the remainder of my Days with cheerfulness & Content. The Necessaries of Life lay in a small Compass, & what ever share I may have of them, may I learn to be contented with them. If I should be reduc'd to a low Condition, my acquaintance may shun my Company & my Friends grow [f.76v] very cold towards me, yet while I enjoy the Testimony of a good Conscience, & if I don't, its my own Fault, I should[22] not be dejected at such sort of Treatment.

If Adversaties of various sorts should invade me at once, & bear very hard on me, yet let me wait with Patience for a removal of them. Death is a sovereign Remedy for all the Evil of Human Life, & for our Comfort, we know it may[23] chance to be near at hand, & then if we have made our Peace with God, (as I trust I have done) we may give Him an hearty welcome when ever he shall call us hence, & this I hope I shall do, & leave the World without any Reluctance.

[f.77r]

Monday, the 29th Sent Henry with Mr Oldworth as far as Nettlebed & Lyon flung him on his return & damag'd Himself, but Henry escap'd very well. A Letter from Sister Rock. Vetches sow'd on the hanging Lands. Read the News at the Golden Ball, & gave a poor man there a pint of Ale.

Tuesday, the 30th Howse draw'd Dung out of the hanging Close into Comb Bottom. Thomas Williams would not undertake the Cure of old Brown. Sent four of the Asses to Forewood.

Wednesday, the 31st Sent to the House rearing[24] a five Gallon Vessel of Ale & after Din the Carpenters came to my House [f.77v] with two Fiddles & the black Jack was fill'd thrice[25] for them. Thomas Williams[26] brought three Bushel of Malt from Littlemore. Jackson mow'd Grass in the Garden for the Horse.

Notes

1 The Bear is still in the square. See Pevsner and Sherwood, *Oxfordshire*, p. 858.

2 This is the park at Blenheim Palace. JN would not, of course, have witnessed the present landscape, laid out by Lancelot Brown, *c.*1764–74, but would have seen the original design by Vanbrugh and Henry Wise in a more formal style with intersecting avenues. See *ibid.*, pp. 472–4. Vanbrugh's grand bridge was there, but flowing under it was a formal canal terminating in a round pool. Rather more of the bridge was showing than today, as Capability Brown raised the water level by fifteen feet when he made the present lake. The bridge was considered too overbearing. Horace Walpole described the scene in his waspish style some nine months before JN's visit: '. . . the bridge, like the beggars at the old Duchess's gate, begs for a drop of water, and is refused.' See H. Walpole, *Selected Letters*, W. Hadley (ed.) (1926), p. 125.

3 William Nicholls was the parish clerk. This is another instance of JN's benevolent nature.

4 The Abingdon Fair is still held in the town each Autumn.

5 Another unexplained gap in the text.

6 This was The Hynd's Head in Old Butcher Row.

7 'Drag Harow'd the Crofts' was crossed out in the text.

8 Michaelmas Day, 29 September 1759, had in fact occurred eleven days earlier. In Great Britain the calendar was changed in 1752 from the Julian (old style) to the Gregorian (new style). This necessitated a loss of eleven days in September 1752, 2 September being followed by 14 September. Although dating his Diary in the New Style, with the year beginning on 1 January, JN here refers to Michaelmas under the old style. Again in 1761, JN calls 10 October 'Old Michaelmas Day'. See later entry.

9 There is no reference to this baptism in the Nuneham *Registers*.

10 This is a whitish, semi-transparent and very pure form of gelatine used for clarifying liquors. See *OED*.

11 This is possibly Fifield Manor, about a mile from Benson. For full details see Pevsner and Sherwood, *Oxfordshire*, p. 451.

12 The Archdeacon of Oxford from 1741 to 1767 was John Potter.

13 St Mary's was the parish church of Oxford. For full details see Pevsner and Sherwood, *Oxfordshire*, pp. 283–7.

14 This was Isaac Lawrence's, a grocer's shop in Cornmarket.

15 'Famery cheeses' is crossed out in the text.

16 Mould is surface soil which is easily broken up, often used to cover seeds or young plants. See *OED*.

17 The church referred to was that of St Peter and St Paul, Wantage. It was a cruciform building with a large tower. See Pevsner, *Berkshire*, pp. 252–3.

18 The capture of Quebec by General Wolfe was one of the outstanding victories of 1759, the so-called *Annus mirabilis*, when British fortunes changed

during the Seven Years' War. Quebec was attacked on 13 September, sur rendering finally on the 18 September. As a result, Britain gained Canada at the Peace of Paris which closed the war in 1763. JN was following common practice in having his church bells rung in celebration. The next day Horace Walpole wrote to a friend: 'Our bells are worn threadbare with ringing for victories.' See *Selected Letters*, p. 359.

19 This was JN's forty-sixth birthday, a perfect excuse for some moral reflections. It is interesting to note that in 1761, JN refers to 29 October as his birthday. See later entry.

20 'of' is crossed out in the text.

21 'O my God' is inserted above the line.

22 'shall not' is crossed out in the text.

23 'cannot be at' is crossed out in the text.

24 i.e. house building.

25 'twice' is crossed out in the text.

26 'Silvester' is crossed out in the text. Thomas Silvester was a former servant, having left JN's service on 3 August 1759. This was perhaps a momentary lapse of memory.

November 1759

Thursday, the 1st Went in my Landau to St Clements & there got out at the Hatters to have a Loop put to my Hat.[1] Bought 4 Sorts of Oyl for Horses. Br at the Cofe & had there some Conversation with one of Pembroke College. Wrote to Sister Rock & Easome. Left an Advertisement at the Printer's for two Servants. M.P. near Pembroke College. Mr Lawrence desir'd I would [f.78^{r}] leave the Room as he wanted to speak to a Woman. Saucages for Din near Carfax Church.[2] Cabbage Plants sent from Paradise[3] to Noah's Ark.[4] Got Home time enough for Tea.

Friday, the 2nd Winnow'd Wheat & Oats. Draw'd Straw out of the upper Rick Yard into the Backside. Begun brewing small Beer. Self feed the Pidgeons & Gave the Dogs fresh Straw. One of the men at my new House not well & One of them sent for Ale & went without it. A man spoke to me about being married to morrow.

Saturday, the 3rd Married Daniel Monk & Mary Wilkins.[5] Self & George Brookes went to Caldecot & found the ———[6] [f.78^{v}] had been greatly Damag'd. Bought some Butcher's Meat. Thomas Williams sold at Oxford four Quarter of Wheat. Howse burn't the Hain in Broadmore Close.

Sunday, the 4th Read a Brief for Rebuilding a Church in Westphalia.[7] The Monkey got Loose. James Hoare din'd here & went with me to my New house. A Letter from Sister Rock.[8]

Monday, the 5th The Abingdon Butcher sent the Meat Home. A boil Fowl & Pig meat for Din & done too much. A Bailiff near Thame offer'd his Service, but he seemn'd too upish. Howse feloniously drank some Ale in the [f.79^{r}] Kitchen & then burn't the Hain in broadmore Close. Gave the Boys leave to take as much Wood as they could carry for their Bonfire.

Tuesday, the 6th Took the Wheat Rick in & abundance of Mice were kill'd by Tyger & others & they had damag'd it extreamly much. James Quartermain of Ensham [Eynsham] offer'd his Service & Self shew'd him my new Glebe. Leg & Shin of Beef for Din.

Wednesday, the 7th Messrs Bush & Beacon din'd here on Leg of Mutton & a Goose. George Brookes much discompos'd because they gave Him nothing.

Thursday, the 8th Brought the Hay away from [f.79^{v}] Caldecot & spoke to Mr Birch about given him Trouble if he did not make good the Damage his Cattle had done to the Hay. Rode Home by the Way of the Golden Ball. Hash'd Mutton for Dinner.

Friday, the 9th Br with Mr Meck at the Cofe Oxford. M.P. near Bocards,[9] & the Clarke thought I was come to read Prayers. Call'd on Mrs Rock. Din'd with my Neice. Went about the Town to sell Straw but could not.

Saturday, the 10th Thomas Williams sold a Load of Straw at Oxford. The Hay from Caldecot put into the two Stables. Howse & Self to the New Glebe [f.80^{r}] & by the Golden Ball through Forewood. Bad Giblets for Din. Lord Harcourt rode by Bab Whyatt's while Self was there.

Sunday, the 11th Turn'd the three Cows & two Calves into Forewood, & eight Horses into Long Mead. Paid Nickols James Lawrence's Marriage Fee. After M.P. Self & George went to Forewood & the new Glebe. Spoke to Henry Bricknal for being saucy to my Housekeeper. A Letter from Robert Esome. Spoke to Clarke about removing Sheep into the Town Meads.

Monday, the 12th Howse kill'd a fat Hog. Thomas Williams draw'd[10] a Load of Straw to [f.80^{v}] Oxford & return'd with a Load of Pot ashes. Self Br at the Cofe Oxon & had some Conversation with Mr Speak or Meak. Convers'd with a Fellow going to Oxford to invite[11] a Person to the Funeral of Mr Kirby of Wantage.

Tuesday, the 13th[12] Winnow'd the Wheat & much Chaff but little Wheat. Jackson grumbl'd about mowing the Rushes in Combe bottom. Harry went to Forewood for Field. An Oven Cake for Br. Howse cut out the Hog.

Wednesday, the 14th Jackson cut Rushes in [f.81^{r}] Combe Bottom. Several great Tubs fill'd with Chaff, & the Oats winnow'd. Church'd the Joiners Wife.

Thursday, the 15th Draw'd Furze to Forewood Kiln from Ditto. Din'd at Mr Bushnall's at Blewberry [Blewbury] & there saw Miss Oldworth. Reach'd Wantage time enough for Tea. Commissioners or Governors of some Charity met here to Day.

Friday, the 16th Left Wantage after Br & went to Grove to enquire after an Housekeeper, but her Sister in Law spoke very queerly of Her. Enquir'd about the Enclosures at Upton. Din'd at Church Hackburn [East Hagbourne], & the Landlord had buried his Wife the day before. Snub'd Crosse's boy for making [f.81^{V}] a Burn Fire in Forewood near the Hedge & Straw. Hash'd Duck for Supper.

Saturday, the 17th Sent Barly & Wheat to the Mill to be ground.[13] Howse & Self went to the Pond in the Common. A Carriage of Water from the River & much of it run'd out. Harry put Straw at the End of the Barn.

Sunday, the 18th The Dairy Maid's Sister came here & was sent away. Self & George went to Long Mead & three of the Horses went out while we were there. A Sparib for Din. Had Christian Barns & all her Family to Din. The Lawyer North sent his man with a Letter.

Monday, the 19th Br at Oxford Cofe. Sent Mrs Rock [f.82^{r}] a Goose & din'd with Her at my Neice's. A New Member chose for the Town.[14] My Horse ran away with me going Home.

Tuesday, the 20th Kill'd a Porker. Sugar offer'd his Service. Angry with Bett thinking She had told a Lye. Went to the Furze Cutter in Forewood. Edmond's Man saw'd the Hovel door in two. Sent Harry for a Boar Cheek.

Wednesday, the 21st Thomas Williams draw'd a Hurdle over the Dung. Winnow'd Wheat. Howse cut the Porker out. A Handle put to the Grubbing Axe. Finish'd Thanksgiving Sermon.[15]

Thursday, the 22nd Draw'd Furze to Forewood Kiln. Spoke to the Pope's Wife about her Boy going to make a Fire. Went to Parson Davis at Chilton to enquire Sugar's Character, but he was from Home. Din'd at Church Hackburn. John Cummins came to me about Bab Whyatt's Debt.

[f.82^{v}]

Friday, the 23rd Begun grubbing up the Trees in Broadmore Close. Gave the Work People at the new Town[16] 2s. 6d. to Drink. Spoke to the Furze Cutter at Forewood. Sparib roasted too much. Gave Christian Barns some old Cloaths.

Saturday, the 24th Draw'd 6 Quarter of Wheat to Oxford, & Christian Barns & two of her Children were to have went in it, but She was too late. Self spoke to Mr Waiste on the Road & Br at Cofe Oxon. Bought 200 weight of Plumbs, two Gallons of Brandy of Mr Lawrance, & din'd with Him.

Sunday, the 25th After M.P. Self & George went to Forewood. A Chick & Hog's Cheek for Din & Sent Bab Whyatt [f.83^{r}] Part of Both. Went to the New Rectory House before Tea. N. Call'd on Bab Whyatt, & saw her New Maid.

Monday, the 26th Self & Howse went to the New Glebe & John Clarke the Shephard had got my Lord's Sheep there. Thomas Williams went to the Mill with Corn for Grinding. Treated Howse with a Pint of Ale at the Golden Ball. Pork not boil'd enough for Din. Mr Bowly sent a Letter for me to write out my Furze Bill.

Tuesday, the 27th Howse kill'd the great black Sow. Two Letters from Polly & one from the Rev'^{d} Mr Davies of Chilton. Howse repair'd the Hovel in Long Mead. Gave some of my [f.83^{v}] Parishioners good Advice. Gave Tom Chapman a Pint of Ale. Edmond Baker put up the Mounding [in] the Backside. The Pidgeons got out of the Cock Loft.

Wednesday, the 28th Gave several Lotts of the old Sow to the Poor. Paid down 14s. 9½d. for the Payment of Bab Whyatt's Debts & to make her Easy & Comfortable. Gave some of my Parish good Counsel. Thomas Williams brought from Sandford Mill the grounded Corn. Pork Griskins done too much.[17] Cork'd & Bottl'd some Wine for Mrs Rock & her Landerdess. Order'd Dame Andrews a Black Pudding.

[f.84^r]

Thursday, the 29th This being the Thanksgiving[18] Self preach'd a New Sermon on the Occasion. Treated at the Locks the Work People belonging to the Parsonage & also the Quicksetters[19] & at my House the Ringers & my Labourers. Took to Bab Whyatt a Quart of Ale & a Pint of Wine. The Leg of Pork for Dinner, not done enough. Begun a Sermon for Christmas Day.

Friday, the 30th Br at Oxford Cofe & din'd near Carfax. Sent the Wine for London & some for Mrs Rock & her Landerdess, & draw'd away a Load of Pot of Ashes. M.P. St Tabbs.[20] Mr [f.84^V] Ward gone out of Town. Secur'd One to take Care of Newnham in my Absence.[21] Thre Hoops put on a Vessel.

Notes

1 John Green was a hatter in St Clement's. See *Jackson's* index.

2 The church referred to was St Martin's church in Carfax.

3 This is the market garden in Paradise Square. For full details see August 1759, note 11.

4 Noah's Ark was a major posting inn at the corner of Rose Lane and High Street, now the forecourt of the Botanical Gardens. It had a large stable and a yard.

5 This marriage is confirmed by the Nuneham *Registers*. Mary Wilkins came from Cirencester.

6 JN left a blank as he turned the page, and omitted the object of the sentence.

7 This is an interesting topic, as JN's own church was to be demolished and rebuilt in 1764. Did he know at this time what was afoot?

8 This letter may have been in answer to JN's of Thursday, 1 November.

9 Bocards was most likely St Michael's at the North Gate. For full details see *Encycl. Oxford*, pp. 416–8. Bocardo was the name of a prison that stood at the North gate of the city until 1771. See *ibid.*, p. 49.

10 'sold' is crossed out in the text.

11 'give' is crossed out in the text.

12 At this point the following entry, dated 13 November, is crossed through: 'A Load of Pot Ashes laid in Combe bottom. Jackson mow'd some of the Rushes. Harry went to Forewood.' See entry for 12 November 1759. The text then continues with a fresh entry for 13 November.

13 The will referred to was at Sandford .

14 The new Member was Sir Thomas Stapleton of Bray, Berkshire. He was the eldest son of Sir William Stapleton whom he succeeded as 5th Baronet on 13

January 1740. He was born on 24 February 1727 and died on 13 January 1781. He matriculated at St Edmund Hall, Oxford, 27 February 1744; D.C.L. 3 July 1754; married Mary Fane 27 November 1765. Sir Thomas sat for Oxford 1759–68. See W.R. Williams, *Members for Oxfordshire* (1899), p. 127.

15 This sermon was preached on Thursday 29 November. See entry for that day.

16 The construction of the new village along the Oxford–Henley road was now well forward.

17 Griskins are the lean parts of the loin of a bacon pig.

18 Public acts of Thanksgiving were common during the eighteenth century so that gratitude for Divine favours, victories in war or deliverance from disaster could be acknowledged. This occasion was to celebrate recent victories in the Seven Years' War.

19 The Quicksetters were those planting the new hedges as a result of the recent boundary changes within the estate. See *OED*.

20 This is St Ebbe's in Oxford. For full details see January 1759, note 27.

21 JN was always good about ensuring that his parochial duties were covered while he was away. He often employed the Reverend Mr Skinner of Corpus Christi College.

December 1759

Saturday, the 1st Br at the great House. Lord Harcourt & Self went to the new Parsonage House about Laying out the Garden.[1] Spoke to Sugar in a Barn at Shillingford about entering my Service. Complimented Lord Harcourt about Mr Hoare's officiating for me in my Absence.

Sunday, the 2nd Din'd at the great House after Ev. Service. Lord Harcourt shew'd me a Letter about the Destruction of the Brest Fleet.[2] Thanks [f.85^{r}] be to God for this good News. Paid Henry Bricknal 16s.

Monday, the 3rd Put the Plumbs to soak for Wine. Lyon rough shod. Treated Howse with a Pint of Ale at the Golden Ball. Spoke to the Furze Cutter at Forewood. An old Hen Turkey for Din. Thomas Williams begun mowing the rough Stuff in Combe Bottom. Water'd Trees in the Hall.

Tuesday, the 4th Order'd the Work People about the Parsonage to drink out at the Locks Five Shillings, & treated the Ringers at My House for the joyfull & good News of Admiral Hawke's Victory over the Brest Fleets. And I hope God's Goodness to us [f.85^{v}] will lead us to Repentance & Reformation of Manners. Gave several of my Parishioners good Advice. Goody Auger displeas'd about the Widows Money. I secur'd one of William Clarke's Girls to wait on Bab Whyatt. Self broke a Bottle of Wine & a Glass. Paid the Collar Maker.

Wednesday, the 5th Horse whipt George Brooks. Mr Isaac came about Milk. The little Cow calv'd a mighty small Calf. Took two Guinea Hens to my Lady Harcourt, but She declin'd accepting of Them. Sent my Cloak Bag for the Coach by Howse.

Thursday, the 6th After Br. Self set out for London. Din'd at Henly. Laid near Maiden Head.

[Two missing folios][3]

[f.88r]

[Tuesday, the 11th] . . . on Riches, but be thankfull to Providence for the Share I have got &, make a good Use of it. N.P. St Anne's.

Wednesday, the 12th Try'd Br[eeches] & Waistcoat. Bought John a Pair of Gloves. Went to Blue Anchor Ally & rec'd some Money. The late Fire was pretty near one of my Houses there, but Providentially it did it no Damage, except the Loss of the Pailing. A very good Beef Stake for Din at the White Horse.[4]

Thursday, the 13th Had little John's Hair cut at the three Pidgeons. Din'd at Robin Hood[5] & little John & Tumbl'd down Stairs, but providentially receiv'd no Damage & I think it was a great Mercy & am thankfull [f.88v] to Providence for my Preservation. Alas, how many are kill'd by Fall, or miserably damag'd, but I came off without any Damage & thanks be to God for his Goodness towards [me]. May I always enjoy a gratefull & thankfull Heart & never omit the easy & pleasant Duty of Praise, & [be] Thankfull for any interpretation of thine in my Favour. To be thankfull for past Mercies is a comfortable Employment, & to be silent on such Occasions argus not only a base but also an[6] ungratefull Temper, & may I never be guilty of it.

Drank a Pint of Madeira Wine at the Turk's Head Cofe. Went [f.89r] to see Mr Cor at Saville House,[7] but did not find Him. Drank Tea with W——— near Leicester Fields.[8]

Friday, the 14th M.P. St Anne's. Met Mr Cowden at Mr Cor's. Call'd near Leicester Fields. Din'd at Dolly's.[9] A Pint of red Wine at the Turk's Head Cofe.

Saturday, the 15th Went to several Coach makers about my Sister's Chariot. Mr Matthews not at Home. Spoke to Mr Gordon at the Royal Exchange. Saw the Tickets drawn at Guild Hall.[10] Took out a £10 Bank Note. Drank Tea in Crown Court.[11] No Letters at the Cofe.

Sunday, the 16th M.P. The Foundling Hospital. Lucinda Baily[12] had got one to Dine with Her, when I went in, [f.89v] and another Came, call'd the Dr. N.P. St George's & saw Miss Dashiere there.

Monday, the 17th Went to Mrs Hill about Sisters Chariot & agree'd for a Post Chariot for Myself. Bought a great Quantity of Tea & Coffee at

Twinings & Carter's.[13] Mrs Pickering paid some Rent. Treated several with Tea near Princes St Cofe.

Tuesday, the 18th Went to Mr Matthews of Grey's Inn. Mrs Hill's Foreman look'd at Sister's Chariot & the Painter brought his Patterns & Sister Rock fixt on One for Me. Paid for Horse keeping.

Wednesday, the 19th Saw a parcel[14] of Fellows drawing a Boat cover'd with black [f.90^{r}] Cloath in Cavendish Square. Sent my Cloak Bag to the Hog in the Pound by the Oystler. Saw Water sold in Oxford Road. After Br Self set out for Newnham & din'd at Slow, & Laid at the Fleece beyond Maidenhead.

Thursday, the 20th Set out after Br. Had some Conversation with one of Luggering's rough Riders & gave him 2d. Din'd at Benson & the Landlord broke his Leg some years past by falling from a Horse, he was showing to the late Mr Lowe of Brightwell. And he had likewise some Knowledge of Mr Ratcliffe, who married Fanny Anderson, One of my first [f.90^{V}] Flames, & though She did not fall to my Lott, all things consider'd, I trust, it was for the Best. Its not my Desire to have my own Will in all things, but rather that God's will may take Place. I know not my real Interest so well as he doth, & therefore its better for me that he should choose for me than I for Myself.

Friday, the 21st Br at the great House, & invited the Family to dine with me the Thursday following. Winnow'd Barly.

Saturday, the 22nd Br at Oxford. Henry Bricknal went there with a Cart & brought Home four Vessels, but the Cloak [f.91^{r}] was not forthcoming. Call'd on my Neice & her Aunt. Bought Candles. Gave the People at the New Parsonage House a Black Jack of Ale.

Sunday, the 23rd Lord Harcourt invited me to Din, but Self did not go. Had some Conversation with Mr Cowden before M[orning] Service. Giblets for Din. Gave John Deadman 6d to hansell[15] his new Coat.

Monday, the 24th Prayers twice to Day. Self & Howse went to the further end of the Common for Holly, & gave Mrs Deane some of it, & some Self put up in my House.

[f.91^{V}]

Tuesday, the 25th [Christmas Day] Mr Cowden walkt with me on the Terras before Morning Ser. Lord Harcourt did not Communicate but my Lady & Daughter did.[16] Self administer's the holy Sacrament to Bab Whyatt at her House. A Goose for Din.

This Day Twelvemonth my Dearest Brother Samuel Rock expir'd[17] & I trust he is at Rest, God grant, I may be so, when I shall be number'd among the Dead.

[f.92^{r}]

To Make great Lamentation & Mourning for Him now is vain & unprofitable, it can be of no Service to him, & therefore its much better not to give way to it. He was not taken of in the full Prime & Vigour of his Life, but was far advanc'd in Years, & therefore it behoves me to be more easy under the Loss of Him. To dye is common to all men & we have daily instances of Mortality, & this should teach us to be ever prepar'd for our own Death & the Death of our Friends & Relatives, & then the Shock will be the less.

[f.92^{v}]

Wednesday, the 26th Baptised a Child at Church.[18] Spoke to Mr Braine about a Jack. Gave the Clarke 2s. 6d for the Ringers.

Thursday, the 27th Lewis of Oxford[19] like a Rogue charg'd 6d to Pound for a fillet of Veal. Mrs Braine drest at my House a Jack. Lord Harcourt din'd with me, & afterwards drank Tea.

Friday, the 28th Four Geese kill'd, & pick'd. Ten Bushel of Malt sent Home to me. Sent George to the Locks with Plates.

Saturday, the 29th Thomas Williams sold at Oxford two Geese & Self gave to Mrs Rock & my Neice two Geese, & to the former, Dust Tea 1/4 Pound. Br at the Coffee House. Bought some things of Austin.

[f.93^{r}]

Sunday, the 30th Fillet of Veal for Din. Went towards my new Parsonage, but return'd again on account of the Rain. Spoke to Nickolls about singing more than *Gloria Patri* after Sermon. Gave Howse One Bottle of Brand[y], three of Cyder & Sugar as a Treat as his Child's Christening.[20]

Monday, the 31st A Pig Merchant look'd at the Pigs but Self sold None. Thomas Williams went to the Mill with six & twenty Bushels of Corn for Grinding.

Notes

1 JN was a keen gardener and the garden was to become a major feature of the new rectory. See Introduction.

2 The 'Destruction of the Brest Fleet' was yet another British victory of 1759. Conflans' fleet of twenty-six ships sailed from Brest in November to escort across to England French troops gathered at Quiberon. Admiral Hawke was soon upon them 'with the swiftness of a bird of prey'. He forced them into Quiberon Bay, where the French were caught in a trap. Many ships were destroyed, others were wrecked in the mud. See B. Williams, *The Whig Supremacy* (2nd edn, Oxford, 1962), p. 366.

3 Two folios are missing from the volume. Four whole days are lost: 7–10 December, Friday to Monday inclusive. The diary recommences in the latter part of Tuesday 11 December with, perhaps, the final sentences of one of his textual reflections, this time on the subject of wealth.

4 The White Horse may have been his usual haunt in Piccadilly. For full details see January 1759, note 25.

5 The Robin Hood in Butcher Row in Temple Bar, near St Clement's. See Lillywhite, *Coffee Houses*, pp. 727–8.

6 An ampersand is crossed out in the text and 'but also an' is superscribed.

7 Savile House was built in *c.*1683 and destroyed by fire in 1865. Prince George lived there until he came to the throne as George III in 1760. For full details see *London Encycl.*, pp. 771–2.

8 The blank may indicate yet another secretive encounter in an area of the *demi-monde*.

9 This was Dolly's Chop House in Paternoster Row, a popular eating place in London. Boswell often dined there 'comfortably'. The house dated from the reign of Queen Anne taking its name from Dolly, the cook of the establishment whom Gainsborough painted. See Lillywhite, *Coffee Houses*, pp. 692–3.

10 For full details of the Guildhall see *London Encycl.*, pp. 343–5.

11 It is difficult to be precise here since there are many Crown Courts. If JN remained in the area of the Guildhall, then Crown Court just off Coleman Street is a strong possibility.

12 Lucinda Baily may have been one of JN's mysterious lady-friends. If so, why did he name her?

13 Twining & Carter were 'teamen' in Devereux Court, Fleet Street. See Mortimer, *Universal Director*, Part III, p. 159.

14 By 'parcel' JN meant a small group.
15 To Han(d)sel meant to try for the first time. See *OED*.
16 This is the first mention of JN celebrating Holy Communion. The Harcourts spent their first Christmas in their new house. The 'daughter' referred to was Lady Elizabeth Harcourt.
17 It was at Samuel Rock's funeral that the *Diary* began. See entry for New Year's Day 1759.
18 The child was Edward, son of William and Mary Turner.
19 This was Francis Lewis, a butcher in George Lane. See *Jackson's* index.
20 The child was Howse's daughter, Sarah.

[f.93v]

January 1760[1]

Tuesday, the 1st This Day twelvemonth was deposited in Newnham Church the Corpse of my dearest Brother in Law Samuel Rock & his Wife scream'd out most outragiously & was so much alter'd, that I knew her not.[2] God grand that no Loss, or Calamity of any sort may[3] transport me in such a manner. May I ever retain a sincere & gratefull Memory of Him, but not offend thee, O my God, by grieving too much for his Death. While I think on the Debt of Nature, he has paid, may [f.94r] I indeavour to prepare myself against the time, I shall be call'd upon to do the same. As I often meditate on my latter [end], I trust, when that solemn Event shall happen, that I shall be in readiness for it, & dye in Peace.

The Time of my Departure is uncertain, yet through God's Grace & Assistance, I will spend all my Days well & then a sudden Death will do me no Harm. As it is my Desire to please God, & the Practice of Virtue & Goodness is most agreeable & delectable to me, I may rest safe & Contented for no Harm can happen to ye Detrement of my Salvation.[4]
[f.94v]

The Clifton Cooper did some Jobbs this Day as well as the Day before. Henry Bricknal brought the Grist from the Mill. Took Howse with me to the Baldwin Taylor & he carried a great Parcel of Cloath's.

Wednesday, the 2nd Thomas Willams rec'd at Shillingford Money due for Barly. Spoke to Mr Cowden about a Gateway from the Common. The Men begun making the dead Hedge round my Garden. Draw'd rich Mold from the Crofts into Combe Bottom.[5]

[f.95r]

Thursday, the 3rd Br at the great House & Mr Blackhall was there. Spoke to my Lord Harcourt about carrying the Mound round the House. Found the old Cock Turkey dead in the upper Rick Yard & as the Puppy

Dogs were suspected to have done the Jobb, Jackson was order'd to hang the young Bitch. Rec'd of Peeds a Year's Rent. Sent a Basket by Howse for the Coach to morrow.

Friday, the 4th Br at Oxford. Bought Materials for a Coat & Waistcoat. M.P. at the New Church, High Street. My Neice not at Home.

[f.95v]

Saturday, the 5th Intended to have went to Dung Cart, but did not, as we could not have two carts. Thomas Williams & Henry grub'd up the Bushes in Combe Bottom, & Howse begun the Trenching. Self & George went to the Baldwin Taylor with Cloath etc for a Coat & Breeches. William Clarke gave his Daughter Patr[icia] a beating bout for stealing a pair of Pattens[6] from my Lord's House. Gave Bab Whyatt some Tea Dust.

Sunday, the 6th [Epiphany] A very wet Day. Lord Harcourt & Lady not at Church. Turner paid for a Tythe Pig. Mr Hall kill'd a Pig from Farmer Fields. Read a Brief.

[f.96r]

Monday, the 7th Thomas Williams sold six Pigs at Abingdon. Mr Ward appraised my Sister Rocks Things & din'd with Me.

Tuesday, the 8th As Thame the Butcher from Abingdon did not come, Self had the Balwin Butcher to kill my Bull, & he jumpt over the Backside gate, before he came.[7]

Wednesday, the 9th Gave the Clarke a Leg of the Bull. The Butcher cut him out & Self paid him 2s. 6d. Met Lord Harcourt as Self & George were going to Baldwin. Mrs Hall bak'd Bread & the Bull's Cheeks. Self had Petty Toes for Din.[8]

[f.96v]

Thursday, the 10th Self Br at Oxford Cofe & found it extreamly cold & was glad I had put on two Waistcoats.[9] Sent two Baskets to Oxford for

Mortimer Street & draw'd away a Load of Soap Ashes. Return'd Home to Din. Bought Russia Drab[10] for George & Cloath for Bett.

Friday, the 11th Self Br at my Lord's with Mr Backall. Self bought from the Taylor my Waistcoat & left Russia Drab for George's Frock.[11] Burn't the rough Grass among the Thorns in Combe Bottom.

Saturday, the 12th Consulted with my Lord at the new Parsonage House about the [f.97^{r}] Cellar Stairs & Doors. Din'd at the great House with Dr Sipthorpe & the Abingdon Lawyer. Bett did not come Home till after 6 at Night. Paid Thomas Williams a Year's Wages due last Mich. old Stile.

Sunday, the 13th Cows & Horses turn'd into the Orchard. After M. Service Self & Thomas Williams went to my New House. Roast Bull Beef for Din. Spoke to Henry about wearing great Coat. Farmer Wright's Housekeeper brought a yound Woman to be hir'd, but She was not. Gave Bull Beef [f.97^{v}] to several poor People, a Letter from Polly.

Monday, the 14th Measur'd my Pailing & did intend to have set it up at my new Garden, but my Lord Harcourt was not willing, & so I am rewarded for my great Condescension, but I hope greater Disappointments than this will make not much Impression on the Peace & Harmony of my Mind. Spoke to Mr Cowden about Mrs Rock Money. Read the News at the Golden Ball. Sent George to Abingdon with a Letter for Polly.

Tuesday, the 15th Ballanc'd Accounts with Mr [f.98^{r}] Edmond Baker, & there was Money due to Him.

Wednesday, the 16th Draw'd Furze Faggots from Forewood to the Kiln & half an hundred to George Sparrow. A Load of Wheat Straw laid up for Clarke of Littlemore.

Thursday, the 17th Sent a Load of Straw to Littlemore & brought from Oxford a Load of Soap Ashes. Self Br at Cofe. Return'd Home to Din.

Friday, the 18th Thomas Williams went with his Sons in Law to Abingdon, & they were treated at my House at Night. Howse shot one or two Pidgeons, if not more.

[f.98v]

Saturday, the 19th Thomas Williams took Six roasting Pigs to Oxford & sold only One. Self Br at Cofe. Bought Shalloon for a furr'd Coat.[12] Call'd on Neice & Mrs Rock. Seven Pidgeons Potted.

Sunday, the 20th After M.P. Self & Thomas Williams went to Forewood. Part of a hash'd Duck for Din. Field & Moulder din'd here & had two Glasses of Wine. Wrote a Letter for Polly.

Monday, the 21st Begun drawing the Timber out of Broadmore Close. Henry trench'd at Combe Bottom. Sent a Letter to Abingdon by Dame Baker. Jackson stopt two Gaps in the Orchard.

[f.99r]

Tuesday, the 22nd Took in the Beans & Vetches. Tun'd up the Wine. A Roast Fowl for Din. Took to Bab Whyatt Wine & Ale. Sold two Calves for £2 5s., to young Haynes.

Wednesday, the 23rd Howse shot some Pidgeons. Boil Bull Beef for Din. Edmond Baker examin'd the Carriage Wheels & found they would not Do, for the Landau. Pack't up Baggage.

Thursday, the 24th Howse knock'd down at one Shoot 9 Pidgeons. Set out in my Landau for London after Br. Din'd at Nettlebed. Laid at Maidenhead Bridge.

Friday, the 25th Br at Cranford Bridge. Got [f.99v] to Mortimer Street by Dinner Time & the Horses were much tired. N.P. St George's Hanover Square.

Saturday, the 26th E.M.P. St James. Strol'd about Covent Garden before Br. No Letters at the Cofe. Went to the Coachmaker. Bought 24 Trusses of Hay. No Books sold at Sandby's.[13] Search'd my Thirteen Lottery Tickets at two Offices & found they were all Blanks, but I am thankfull to Providence for what the Blanks will Produce.

Had a great Prise fallen to my [f.100r] Lott, its possible I might have missapply'd it, (but I trust I should) if so its better for me to be without it & I am content & I dont set my Heart upon Riches, but on the Service of

God & may I ever continue so to Do. A great Fortune wont make a Man Happy. For its often seen that those who abound in Riches abound in many Wants as well as the poor & indigent. Let us suit our Minds to our Fortunes & moderate our Desires & then both Rich & Poor may do tollerably Well.

The Loss I am likely to suffer [f.100^{v}] out of the Profits of my Living,[14] I Hope, by the Blessing of God, will make no Breach on the Peace & Harmony of Mind, but that I shall be easy[15] & quite contented under that Misfortune.

To expect to live free from Misfortune, is romantic, & if we live flatter[ing] ourselves with that Conceit, we shall ere long be experimentally convinc'd of our Error. Crosses & Disappointments will happen, & when they Do its our Duty to bear them with Patience & Resignation to ye Divine Will.

[f.101^{r}]

Sunday, the 27th Sacrament at the Foundling Hospital, & follow'd a Woman Self lik'd to her Home in Red Lyon Square.[16] A roast Pig for Din. N.P. Mary Bonne. Mrs Pickering was expected here but did not Come.

Monday, the 28th M.P. Berwick Chapple. Went into a Shop in Leicester field because of the Rain & then bought a Ribbon Cane. Read News at Slaughter's Cofe. Call'd on Dunning[17] but no Money. Din'd near the Royal Exchange. Saw a Post Chariot. Taken with a violent Beating at Night.

Tuesday, the 29th Rec'^{d} upwards of £25 of Polly as my Share. Compos'd Part of a Sermon pretty readily, & I [f.101^{v}] am thankfull to God that I was able to do so. Stay'd at Home all Day. Rec'^{d} a Letter from Mrs Rock.

Wednesday, the 30th Harry rode out with the Horses after Din. Compos'd part of a Sermon. Stay'd at Home all Day. Laid the Carpets on the Floor. Last Sunday was the first day of wearing my new Grey Coat & as for the black Waistcoat I wore that, about ten Days before that time.

Thursday, the 31st E.M.P. St Annes. Hunted about for a Green Surtut Coat for George. Stay'd at Home all the Day after Br. Finis'd Sermon. A Buttock of the Bull Beef for Din.

Notes

1 The date was written originally as 175–. The 5 is crossed out in the text and nothing has been superscribed. The year is, however, definitely 1760, as con firmed by the date given for subsequent months.

2 The recollection of these events, recorded at the beginning of the *Diary*, provides JN with a good excuse for some philosophizing.

3 'not' is crossed out in the text.

4 The following entry is crossed through: '2 Thomas Williams rec'd at Shillingford Money due for Barly.' It follows in the entry for 2 January. This provides further evidence that JN sometimes wrote up his diary several days at a time.

5 'Sent a Basket to ye new' is crossed out in the text. 'I opt for London' is superscribed and crossed out.

6 Pattens were a pair of wooden shoes or clogs, or a pair of overshoes to raise ordinary shoes out of the mud. See *OED*.

7 The bull's bid for freedom failed to save his skin, as the opening of the next entry suggests.

8 Pettitoes are the trotters or outer part of the hoof. See *OED*.

9 The extremely cold weather was noted in the press. The frosty conditions caused accidents, as at least two people slipped in the streets and broke their legs. See *Jackson's*, Saturday 19 January 1760.

10 Russia Drab was a type of red cloth.

11 By 'Frock' JN meant frock coat.

12 Shalloon was a closely woven woollen material chiefly used for trimmings and linings. See *OED*.

13 William Sandby was a bookseller in Fleet Street opposite St Dunstan's church. See Mortimer, *Universal Director*, Part III, p. 169.

14 JN may be commenting on the changes afoot at Nuneham which he saw as affecting his income.

15 'enjoy' is crossed out in the text.

16 Red Lion Square was laid out in 1684 by Nicholas Barbon. It was built after fierce battles with neighbouring Gray's Inn lawyers who objected to losing their rural vistas when the houses were erected. For full details see *London Encycl.*, pp. 639–40.

17 Dunning was one of JN's tenants.

[f.102^{r}]

February 1760

Friday, the 1st Late at M.P. Gray's Inn.[1] Left an Advertisement for the Post Landau. Went to Mr Fitzgerald's Auction of Goods. See the uncertaintly of human Greatness! he who lately was in high Credit, & a flourishing Condition is reduc'd to great Straits. May such Instances of the Misfortunes of Others, teach me patiently to bear Losses & disappointment & not to lay them too much at Heart.

Din'd near Ludgate. Punch at [f.102^{v}] Ashley's. Could not meet with a proper pair of double Channel Pumps. Got Home time enough for Tea.

Saturday, the 2nd E.M.P. Covent Garden.[2] Left a Letter for J N. at the Royal Point. Bought a pair of Shoes & Buckles. Br at Lord Harcourt's. Went to the Coach Maker's. Saw Mrs Adderly at the Auction. Spoke to Mr Piggot in Pall Mall. Mr Cowden drank Tea & paid me on Mrs Ann Rock Account £18 15s. Wrote to Mr Ward offering him the Goods at his own Valuation. The House opposite the Chapple is not to be Lett.

[f.103^{r}]

Sunday, the 3rd St George's Ch. Queen's Sq Sac^{rt} & afterwards went to the Foundling. One of Newnham Hams for Dinner. N.P. Marybonne. Bought one of Miss Truffler's Cakes. John Woods went Home with his Mother to be tann'd by his Father.

Monday, the 4th E.P. St James's. Bought a hard Brush. Went to the Coach maker's & much displeas'd at the Crest. Costard, late Servant of Edmond Baker spoke to me near Westminster Hall. Din'd over the Bridge. Treated Eli Norris with Wine. George brought a Basket of Provision from the Inn out of the Country.

[f.103^{v}]

Tuesday, the 5th Left word at the Coach Makers, that if the Chariot was not done in a proper Manner the next time I should send for it, that then I might not take to it. M.P. Conduit St. No Money from Dunning. No Letter at the Turk's Head from J.N. Call'd at Mr Wood's about his son John. A Newnham Pig for Din. N.P. St George's.

Wednesday, the 6th Cob the Coach Painter came about the Crest being badly done, & Self agree'd to send for the Chariot next Friday. Little John Wood went Home with a bad Head, & Self gave Him 2d.

Thursday, the 7th Wrote on my Dearest Mothers Death & Burial. N.P. St Georges Hanover Square.

[f.104^{r}]

Friday, the 8th Went to the Coachmakers for the Post Chariot & the Horses were put to, but came away without it, as it was not finish'd according to my Mind. Call'd at John Wood's & he was gone for Mortimer St. Had George with me to Pater Noster Row for a Leg of Mutton cut out Venison Fashion, but there was not then One ready. Din'd near Ludgate.

Saturday, the 9th E.M.P. St Anne's. Proll'd about Covent Garden. Polly went with me to the Coachmaker's. No Rent of Dunning. Took out a fresh Licence for my Carriage. Din'd near Ludgate & then went to the Punch House. Got home by Tea time.

[f.104^{v}]

Sunday, the 10th Sacr^{t} St George's Queen Square & but a small Number of Communicants indeed. A very large Ham from Newnham for Din. N.P. St Mary le bone.

Monday, the 11th Cobb, the Painter sent to me to see the Painting. E.M.P. St James's Ch. George brought a Basket from Piccadilly, from Newnham. Mary Hall in her Letter gives Notice of quitting my Service.

Tuesday, the 12th Self & Polly examin'd the Arms on the Chariot. Took George with me to the Butcher's, but he went without the Leg of Mutton. Din'd near Fleet Street. A Pint of Porter near Covent Garden.

Bedford [f.105r] Cofe.[3] Saw the Beggar's Opera[4] & two were not willing to have me to set between them, but Self did.

Wednesday, the 13th Advertiz'd for an Housekeeper etc. E.M.P. St James's. compos'd part of a Sermon. A Pig roasted very badly.

Thursday, the 14th E.M.P. St James's. One offer'd her Service for an Housekeeper but was not accepted. A Leg of Mutton for Din, but Self din'd chiefly on Sprats. The Plate was divided.

Friday, the 15th E.M.P. St James's. Fish very badly drest. Some Tiles fell down from the Dining room Chimney, [f.105v] & as no one in the Family receiv'd any Damage considering how very tempestuous the Weather was,[5] I am thankfull to Providence for his Goodness to us, & may I ever enjoy a truly gratefull Soul. If I consider how ma[n]y Souls by Sea & Land have perish'd this day, as it must or ought naturally to give me some trouble & uneasiness, yet likewise should it make me very thankfull to God for being so very kind to all of this Family for receiving no Bodily Hurt. When our Neighbours suffer by Sea & Land & we escape unhurt, let us [f.106r] not neglect to return ye Homage of Praise & Thanksgiving to God for the Same. When Storms & Tempests arise, & we find ourselves in much Danger, how naturally do we call upon God for his Protection, & when we find our Selves out of Danger, should we not be thankfull to him for the same?[6] Most certainly we should.

Saturday, the 16th E.M.P. St James's. No Rent of Dunning. Saw a Coach horse fall down in Fleet St. Such accidents will happen but Providence governs all Things. Enquir'd after Emery. Went to the East [f.106v] India House. Insur'd my Parsonage House Goods etc. Din'd near the Mansion House.[7] Call'd on Watts the Wig Maker.[8] Brought my dearest Mother's Watch Home.

Sunday, the 17th M.P. Foundling Hospital & Self let into my Pew Dr Oliver & his Daughter. Mr Murden Preach'd above One Hour. N.P. Marybone.

Monday, the 18th E.M.P. St James's. Went to the Royal Exchange & din'd near the Mansion House & a man play'd [ ] on a Jew.[9] May I have always more good Nature & humanity towards those I converse with,

[than] to indeavour to give sport to others by treating [f.107^{r}] my Neighbours out of Character, may I not expose their Faults & Failing with any secret Pleasure & delight, but rather cast a veil over them & reflect on them in the most favourable manner. Bought a Pair of single Channel Pumps & Corks.[10]

Tuesday, the 19th [Shrove Tuesday] E.M.P. St James's. Gave Harry good Advice. Much delighted with Howell's Letters. Enquir'd into Margaret Camel's Character. Mr Dunning sent a Quarter's Rent due 25 of last Decr. Receiv'd my Policy.

Wednesday, the 20th [Ash Wednesday] E.M.P. St James's. N. Conduit St Chapple. Call'd at Gray's in Queen Street but not at Home. Fasted all the Day.

Thursday, the 21st E.M.P. St James's. Went [f.107^{v}] with my Sister Rock to the East India House in Admiral Long's Chariot. Din'd at the Widow Gould's.

Friday, the 22nd E.M.P. St James's. Enquir'd after Counsellor Harley in Lincoln's Inn Fields instead of Lincoln's Inn & so did not find Him.[11] Went to Westminster Abby. Dish of Chocolate at Slaughter's. Din'd at the Widow Goulds.

Saturday, the 23rd E.M.P. St James's. Went to Counsellor Harly. Met the Coachmaker just as I came from my Lord Harcourt's. Spoke to the Cane Maker about George Brooks. Din'd at the 3 Cups in Holborn. Punch & Wine at the White Hart.[12] Took a Coach near Bloomsbury Sq.

[f.108^{r}]

Sunday, the 24th Sacr^{t} at the Foundling Hospital. N.P. St Mary le Bonne.

Monday, the 25th E.M.P. St James's. Self deliver'd in at the Exchequer all my Lottery Tickets, being thirteen Blanks. Took a Turn in Westminster Abby. Sprats for Din. N.P. Conduit Chapple. Spoke to the Farrier about his Bill.

Tuesday, the 26th Bought three Bottles of Olives in Pudding Lane near the Monument & George Carried them. Call'd at the Cane Maker over London Bridge & told Him how the Case stood with me & George Brookes. Return'd Home to Br over Westmi[nster] [f.108^{v}] Bridge. Dr Sipthorpe Br with me & one of my large Herbals. George's Mother came for Him & took him away without a Coat.

Wednesday, the 27th After Br Self set out for Newnham & din'd at Colebrook, & got to Maiden Head Bridge by Tea time & had an Eel for Supper. The Landlord was lately hurt by falling from his Horse but is in a fair Way of doing Well. May God sanctifie his Hurt to his spiritual Go[o]d, & may I ever be prepared against a sudden Death. When he little expect any Danger he was in danger of being kill'd on the Spot, so that in truth we are continually in the Neighbourhood of Death.

[f.109^{r}]

Thursday, the 28th After Br Self set out & din'd at Nettlebed & there met with William Baites whose father lately kept the Bull[13] of the same Place, but is now greatly reduc'd, perhaps it may be for his everlasting Welfare & cause a thorough Reformation in his Manners. Some get Rich & some Poor & so the world goes on, but that is the best State which makes us better. As for my part I am altogether resign'd to the Will of God and trust that he will order all things most for my Profit, if I am not wanting on my Part, & therefore in every State may bless & praise his holy [f.109^{v}] Name & say the Will of the Lord be done. Reach'd Newnham about 6'o Clock at Night Safe & in Good Health, for wch Mercy I am thankfull to my most gracious & mercifull good God.

Friday, the 29th Winnow'd Wheat. Fasted the Boar Stag. Howse shot some Pidgeons.

Notes

1 Gray's Inn was one of the four Inns of Court. JN worshipped in the chapel which has been on the same site since 1315. It was rebuilt in 1689 and further restoration took place in 1893. The original building was destroyed in 1941, but the chapel was reconstructed after the war with much of the original stained glass. For full details see *London Encycl.*, pp. 321–2.

2 This was St Paul's church, Covent Garden, designed by Inigo Jones for Francis Russell, 4th Earl of Bedford. It was built in 1631–3, renovated in 1788 and restored after a fire in 1795. Further alterations took place in 1871. For full details see *ibid.*, pp. 754–5.

3 The Bedford coffee house, 'under the Piazza Covent Garden', was first mentioned in 1730. Garrick had letters addressed to himself there in 1744. Other frequenters included Fielding, Pope and Horace Walpole. For full details see Lillywhite, *Coffee Houses*, pp. 114–5.

4 This was a ballad opera by John Gay. It was first performed in London in 1728. It consists of a play interspersed with about seventy songs set to popular tunes of the time.

5 There were storms across the country. Violent winds did much damage to property in Oxford, but there was no loss of life. See *Jackson's*, Friday 15 February 1760.

6 'If we are' is crossed through in the text.

7 The Mansion House was the official residence of the Lord Mayor of London during his year of office. The building was quite new to JN. After a lot of discussion, George Dance, Clerk of the City Works, was asked to produce designs in 1735. The foundation stone was laid in 1739. For full details see *London Encycl.*, pp. 493–4.

8 This was George Watt of St Martin's Court, St Martin's Lane. See Mortimer, *Universal Director*, Part II, p. 26.

9 Judging by the context, a man may have played a trick on a Jew.

10 These were not the best quality shoes, as 'single channel pumps' only had one row of stitching fixing the upper to the sole. Compare with 'double channel pumps' mentioned in the entry for 28 February 1759 and note 24.

11 Lincoln's Inn was one of the four Inns of Court. For full details of this and of Lincoln's Inn Fields see *London Encycl.*, pp. 457–60.

12 The White Hart without Bishopsgate was an ancient inn. It was a favourite haunt of Quakers and Masons. See Lillywhite, *Coffee Houses*, pp. 644–5.

13 This was the Bull Inn, an early Georgian building with a central pediment enclosing a lunette. See Sherwood and Pevsner, *Oxfordshire*, p. 714.

March 1760

Saturday, the 1st Thomas Williams draw'd six Qu[arter] of Wheat to Oxford & brought Home Candles, Hops etc. Bak'd. Howse kill'd the Boar Stag.

Sunday, the 2nd Self & Thomas Williams went to Forewood after M. S[ervice] & there saw a dead Ass. Mr Bowly drank Tea with me.

[f.110^r]

Monday, the 3rd Lord & Lady Harcourt came to Newnham. William Baites of Nettlebed enter'd my Service.[1]

Tuesday, the 4th Henry Bricknall begun brewing but left it because Mrs Hall discompos'd Him.

Wednesday, the 5th Draw'd Furze Faggots from Forewood to Kiln D$^{o.}$ Br at Lord Harcourt's. Employ'd Howse in Combe Bottom.

Thursday, the 6th Howse cut down the Wood on my late Furze Plant. Black Moll brought me a Letter from Polly as I was with Him. Draw'd more Furze Faggots to the Kiln in Forewood.

Friday, the 7th Rec'd a Letter from Polly giving [f.110^v] a bad Account of Margaret Camel.[2] Self sent Henry to Oxford with one Letter for Polly, & another for (Mary) Camel & an Advertisement for an Housekeeper & also for the Sale of my Chaise & Chair. Howse begun cutting Furze Faggots in Forewood.

Saturday, the 8th Br at Oxford & took William Betts[3] with me on the little Mare. Paid Mrs Rock her Money. Call'd on my Neice. Found no Housekeepers had made any Enquiry after my Place.

Sunday, the 9th After M.P. Self & Thomas Williams went to Forewood & found my Sheep & Cows had got into my [f.111^r] Lord's

Grounds, the Shephard being gone from them. Sent Bab Whyatt some Calves Head hash'd.

Monday, the 10th After Br set out for Oxford & convers'd with Mr Warde about his Bill. Din'd near Carfax & the Woman who kept it when I was there last hath Lett it, [to] her Maid & Oystler who are now married, & She retir'd from Business, God bless them & may they spend the remainder of their Days to the Honour & Glory of God, & dye with Peace & a good Conscience. Laid at Staple [f.111^{v}] Hall at Whitney[4] & the Landlord has had 24 Children & both he & his Wife are very hearty. Children are a great Blessing when they Prove Loving & dutifull to their Parents & take to good Ways, & when they do not its too often owing to their Parents neglecting to instruct them in the Principles of Virtue & Religion in their youthfull Days. The neglect of which is very dreadfull both for the Parents as well as their Children.

An Oxford Buck got terrible drunk, a shamefull thing, & [f.112^{r}] may I never be in such a Condition.

Tuesday, the 11th Some Oxford Scholars had Wine for Br. Call'd at Marriott, the Wool Dealer but not at Home. Walk'd about the Church Yard.[5] Knock'd twice at Mrs Cole's Door & retir'd again as no one came to me. Should it be my Lott to marry her Daughter, I trust through the Blessing of God, to live very easy & comfortable & above all to spend my Days after a very holy & religious manner, & to encour[ag]e one another [f.112^{v}] in the Progress of Virtue & Religion & to make that our chiefest Study & Delight.

Din'd at Ensome Ferry on a Jack.[6] Many Years ago Self & James Taylor was at this Place in my Way to Bath. I am alive, the other is Dead, & I am thankfull to Providence for the Prolongation of my Life. My Business in that Expedition was to trye my Fortune with Miss Longman, but after I had waited on her Father, I found it would not do, & if she kill'd her Self with Drinking, what [f.113^{r}] Pleasure could such a Wife have given Me, so that all things consider'd, may I ever conclude, that Providence always orders all my Affairs after the best manner for my spiritual Interest, & therefore may his Will & not mine always take. Spoke to Mr Patten. Got home in good Time.

Wednesday, the 12th Self & William rode to Dorchester & left a Letter there for Polly & bespoke Nails for my Landau. Thomas Williams sold nothing at Shillingford. Sent Dame Andrews a good [f.113^{v}] Commons of Calves Head. One of the Workmen came to me to met Bowly at my New House, but he was not there when I came.

Thursday, the 13th Thomas Williams[7] mightily discompos'd because Will was sent to take Moll's Place in the Barn. Sent Straw & Cavings to my Lord's.[8] Went to the Collar Maker.

Friday, the 14th Self fasted all the Day.[9] The Sheep & Cows got into my Lord's Grounds. Went to Forewood. A thine Congregation at N.P.

Saturday, the 15th Barly, Butter & Eggs sold at Oxford. Took my Grandfather's Manuscripts of the Herbal to Dr Sipthorpe's & saw his Wife who was mighty [f.114^{r}] dirty.[10] Paid the Tinman's Bill. Call'd on my Neice. Rec'^{d} a Letter at the Printer's about an Housekeeper. Spoke to Mr Trollope. Bought several things. Took Breeches to be clean'd. Gave the Men at the new Parsonage One Shilling.

Sunday, the 16th Self, Bett & Thomas Williams got some Asses Home from Forewood. William Betts undertook the Care of the Sheep, as Clark's Boy forsook them. Brown & the Mare got out of the Orchard. Thomas Williams fodder'd the Sheep at Night. No singing at N.P.

Monday, the 17th Spoke to Mr Bush at Abingdon. Enquir'd after the Wooll Merchant. [f.114^{v}] Bought a Leg of Mutton. Return'd to Din. Sent Henry Bricknall away who wanted to be paid for the wearing of his Cloath, but was not.

Tuesday, the 18th Sold all my Wool. Went to Little Milton[11] after a Cock Turkey but to no Purpose.

Wednesday, the 19th Br at Witney. M.P. D^{o}. Conversed with an Elderly man who was acquainted with Dr Halloway. Miss Cole I found by him had been cross'd in Love, & did not frequent the Church as She was want to have done, a Melancholy Affair!

Give me Grace, O my God, to keep close to my Duty, & not to suffer [f.115^{r}] Crosses & Disappointments to render me remiss in the Discharge of it. As long as I live I must expect to meet with Troubles & Afflictions, but may they not make such a deep Impression on my Mind, as to render it irreligious or unmindfull of what is lawfull & right. If I cannot bear with a tollerable degree of Patience the common Misfortunes & Calamities of Life, my Condition is bad, but I trust I shall not be too much dejected in the most Adverse State, And that I shall always enjoy the Blessing of a good Conscience, & then I may hold out [f.115^{v}] unto the End with Patience.

Din'd at Ensome[12] & a Farmer came in, seeming in a bad State of Health to sell Furze Faggots to One who knew me. Got Home in good Time.

Thursday, the 20th Went to the Lamb at Abingdon, but the goods were very indifferent. Came home to Din by Long Whittenham.[13] Spoke to Stevenson ab[out] Clarke's Boy. In leading the Horse through the Gate the Stirrup caught in the Catch & the Saddle came off, the two Girth Straps breaking.

[f.116^{r}]

Friday, the 21st Found Christian Barns in Bed. Gave Bab Whyatt a Quart of Ale. Spoke about having some Things done in my new Parsonage House. Went to the Furze Cutter. Paid Clarke some Parish Taxes.

Saturday, the 22nd Br at Oxford. M.P. Carfax. My Neice was this day safely deliver'd of a Girl.[14] Praised be God for this Mercy & may She live to be a Comfort to her Parents & become a very good Christian. Married People naturally desire to have Children & are uneasy if they have none, though they too often find more Trouble & Vexation [f.116^{v}] from them than Pleasure & Delight. Should Self enter into the holy State of Matrimony, may not earnestly desire to have Children, but be quite easy as to that Affair whether I have any or not.

Went to Paradise. Din'd at the New Inn. Heard of a manservant who now lives with Dr Cooper, & late with Mr Austin. Sent Sister Rock a Letter. Brandy & Rum at the Mayor's.[15] Got home to Tea.

Sunday, the 23rd Paid the Clifton Furze Cutter & he had a pair of old Boots instead of 2s. Howse went away discontented. After M.P. Self & Thomas [f.117^{r}] Williams went to Forewood. A Leg of roast Mutton & Dandylyon for Din. A Married Woman offer'd her Service but I believe She wont do.

Monday, the 24th Mrs Hall & Black Moll went to Abingdon with Butter, Eggs & Cheese. Went to Howse at Forewood who was cutting the rough Bushes. The Whitenham Tasker enter'd for the first Day.[16] Cold Mutton & Dandeleon for Din.

Tuesday, the 25th Jackson shot two Wood Pidgeons. Howse went off after he had cut 3/4 of Hundred of Furze Faggots. Hash'd Mutton for Din. Gave Dame Whyatt's Maid good Advice. [f.117^{V}] Mrs Cummins sent her Son John to desire me to write to my Sister Rock & to beg of her to advise her Eldest Son to return Home should he call upon Her. A sad thing indeed for a Son to give his Parents so much Trouble & Vexation, who should rather make it one of his chiefest Delights to make them as easy & as comfortable, as Possible.

Wednesday, the 26th Sent Polly a Letter. M.P. Abingdon. Call'd at the Wooll Merchant's. Return'd Home to Din. Howse cut down some Boughs in Long Mead. The Sheep were pounded. A troublesome Job to get them into the Fold.

Thursday, the 27th A Load of Bushes drawn from Forewood to my new Glebe & . . .

Notes

1 William Baites's father had lately kept The Bull at Nettlebed. See entry for 28 February 1760.

2 Margaret Camel was a possible candidate to replace Mary Hall as JN's housekeeper.

3 JN meant William Baites.

4 This is the Staple Hall at 32 Bridge Street, Witney. The present building dates from the sixteenth and seventeenth centuries. The first structure is said to have been erected by Roger de Stapleton in the early fourteenth century at the same time as Exeter College. For full details see Sherwood and Pevsner, *Oxfordshire*, p. 850.

5 The churchyard referred to is that of St Mary's church, Witney. This is a large church with a handsome central tower. For full details see *ibid.*, pp. 843–4.

6 Eynsham Ferry was the crossing point of the Thames at Eynsham. It has now been replaced by a toll bridge.

7 'Silvester' is crossed out in the text.

8 'Cavings' were a mixture of straw and chaff.

9 This was recorded as a 'Day of Solemn Fast' in the press. See *Jackson's*, Friday 14 March 1760.

10 The 'Herbal' referred to is: *A Compleat Herbal of the late James Newton M.D., containing the Prints and the English Names of Several thousand Trees, Plants, Shrubs, Flowers, Exotics, etc., All Curiously engraved on Copper Plates*, (London 1752, 8vo.). Dr Newton (1678–1750), JN's father, was a botanist who kept a private lunatic asylum by the Islington Turnpike. He is traditionally supposed to have written the herbal, but, if JN is to be trusted, this would not appear to be the case. Furthermore, the work is believed to date from about 1680, thus ruling out his father as the author. JN's grandfather was also called James and it seems likely that the work was in fact his. Only a portion of the herbal appeared during his lifetime and JN clearly had a hand in its later publication. The 1752 edition bears an engraved portrait of the author and a dedication to Earl Harcourt by 'James Newton, Rector of Newnham in Oxfordshire'. See W.I. Pinks, *The History of Clerkenwell* (1865), p. 274; *Dictionary of National Biography*, L. Stephen and S. Lee (eds.) (Oxford, 1921–2), XIV, pp. 393–4.

11 Little Milton is a village about five miles east of Nuneham.

12 JN meant Eynsham.

13 JN meant Long Wittenham

14 In another hand in the text at this point is written, 'Dorothy', afterwards Mrs J.W. Moss.

15 The Mayor was Sir Thomas Munday.

16 'Jackson shot two wood' is crossed out in the text.

Diary: Volume II

[f.1r]

April 1761

Sunday, the 5th[1] **[Old Lady Day]** Self & Bullock[2] went over the Glebe before Br. Preach'd one of my first Sermons. Pray'd by Dame Well's Mother & sent Her Plumb Pudding & some Rabbit. Bullock displeas'd at my speaking to Him about leaving the Key in the Barn Door.

Monday, the 6th Two of Edmond's Men begun hewing out the Timber. Bullock wanted to have more Wages. Begun removing Earth to the forepart of the House with the Dutch Carts. Fastened the Puppy to the House.

Tuesday, the 7th Busy in getting Things in readiness for my Bath Journey. Part [f.1v] of a cold Rabbit for Din. Self got Greens & Radishes from my Lord's Garden. Made use of the two Dutch Carts for removing Earth towards[3] the Front of the House.

Wednesday, the 8th Pray'd by Dame Wells & her Mother. Intended to have set out for Bath but was prevented by the Rain. Wells brought from Abingdon a Yoke & Seeds. No Milk from the Upper Farm & Nineveh.

Thursday, the 9th Tythe Milk from the Upper Farm & Nineveh. Self & Giles set out after Br for Bath. Pray'd by Dame Wells & her Mother & the old Woman is likely to dye & may the Lord have Mercy on her Soul. Din'd at Farringdon [f.2r] & Laid at Leachlade & had cold boil Beef for Supper.

Friday, the 10th The Oystler offer'd his Service for a Postillion. Br at the Bull at Cirencester, & then went to Morning Prayer,[4] where I saw a

Woman I lik'd tollerable well for a Wife & her Name is Web.

Strol'd about the Park.[5] Had Saddle & Bridle rectified. After Din set out for Tendbury [Tetbury] & there made use of my own Tea & Br[ead] in Bed Chamber.

Saturday, the 11th Br at the half-Way House with a Stranger. Gave the Smart little footboy 6d. who lives at Wells & came with me from Tebbury [Tetbury]. Reach'd the Saracen's Head at Bath[6] by Din time & din'd on a Shoulder of Veal. N.P. St Michael.[7] Bought a New Hat for 17s.

I am thankfull to thee, O my God, [f.2^{V}] for bringing me once more safe to this Place, this Place I have so often frequented in my more juvenile Days,[8] & I hope innocently too, & may I still continue so to do wherever I am, or what State soever I shall be in, for it's my hearty desire to please thee & to serve thee with all my Might.

Sunday, the 12th M. & N.P. Abby. Walk'd about with Fowel. Saw a great number of Communicants coming from the Square Chapple.[9] Subscrib'd at Morgan's & drank Tea there.

Monday, the 13th M.P. Abby. Hunted about after a Lodging & at last went to my old Quarters in King's Mead Street[10] & took a Woman with me who took the second Floor. Beef Stake for Din. Tea at Morgan's.

[f.3^{r}]

Tuesday, the 14th Marketted & bought a Fowl, Beacon, Crab etc. Stay'd a short time in the Rooms at Morning.[11] M. & N.P. Chapple. Call'd on my old Washerwoman. Went to the Ball & return'd Home about 9. Snub'd Giles for not riding in the Square till Self came to Him. Gave the Chamber Maid & the Tapster something at my Inn.

Wednesday, the 15th M. & N.P. Chapple. A very rainy Day. Self brought Home three Books from Leake's. Spoke to Sir George Cobb in the Fish Market. Bought some Anchovies. Bespoke a Brown Loaf. Giles Laid for the first Night at my Lodgings.

Thursday, the 16th M.P. Chapple. Self & Giles din'd on cold Provision at Lincome.[12] Lost at Lottery 2s.

[f.3^{v}]

Friday, the 17th M. & N.P. Chapple. Rode out. Din'd with a Gentleman whose Name I know not, & went with him to see Russel's Garden.

Saturday, the 18th M.P. the Chapple. Had much Conversation with a Man about some of my old Aquaintance of Bradford [-on-Avon] in my way there. Din'd at Holt. A bad road Home.

Sunday, the 19th M. & N.P. Abby & Sacr^{t}. A roast Fowl & Beacon for Dinner. Drank Tea at the Rooms being a general Treat.

Monday, the 20th M. & N.P. Abby. Rode toward Bristol with a Doctor & retun'd the upper Way, & then rode in the London Road. Din'd at the Beef Stake House. Saw Miss Payne at the Rooms in the Evening, & its possible She may [f.4^{r}] become my Wife, but God's Will be done in this Affair & all others.

May I be easy in every Condition of Life, & with Patience & Resignation submit to Providence[13] in all Things, in Adversity as well as Prosperity.

Tuesday, the 21st Went to the Pump Room[14] before Br. M. & N.P. Abby. Rode in the Bath & London Road. Cold Provision for Din. Went to the Ball.

Wednesday, the 22nd Rode out. Cold Provision for Din.

Thursday, the 23rd Convers'd with a Lady on Lincomb Mount. Din'd at the Florist Feast.

Friday, the 24th A Mackerel for Dinner. Rode out. Bought a Crab.

Saturday, the 25th M.P. Chapple. Tripe for Din. Play'd at Lottery.

Sunday, the 26th M. & N.P. Abby. Spoke to Miss [f.4^{v}] Payne at the Rooms Evening & She was mighty Shuff.[15] Tripe for Supper.

Monday, the 27th M.P. Chapple. Din'd at Lincomb & drank Tea at the Spar. Convers'd with the Lady's Maid. Gave Giles & Will each of them a Plumb Cake.

Tuesday, the 28th Br at Lincomb. Got acquainted with several People there. Mackerel for Din.[16] Met one at the White Hart[17] who knew my late Brother Rock.

Wednesday, the 29th Br at Lincomb, & the Lady came into the Room before I had done. Rode in the London & Bath Road. Mackerel & Beacon for Din.

Thursday, the 30th [Ascension Day] Convers'd much with Miss Payne in the Pump Room & She seems mighty Shye. Din'd at Holt & met with much Rain.

Notes

1 JN still refers to the old style calendar which was eleven days behind the Gregorian calendar in use after 1752. Thus 5 April new style was 25 March old style, i.e. Old Lady Day.

2 Bullock was JN's farm manager.

3 'before' is crossed out in the text.

4 The Bull was on the south side of the market place most of which was rebuilt in the nineteenth century. JN attended Morning Prayer in St John the Baptist, 'the largest parish church in Gloucestershire and one of the most spacious in England.' See D. Verey, *Gloucestershire: The Cotswolds* (1970), pp. 161–172.

5 The park referred to surrounds The Mansion or Cirencester House, built in 1714–18 by Allen, 1st Earl Bathurst. It is the finest example in England of planting in the pre-landscape manner. It was begun just when geometrical avenues were becoming old-fashioned and continued until 1775 when Capability Brown's own 'natural' parks were themselves being called into question. For full details see *ibid.*, pp. 184–7.

6 The Saracen's Head was in Broad Street, Bath. For full details see January 1759, note 26.

7 This was St Michael's church, Bath. According to Wood it was 'a very neat and light building' erected by Mr Killigrew around 1728; a 'whimsical Fabrick' sixty-three feet by thirty-seven feet with only a timber floor 'to separate the Living from the Dead'. The church was in fact constructed by John Harvey in 1734 and demolished in 1830. See Wood, *Description of Bath*, p. 308; W. Ison, *The Georgian Buildings of Bath* (Revised edn, Bath, 1980), p. 53.

8 JN had been a regular visitor to Bath since the 1730s. In this volume of the *Diary* he makes two journeys there. On the first occasion he remained for three weeks and three days, from 9 April to 6 May. Later he stayed for another three-week period from 14 May to 7 June. His main purpose seems

to have been pleasure, enjoying all the facilities of the Pump and Assembly Rooms and even indulging in some mild gambling, as well as trying to find a wife. Throughout the *Diary*, he seems very interested in the ladies, but there is no evidence that he ever married despite all his efforts and his natural inclinations. Bath was one of the principal social centres of the eighteenth century. For details of the activities see M. Girouard, *The English Town* (Yale, 1990), Interlude I, and Chapters 7 & 8; J. Penrose, *Letters from Bath, 1766–67* (Gloucester, 1983); A. Barbeau, *Life and Letters at Bath in the Eighteenth Century* (1904); J. Lees-Milne and D. Ford, *Images of Bath* (1982).

9 This was St Mary's by Queen's Square, built by John Wood and opened with great pomp on 25 December 1734. On this occasion there was a concert 'of vocal and instrumental Music and an Anthem composed and set to music by Mr Chilcot based on psalm 84'. Services were held daily at 11 a.m., and on Sundays at 11 a.m. and 5 p.m. See P. Thicknesse, *New Prose Bath Guide* (1778), p. 34; Wood, *Description of Bath*, p. 314.

10 This street was thirty-two feet wide and contained thirty-six houses with four good ones. 'But for the rest, little can be said to draw ones Notice.' See *ibid.*, p. 336.

11 'The Rooms' JN frequented were the Lower Rooms to distinguish them from the Upper Rooms, built by John Wood jnr and opened in 1771. Until about that date, social life centred around the lower end of the town. The Lower Rooms were gutted by fire in 1820 and demolished in 1933. The first room to be built was Harrison's, dating from 1708. A ballroom was added in 1720, followed by a further suite of rooms in 1749–50, during Simpson's tenancy. By 1766 the Rooms were known as Simpson's. The ballroom of 1750 measured ninety feet by thirty-six feet and was thirty-four feet high. According to a guide of 1792, it was 'one of the pleasantest morning rooms in the Kingdom'. Next to it was a card room with a coved ceiling. There were also two tea rooms. Lindsey's Room, afterwards Wilshire's, was opened in 1730. The *New Bath Guide* described this in 1763 as 'a very neat Room' decorated with 'many curious Landscapes'. For full details see Ison, *Bath*, pp. 25–6. The general routine at Bath seemed to be a visit to the Pump Room in the early morning, then breakfast at home or in public, for example at Spring Gardens. This was then perhaps followed by a church service and a stroll along the Parades, built by John Wood in 1740–43. In the evening there were balls, card parties, concerts and various theatrical entertainments, as well as the socializing in the Assembly Rooms.

12 Lincombe Spa was a suburb of Bath.

13 'God' is crossed out in the text.

14 The Pump Room was built in 1706 by John Harvey. This was a simple one-storey building for the convenience of those who came to drink the waters. It was enriched with Corinthian columns and pilasters, with a gallery at one end to hold a small band of musicians for the entertainment of the water drinkers. Waiters handed out glasses of water to those wishing to drink. See

Ison, *Bath*, pp. 38–45.
15 By 'Shuff' JN means shy.
16 'and Beacon' is crossed out in the text.
17 This was The White Hart in Stall Street, Bath.

[f.5^{r}]

May 1761

Friday, the 1st A Gentleman scrap't acquaintance with Me in the Pump Room who knows Mrs Brocas. Br at Lincomb expecting to have found much Rabble there but they were gone. M. & N.P. Abby. A Bottle of Rum from the White Hart & Giles gave me some of it instead of small Beer.

Saturday, the 2nd Marketted before Br & then went to the Pump Room. M.P. Abby & N.P. & Bath. The Washerwoman's Boy was hurt yesterday very much by falling out of a Cart. Giles rode the horses out.

Sunday, the 3rd M. & N.P. Abby & Sac^{rt}. Boil Pidgeon & Beacon for Din. Went to the Rooms in Evening.

[f.5^{v}]

Monday, the 4th M.P. Abby. Agreeably surpris'd with the Garden belonging to the House where the Sale of Goods is. Saw the Post Chaise that was terribly damag'd coming down Clarken Down Hill, & so were all the three Women Passengers & the Postillion, God grant they may survive this Misfortune & make a good use of it, & learn to grow better & to be ever in readiness for their latter End. Din'd at the Beef Stake House & then went to the White Hart. Spoke to Mr Stonehouse at the Rooms & made several Betts with Him.

Tuesday, the 5th Paid my Taylor's Bill. Dock'd Dame Hill.[1]

[f.6^{r}]

Wednesday, the 6th M.P. Abby. Set out from Bath about twelve Clock M. & Din'd at the half Way House & met with good Ale Beer.

New Cheese for Supper at Tedbury & the Landlord laid on a Couch by the Fire having galled himself in riding.

Thursday, the 7th[2] Reach'd Cirencester in good Time for M.P. & there saw Miss Webb. Before Din Self went into the Park. Mutton Chops for Din & after Tea, Set out for Leachlade. Enquir'd after the young Oystler & he was gone, & had left no very good Character behind Him.[3] Cold Mutton & Cheese for Sup.

Friday, the 8th Breakfasted at the Lamb, & the Landlord told me of a Postillion. Call'd at Cross at Abingdon but [f.6^{v}] not at Home, neither was Howse. Reach'd Newnham to Dinner & in good Health for wch Blessing I am truly thankfull to my God whom I love with all my Heart.

Saturday, the 9th M. & N.P. Bowly came to me about the Tythe Lambs & the Church Yard. Tom Anderson paid for his Lambs. took the Tythe of his Cows & Calves up to Ladyday next. Winnow'd Wheat. Pray'd by Dame Pearce.

Sunday, the 10th [Whit Sunday] Administer'd the Sacrament at the New Town[4] to Dame Andrews, Wells & her Aunt. Lord & Lady Harcourt went to Cockthropt [Cokethorpe] instead of going to Church. Joe set off for Cheltenham for to see his Father.

[f.7^{r}]

Monday, the 11th Self & Bullock took a View of my Lord's Lambs & some of them are in very bad Order. Kill'd the Boar Stag & gave part of him to several poor People. After Din Self went to Oxford. Drank Tea with my Neice & Mrs Weston was there, but my Neice's Conduct towards her Children is very faulty & that in the too indulgent & humouring Way. Enquir'd after a Postillion.

Tuesday, the 12th Went to M.P. in the Rain. Gillet cut out the Boar Stag. Agree'd with Bowly for the Tythe Lambs. Put Locks to several Gates. Howse taken Ill with the Ague.

Wednesday, the 13th Br at Oxford & Din'd at the Visitation. Tea at Cofe. N. Spoke [f.7^{v}] to Mr Skinner in the Street to take Care of my Church. Bullock sold ten Quarter of Wheat at Shillingford.

Thursday, the 14th Baptized Dame Andrew's Child at Home.[5] Press'd the Plumbs & tun'd up the Wine. Set out about Eleven o'Clock for Bath & din'd at the Lamb. Got to Leachlade about 9 nt.

Friday, the 15th Reach'd Cirencester to Br. M.P. but Miss Webb was not there. Visited the Park & gave the Porter 1s. After Din set out for Tedbury, & there laid.

Saturday, the 16th Br at the halfway House. [f.8^{r}] It rain'd before Self reach'd Bath. Mr Pearce much displeas'd at a Shock Dog[6] running at one of his little Dogs. Got to the Saracen's Head to Din Safe & Well & am truly thankfull to Providence for this Blessing.

N.P. St Michael's. Books from Leake's. Went to my old Lodgings.

Sunday, the 17th Went to the Angel about Grass.[7] M. & N.P. Abby & Sac^{rt}. Borrow'd Sixpence of Mr Leake. Sent my Housekeeper a Letter. Walk'd on the Parade after 9 o Clock Nt.

Monday, the 18th Went to Lincomb by Holyway Turnpike & the Hill after I had been [f.8^{v}] about Grass for my Beasts. M.P. Abby & shut the Door at the Desire of a Ladyday. Advertis'd Herbal. Elizabeth Overton's Master brought me her Address. Bought a pair of black Buckles.

Tuesday, the 19th M.P. The Chapple. Turn'd the Horse & Mare to Grass & was caught in the Rain. Griggs for Din.[8] N.P. Chapple & but few. Went to the Rooms Evening, & there saw the Woman Self saw at the Chapple.

Wednesday, the 20th M.P. & N. Chapple. A Fish for Dinner. Lost at Lottery 2s. Lobster for Sup. Pint of Rum from a New Place.

Thursday, the 21st M.P. Abby. Went to see the Horses & the Mare continuing very Lame. [f.9^{r}] Pidgeon & Beacon for Din. Went to the White Hart after Dinner. Spoke to Webb on the Parade.

Friday, the 22nd The Rev^{d} Mr Webb Br with me at my Lodgings. M.P. Abby. Found Mr Roberts had been a particular Acquaintance of Mr Way. Walk'd into the Meadows before Din. Drank a Pint of Port at the White Hart. A Gentlemen on the Parade took me for One Fawseet.

Saturday, the 23rd Intended to have set out Early for Bristol but was prevented by the Rain & therefore laid till about 10 o Clock M. wch was a Shamefull thing. Din'd at the White Hart with One who knew Mr Way. Walk'd with Major Pepys [f.9^{v}] on the Parade. At the Rooms Evening. Broke an Empty Bottle where I bought the Rum.

Sunday, the 24th M. & N.P. Abby. One Pidgeon & cold Beacon for Din. Walk'd with Major Pepys on the Parade. View'd my Horses at Grass. Drank Wine & Cyder with Mr Dearing at his House.

Monday, the 25th M.P. Abby. Convers'd with two Ladies in the Pump Room. Walk'd towards Lincomb, Mr Allen's, & to Spring Gardens.[9] Din'd at the White Hart with a Goughty Gentleman & the Person Self din'd with last Satur[day]. A little Girl din'd with us, whose mother, I fancy, I knew from a Girl. Lost at Lottery 3s.

[f.10^{r}]

Tuesday. the 26th Wrote out Part of an old Sermon. Din'd at the White Hart with Earl of Salisbury,[10] Partridge of Turnham Green, Peer William uncle to the Gentleman who was Kill'd at Belleisle. One Dish of Coffee at Morgan's. Went to the Rooms Nt.

Wednesday, the 27th Went to the Pump Room M. with Surtut Coat. Wrote out Part of a Sermon. Mackerel & Shrimps for Din & very late. Sent Giles for a Bottle of Port Wine. M.P. Abby. A Pot of Coffee at Morgan's Nt.

Thursday, the 28th Din'd at the White Hart. Play'd at Lottery at Rooms & Wone about £16.[11] Drank Punch & Wine at Lodgings at Nt. Begun a Sermon.

Friday, the 29th Oaken Boughs set at Many People's Doors.[12] Din'd at the White Hart & Jones was sent for Last Ball Night.

[f.10^{v}]

Saturday, the 30th Went to the Pump Room before Br. Stay'd for the ketching[13] of the Horse. Quarter'd at the Bell at Bristol in St Thomas's

Street. Went to the Hot Wells & the Long Room.[14] Drank Coffee at the little man's Room. Return'd to my Inn & had Bread & Cheese for Sup.

Sunday, the 31st Went to Bett Overton's Master House & she breakfasted with me at the black Horse, but did not behave so well as she ought to have done, but Self gave Her two Shillings & good Advice & may she attend to it. Loin of Veal for Din & the Landlord was not well. Laid at the old Passage.

Notes

1 'Gave my Landress some Provisions' is crossed out in the text.

2 This entry was originally marked 6 May. The '7', is written over it. Likewise the next date, originally written as '7' is changed to '8'.

3 See the entry for Friday 10 April 1761.

4 The 'New Town' was the new village on the Oxford to Henley road. Many of the cottages were evidently occupied by this time.

5 There is no record of this baptism in the Nuneham *Registers*.

6 A 'Shock Dog' is a dog with long, shaggy thick hair. See OED.

7 The Angel Inn was near the old bridge.

8 Grigs are small eels. See OED.

9 'the' is crossed out in the text. Spring Gardens was a place of alfresco entertainments along the lines of Vauxhall and Ranelagh in London. This was a popular feature of the social scene. The gardens were set up in *c.* 1735 and flourished until superseded by the establishment of the Grosvenor and Sydney Gardens during the 1790s. In their heyday they gave great pleasure 'to all Conditions of People', being a great delight yet so close to the city. In them were held public breakfasts on Mondays and Thursdays, from the middle of April throughout the Summer season. There was a good band of musicians. In 1778 the subscription for a whole season was 2s 6d. See Thicknesse, *Prose Bath Guide*, p. 87.

10 James Cecil, 6th Earl of Salisbury, was born on 20 October 1713 and died on 19 September 1780. He was educated at Westminster School (1724–1729). From 7 August 1739 he was a Governor of the Foundling Hospital. See *Complete Peerage*, G.H. White (ed.) (1949), XI, p. 410.

11 This is JN's first recorded win at the lottery.

12 Oak Apple Day is 29 May, the day of the Restoration of Charles II in 1660. The wearing or displaying of oak leaves was in memory of his successfully hiding from his pursuers in an oak tree after defeat at the battle of Worcester in September 1651.

13 By 'Ketching' JN meant catching. The horse had to be caught having been turned out to grass.

14 In Bristol there were two large Assembly rooms 'next to the Wells for balls, concerts, public breakfats etc.,'. They were enlarged in 1755. The rooms became the social centre of the town for the rest of the eighteenth century, although not on the same scale as in Bath. The water from the Hot Wells was well known for its efficacy in dealing with 'the dysentry, spitting of blood, consumption, coughs, diabetis, etc., etc.'. The season for taking the waters lasted from March to September, when the wells were 'much frequented by nobility and gentry'. See W. Ison, *The Georgian Buildings of Bristol* (1952), pp. 108–114; *New Bath Guide*, (R. Cruttwell, 1784), pp. 53–4.

June 1761

Monday, the 1st Us'd my own Tea for Br & the Landeress gave me an Account of [f.11^{r}] Dr Taylor the Oculist & She seems to be a very pretty Sort of a Woman. Strol'd about the Shoar & the Beach.[1] Two Boats with Malitia men came to Shoar before I left the Place. Din'd at the White Lyon[2] at Bristol & had very bad Wine at first, but it was exchang'd for better. Enquir'd about the Cyder. A man for unnatural Practices was ago-ing to the Gallows as Self was going on.[3] I hope he made his Peace with God & dy'd a true Penitent.

Tuesday, the 2nd Walk'd on the Parade before Br with Miss Clarke.[4] M.P. Abby. Giles lead the Mare to Lincomb. Met with Miss Clarke, her Sister & Mr Pemberton & Self went with them by Calibet's Seralio. Shew'd Miss Clarke my Herbals.[5] Lost at Lottery 4s. at Night.

[f.11^{v}]

Wednesday, the 3rd M.P. Abby. Miss Clarke return'd the Herbal. Mr Taylor wanted me to read Prayers but Self declin'd it. Din'd at the White Hart & a young Buck gave an Acc^{t} of a man's breaking his Wife's Arm on Purpose because She struck Him.

Thursday, the 4th M.P. Abby. Self, Miss Clarke, Mr Pemberton & Miss Mapletoff walk'd toward Weston & She did not care to go on because of an harmless Bull & Miss Clarke tore her Ruffle in getting under a Stile. Self din'd at Lincome & Mrs Lancashire would fain have persuaded me that Miss Clarke had din'd lately at her House with a sec-ond Fellow but she was mistaken. Illuminated my Windows & the Town was finely illuminated indeed & Self strol'd [f.12^{r}] about instead of going to the Rooms.[6]

Friday, the 5th M.P. Abby. Went about the House Self lodg'd in for-merly beyond the Turnpike & did not know it at first, & then went on farther intending to have made towards the Wey House but did not hit on the right Way. Did not Eat one whole Mackarel for Din so bad was my Stomach. N.P. Abby. In the Evening Self went to Spring Garden by the Way of King's Mead.

Saturday, the 6th Invited Major Pepys to Mortimer Street & he invited me to Br with Him but Self did not. Paid Mrs Thorpe for Lodging. M.P. Abby. Griggs for Din. Self solo drank Tea at Spring Gardens & was delighted with the Fall of Water, but may my [f.12ᵛ] greatest delight consist in the Service of God. Sent Giles to order the Horses to be in readiness for me in the Morning. Set a pretty while by Miss Clarke as She was at Cards & slear'd off without taking my Leave of Her & its likely She was much displeas'd at my Behaviour. John Taylor came to me in the Evening & wanted an Advance of Wages, but Self did not agree to it, & so he was order'd to come in the morning.

Sunday, the 7th Self call'd Giles & sent Him after John Taylor. Paid for the Horses & gave the Man 6d. At the Turnpike Johns Baggage was taken from the Mare. Br at the Cross Hands & left a [f.13ʳ] Direction with Giles for John. The Landlord went with [me] to the Church & then return'd Home again. The Parson's reading of Prayers was very poorly indeed & without any Piety & Devotion, a fault I hope I shall never fall into. There are four Bells in this Church unhung & one of them broke & the Bell they ring is also crack'd. The Prospect from the Church Yard is very delightfull.

Dʳ Heartly Son, whose Father I knew, for a pious good man I believe he was, has a large Estate here & lately came to Age. God grant he may make a good Use of it & equal his Father in Goodness. [f.13ᵛ] Too late for E.P. After Tea, Self set out for Tedbury & got to my old Quarters in good Time & Safe for wᶜʰ Mercy I am thankfull to Providence.

Monday, the 8th Reach'd Cirencester time enough for M.P. but Miss Webb was not there. After Br rode in my Lord Bathurst's Park & its a very grand One indeed. Gleede made Himself known to me & was about setling a Traffic with another Person. Gave some poor Children a few Halfpence. Spoke to a [man?] hewing Timber near Miss Webb's Ho[use]. Some Woman came to see her a Horseback attended with her Lackay. After Tea Self set out for Leachlade, & after I was come there I [f.14ʳ] went to the Wharfe & into the Meadow behind the Garden. Cold Beef for Supper. Fanny Basset came to see me at my Quarters, & Self treated Her with Cyder.

Tuesday, the 9th Set out about 6 o'Clock M. & Br at the Lamb & Commissioners were to dine there who where appointed to lay out the Common Fields. Met Palmer agoing to his Farm. Reach'd Newnham & had a Fowl for Dinner that had been kill'd by some Vermin, its likely.

I am truly thankfull to Providence for bring[ing me] Safe to this Place & for his Protection of me since I left it. Its my delight to lead a holy & religious Life. God grant I may continue in the right Way till Death.

[f.14^{v}]

Wednesday, the 10th Self Br at my Lord Harcourt's & he was much displeas'd at my Milking his Cows too soon & for my talking to Stewart about the Church Yard[7] & for my Saying he had done every thing to me except cutting my Throat, wh^{ch} last Expression is palpably False, & told him with a Malevolent Design to injure me & to render him my Enemy, but though I may have him for my Enemy, I trust I shall have God for my Friend, & then I hope th[r]ough his Blessing & my own good Conscience I may do very well & spend the Remainder of my Days in Peace & Quietness.
[f.15^{r}]

Went to the Locks & had a Jack from thence for Dinner, but it was along while before the Man could find the Trunk & Self gave him 6d. Wash'd the Sheep. Joe stopt the Gap by the little Gate in Fisher's Green. John Taylor enter'd my Service after the rate of Six Pound a Year.

Thursday, the 11th Self Br at Oxford Cofe. Giles rode Lyon for the first Time. Paid his Mother twenty Shillings for half a Year's Wages. M.P. at her Parish Church, & the Clarke has got several Flowers in the Yard. Din'd at Mr Austin's. N.P. C.C.C.[8] Ingag'd Mr Skinner to supply my Absence. Heard part of an excellent Anthem [f.15^{v}] at Christ Church & when it was over several went away, O shamefull indeed! Basket not come from Bath. Some Micheivous Person cut down the Garden Beans at the King of Prussia Head,[9] may I never be guilty of such a base Action, but rather study to do all offices of good Will toward my Neighbours, Foes as well as Friends.

Friday, the 12th Self & Giles went to the Hay makers before Br. Molly begun washing. Self & Giles went to the Balden Taylor with several things for Raperation. Call'd on Dame Andrews & Wells. A Duck for Dinner.

Saturday, the 13th Settl'd Accounts with the Housekeeper. Bullock shot 8 Pidgeons [f.16^{r}] at one Shoot, & Self gave him one for his Wife & two were roasted for Din. Wrote out Diary for several Days past.

Sunday, the 14th Ask'd two Couple,[10] Preach'd a New Sermon. Boil Pidgeons for Din. Nickolls came to me while Self was Shaving. Tapt a Vessel of Ale.

Monday, the 15th Self married two Couple[11] & one of the Fellows was somewhat in Liquor. Lawrence made Praperation for the Bailiff's Lodge. Self & Giles Smith set out for London & din'd at Nettlebed. Laid at my old Quarters this side Maidenhead & had Br[ead] & Cheese for Sup.

Tuesday, the 16th Much rain before Self reach'd Hounslow to Br. Got to Mortimer Street before Din. Call'd on two People who had been about my Strand House & [f.16^{v}] [one] of them had provided Himself. Left a Tenour[12] [of] an Advertisement for my House. Tea at the Turk's Head Cofe.

Wednesday, the 17th M.P. Berwick St Chapple. Bought Cheshire Cheese & chang'd the Coffee & William went Home with it. Saw Duning & Long on the Royal Exchange. Beef stake near the Exchange. A Seafairing man was much afflicted with the Rheumatism wch seiz'd him for the first time when he was a Prisoner, & a person present gave him a Receipt[13] for it. Bespoke Brand[y] & Rum at Wenman's. Drank Tea with Miss Oldworth. N.P. near her House. Rec'^{d} a Quarter's Rent of Dunning.

Thursday, the 18th M.E.P. St James's. Went to Blue Anchor Ally & call'd on Dame Pickering[14] [f.17^{r}] & Mr Challiner[15] but no rent. Din'd with Admiral Long at his House. N.P. St George's Church. Rode to Chelsea without going through the Turnpike.

Friday, the 19th M.P. Cavendish Square Chapple & spoke to Mrs Summer. Took a Bill to my Strand House & went over it & the Rain hath done some Damage to it. Din'd at the Widow Goulding's. Rode to Chelsea.

Saturday, the 20th M.E.P. St Anne's. Strol'd about Covent Garden & bought Strawberries & Flowers. Din'd at the Admiral's, & lent Him Lyon.

Sunday, the 21st M. & N.P. Harrow on the Hill. A young Woman displeas'd at my being in her Pew & so Self left it. A little boy behav'd very badly towards his Parents [f.17^{v}] at the Ordinary.[16] Two Women who came to the Inn were detected with two Tumblers. Mrs Pickering Paid some Rent.

Monday, the 22nd M.E.P. St James. Went to see the Works at the New Bridge.[17] Call'd at the Strand House & got the Bill paid up. Br at Hungerford Market Cofe[18] & the old Tenant is gone to live at Chelsea. The Admiral wanted me to play at Cards but Self declin'd it & rode out to Chelsea & Brown did not care to pass by the Machine but did at last.

Tuesday, the 23rd The Admiral sent Lyon Home, his Shoulders being Hurt. Went to Mr Robinson & went [to] met the Admiral at Mr Gibbons who drew up the inten-[f.18^{r}] Intended Notice for Dr Morley, but he thought it would be of no Account. After Din met much Company at the Admiral, & also Mrs Pedigrew, the pretty Widow.

Wednesday, the 24th M.E.P. St James's. Went to Mr Roberson. Call'd on the Bricklayer & he came to me at my Strand Ho. Dunning Paid all his Rent at the Ale House & Self gave him 12s. instead of 6s. but [he] return'd it again. Treated Sister with a Turbet for Din. N.P. St George's & walk'd with Mrs Summer from thence as far as Cavendish Square. In the Evening Rode out.

Thursday, the 25th Met Dunning near St Paul's. Let him have the Key of my Strand House to take away the [f.18^{v}] Remainder of his Things.

Friday, the 26th King & the Bricklayers did some odd Jobs at the Strand House but we waited about an Hour for the Key. Self made a pounding at the three Tuns[19] for the Key but it was not there. Br at Cofe.

Saturday, the 27th Went if I mistake not to the Strand House. The Landress sent Home my Breeches & Waistcoat. Din'd at Home.

Sunday, the 28th Br & Din'd at Richmond. M. & N. Pr.[20] Walk'd into the Park.[21] Low liv'd Company at the Ordinary. Lyon stumbled twice with Giles & he rec'^{d} no Hurt & I am Thankfull to Providence for it. Mr Larcome's Sight contines bad still. Oh, what [f.19^{r}] a Mercy it is that I enjoy my Sight so well – may I long continue so to do. Return'd Home in good Time.

Monday, the 29th M.P. Berwick St & follow'd a Woman from thence almost as far as Lincoln's Inn. Rode to Chelsea in the Evening. Several People came about my Strand House when I was out.

Tuesday, the 30th M.P. Berwick St. Call'd on the Chemist. Bought Cheese in Newgate Street. Took up at the Bank three ten Pound Notes. Saw Mrs Pedigrew at the Admiral's.

Notes

1 The 'e' of 'Shoare' is crossed out in the text. The Quay 'more than half a mile in length, is thought to be the most commodious in England for shipping and landing of goods, having several large cranes which are not to be equalled for the extraordinary dispatch with which they clear the ships'. See Crutwell, *New Bath Guide*, p. 53.

2 The White Lion was in Broad Street. See J. Latimer, *Annals of Bristol in the Eighteenth Century* (1893), p. 17.

3 The man was William D. Sheppard, facing execution for 'unnatural crime'. The gallows were on St Michael's Hill. See *ibid.*, p. 295.

4 JN was by now back in Bath.

5 'my Herbals' was presumably a copy of the Herbal published in 1752. See entry for 15 March 1760 and note 10.

6 Lights were put in the windows to celebrate the twenty-third birthday of the King, George III.

7 This was one of the few disagreements between JN and Lord Harcourt. The churchyard, along with the church, was about to be destroyed and incorporated into the new park. See Introduction.

8 C.C.C. is most likely to be Corpus Christi College, JN's old college, as Mr Skinner was a Fellow there.

9 The King of Prussia was an inn on Rose Hill. During the First World War its name was changed to the Allied Arms.

10 To 'ask' in this context meant to publish the banns of marriage.

11 The couples were William and Mary Smith, and Joseph Dugless and Mary Clarke. See Nuneham *Registers*.

12 By 'Tenour' JN means an exact copy of the document.

13 A 'Receipt' was a formula or statement of the ingredients necessary for the making of some medical preparation. See *OED*.

14 JN owned a house in Blue Anchor Alley. Dame Pickering was his tenant there.

15 'Pickering' is crossed out in the text.

16 An eating-house or a tavern providing food.

17 The new bridge was Blackfriars Bridge, begun in 1760 and designed by Robert Mylne. This bridge was the third to span the Thames in London and cost £230,000. For full details see *London Encycl.*, p. 68.

18 For full details of Hungerford Market Coffee House, see Lillywhite, *Coffee Houses*, pp. 277–8.

19 This was The Three Tuns in the Strand. See *ibid.*, p. 741.

20 The services were at St Mary's church, Richmond. For full details see *London Encycl.*, p. 742.

21 This was Richmond Park. These 2,470 acres of parkland were first enclosed in 1637 by Charles I. For full details see *ibid.*, p. 649.

Plate 11 A west prospect of the city of Oxford; by kind permission of the Bodleian Library (G.A. Oxon. a. 42, p. 19, item 30)

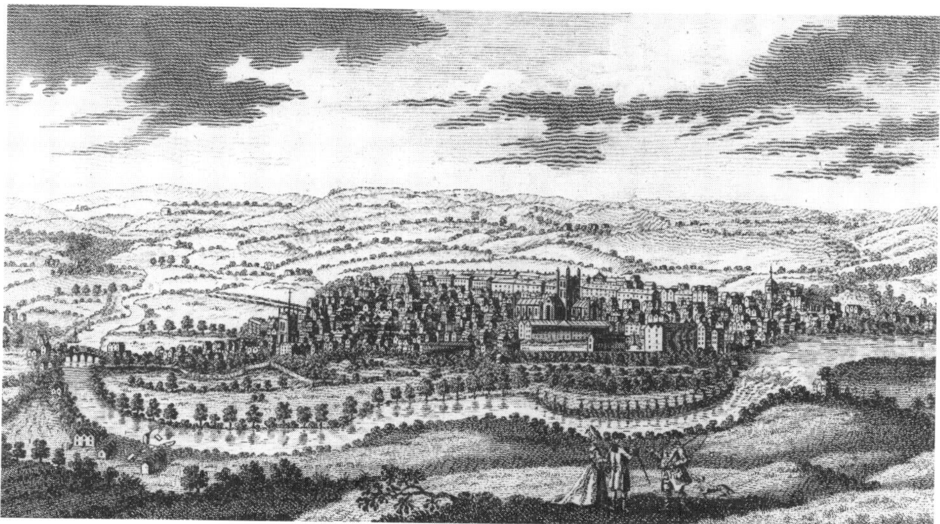

Plate 12 A perspective view of the city of Bath; by kind permission of the Bodleian Library (Gough Maps, 28, fo. 42b)

Plate 13 A west view of London with the bridge; by kind permission of the Bodleian Library (Gough Maps, 21, fo. 34b)

Plate 14 A view of the lake and island at Kew seen from the lawn, from Sir William Chambers, *Plans, Elevations of the Gardens and Buildings at Kew in Surrey* (1763); by kind permission of the Bodleian library (G.A. fo. c. 28, fig. 38)

July 1761

Wednesday, the 1st Br at Tunbridge Wells. M.P. Stoke Newington & then took one turn in Queen Elisabeth Walk.

[f.19^{v}]

Thursday, the 2nd Br at Tunbridge Wells. Went to see Cousin Warren & gave Her Money, Tea & Sugar & Money to two poor Women in the Poor House. Left the Horses by the Turnpike at Bednall Green [Bethnall Green]. Self was in form'd of a Person loosing about seven & twenty Guineas while he was from Home. A great Loss & I am sorry for the Person who lost as well as for the Person who stole for not having more grace – Honesty. Mrs Pickering begun clearing my Strand House. N.P. St George's. Spoke to Mrs Summer.

Friday, the 3rd Went to the Strand House & Dame Pickering & another busy there, & Self treated them with [f.20^{r}] a Pot of Porter. Paid the Glazier at the three Tunns. Went to the Farrier about Shoing Lyon.

Saturday, the 4th M.E.P. St Anne's. Bought at Covent Garden Flowers. Paid for Shoing Lyon. Din'd at the three Tuns. N.P. St Martins.[1] Spoke to the old Lady who liv'd the next Door to the late Colonel Johnston. A scowerer[2] in St Martin's Lane about my House. Bought for Oldworth Coffe 1/4 P[ound]. Went to Vaux Hall Entertainment.[3]

Sunday, the 5th M. & N.P. at the College Chapple Greenwich. Br at the Grey Hound & Din'd by the River. Sent Giles to another House for his Din & [the] Publican would not help him to any. [f.20^{v}] Treated Mr Oldiworth with Tea at a House about half a Mile from Sir Mordent's College.[4] Got Home in good Time. Snub'd a Fellow for Digging.

Monday, the 6th M.P. Berwick. Saw the Woman Hous'd. Call'd on a Fellow about my House but dont like Him so well as the Paper Man. Giles took Provision with him to the Strand House. Self Din'd by the

Waterside & an Oxford man a Shoemaker was there. Call'd on Mrs Harcourt & Mrs Rock.

Tuesday, the 7th M.E.P. St Martin's. Call'd on Maclean about my House. Hunted after Forster a Shoemaker who wants to rent my House but could not find Him. Bought Salts etc at Godfrys.[5] Din'd by the River, [f.21^{r}] & there met with a Woman who had been miserably scalded, but was cur'd at Hyde Park Hospital, & heard of a man who lately thereabouts broke his Leg in three Places, such Misfortunes & calamities we are all subject too & when we see others labouring under them, we should assist them with all our Might & be thankfull to God that we are free from such Dissasters.

In our most prosperous State we are in danger of an adverse Fortune & therefore we should not depend too much on it, but act with Caution & Prudence in all our Affairs & leave the Event[6] of them in the hand of Providence & indeavour to be easy in every Condition of Life.

[f.21^{v}]

Wednesday, the 8th Went after the Stay Maker. Found out Forster the Shoemaker in Drury Lane. Self & Giles at the Strand House. Din'd in the Court next to the Thames & some stole out of the common Room a peice of Cloath belonging to a Waterman. Rode to Chelsea in the Evening & saw Mrs Ayres & her Son.

Thursday, the 9th Went to Bed before Br. Brought up some bitter Stuff. M.P. Berwick Street. Saw the Houses that were burnt near Westminster Bridge a Melancholy Affair & I am thankfull to Providence that I have not suffer'd in that Way. Call'd on Mrs Maw for a Receipt for an Asthma. Intended to have put my Horses up at another Place, but there was not Room for them. Saw a Drunken Cobler near the Place Self [f.22^{r}] din'd & a noisy drunken french Woman in Leicester Fields.

Friday, the 10th Br at Islington Wells. Paid the Plate Duty for my Sister Rock. Giles & Self waited at the Strand House. Din'd in the Court by the Thames. The Excise man came again about the Strand Ho. Put up my Horses nearer Home.

Brown got into a Hole in the Water near Islington Road & had like to have fell down with me, but as I got out without any Bodily Hurt, I am thankfull to Providence for his Goodness towards [me] & may I ever retain a due & gratefull Sense of it. To receive favours from the Hands of God & not to be thankfull for them is very base & [f.22v] ungenerous, God grant, I may never be guilty of it. May my Heart never reproach me for neglecting the Duty of Gratitude towards God or Man, may I perform it with Cheerfullness, & Alacrity, & all the Demonstrations of Sincerity. Put Horses up at a New Place.

Saturday, the 11th A poor Stomack for my Br. Din'd in a Court by the Thames. Rode out. N.P. St George's just over. Lighten'd much before Self got Home. Admiral Long drank Tea here & took Polly with Him in his Chariot.

Sunday, the 12th Br & Din'd at Greenwich. M. & N.P. The Chapple. A Parcel of Jews din'd at our Inn. Two Men caught in the Rain in ferrying over & made some Sport for the Company. Amus'd [f.23r] Self in the Park. Drank Tea near Sir John Mordant's College & treated a Stranger with some. Call'd on my Friend Oldiworth & he shew'd Me their Mistress's House & Garden. Lyon broke his Bridle. Got Home in good Time.

Monday, the 13th Drank some Camamile Tea, & through the Blessing I hope I shall be benefited by it, as I brought up Fleam, if not yellow bitter Stuff. Call'd on Allen the Bricklayer. Went to the Foundling Hospital. Polly din'd with the Admiral. N.P. St George's. Rode to Chelsea.

The Melancholy News of the Death of the King's intended Consort's Mother took Place this Day,[7] & am sorry for it as I am a well wisher to all [f.23v] Mankind, & am ready to Sympathise at the Misfortunes of others.

Its possible She might be too much affected with the Thoughts of her Daughters Exaltation, & of the Honour & Profit arising from her alliance to her Family, but so it is, that some People are no better able to bear Prosperity than Adversity & compleat their Ruin in one State as well as in the other. As for my Part I study to be contented in whatsoever State Providence shall provide for me, & if I find my present Condition not agreeable I indeavour to make it more agreeable[8] & to persuade myself that it will turn out to my Good in the End If I behave after a proper & becoming [f.24r] Manner.

A Man near Lock's Hospital[9] was so much intoxicated with Liquor that he fell into the Ditch & might have soon perish'd had he been got timely out. Alass! how dreadful must it have been for that man to have left the World so little prepaired for his mighty Change. May it be a caution for

Me never to transgress the Bounds of Drinking least I should dye in that deplorable Condition or perpetrate some other greivous Sin & so lay the foundation for much Sorrow & Contrition. How much better is it to observe temperance in our Cups, though excess was not criminal, than to run out into Debauchery [f.24^{v}] & so bring ourselves into a bad State of Health & without that, what signifies all the Riches of the World? If we can't drink with Reason & Moderation & leave the most pleasant Liquor & most delightfull Company without, rather than running into Excess, We offend God & render Ourselves unworthy of the Blessings we enjoy.

Tuesday, the 14th Br at Islington Wells. Rode to Hampstead & Highgate & towards Barnet. Rode to Chelsea in the Evening & was caught in the Whet.

Wednesday, the 15th Br at Islington Wells & had some Conversation with the Widow. Saw a poor man in the Road in a Fit & stay'd with him till he got out of it & gave him a few Halfpence. To see a Fellow Creature in Distress & not to [f.25^{r}] assist Him would be extreamly unkind & argue something base & ungenerous in Us. Can we see any One labouring under any Misfortune & not soften & mitigate it when we have it in our Power? Can we be an Idle Spectator of any one at the near Approach of Death & not use our best Endeavours for his Recovery, I say if we can, Woe be unto Us! for we may reasonably fear some heavy Camality will soon fall upon Us. Met Allen at the Strand House. Call'd on King. M.P. Berwick St Chapple & found Mrs Clarke was Married. N.P. St George's. Rode to Chelsea.

Thursday, the 16th Br at Islington Wells. Went to [f.25^{v}] the Strand House. Din'd at Dolley's & met with One who knew Admiral Long.

Friday, the 17th Br at Islington Wells. Went to the Strand House. Rode to Chelsea. Din'd at Dolley's.

Saturday, the 18th Br at Islington Wells. Went to the Strand House. Din'd at the three Tunns. The Plasterer went off at Dinner. The Upholsterer came to me about my House but to no Purpose. Rode to Chelsea.

Sunday, the 19th Br on Blackheath & the Landerdess overcharg'd for Br but Self did not agree to it. M. & N.P. at Greenwich Hospital Chapple. Saw the House in wch Queen Elizabeth was born[10] & the Lord

Northampton's Hospital[11] [f.26^r] near it. Din'd at the Ordinary. A Boat would most likely have sunk if She had not broke Loose. Tea at Noon at Grace Tosier's & Self had little or no Idea of the Place, tho' he had lain there one Night many Years past. Got Home in good Time.

Monday, the 20th Br Islington Wells & had some Conversation with the Widow. Went to the Strand House. N.P. Conduit St Chapple. Drank Tea at the Admiral's & Mrs Peddigrew was there etc. Bought a Cake at Marybone Gardens. The Guns were fir'd off at the News of taking Pondicherry[12] but the News of our great Loss at Sea was very Melancholy,[13] but so it is, that Prosperity & Adversity often go together [f.26^v] & render it doubtfull, wether we have more Reason to rejoice or to be sad for[14] what hath befallen Us. A Victory may be purchas'd at too dear a Rate, & when that is the Case, what just Cause have we got to Triumph.

Tuesday, the 21st Went to Lord Harcourts & he was for seeing me another Time. Giles & Self were at the Strand House. Went to York Building Walk by the Thames.[15] Spoke to Raye about knowing his Father. Rode to Chelsea. Spoke to Head about painting the Front of my House.

Wednesday, the 22nd Went to Islington Wells & convers'd with the Widow. Br at the old Breakfasting House. Went to the Strand House. Waited on Admiral [f.27^r] Long with the News of the French being Beat in Germany.[16] Mrs Ridly drank Tea here. Took a Walk to Mary bonne in the Evening.

Thursday, the 23rd[17] Went to Lord Harcourt's & he was from Home. Br at Home. Went to the Strand House. Din'd at the three Tunns. Amus'd myself in York Building Walk. A Cat thrown out of [a] Winder into the Thames got up the Spout & so likely escap'd with her Life. Its natural for all living Creatures to struggle hard for Life, & to desire the Prolongation of their Days.

Friday, the 24th Br at Lord Harcourt's & my Lady was Shuff. Saw some of my Lord's fine Cloaths. Went to the Strand House & bought some Locks & Thumb Latches. Spoke to Maclean about [f.27^v] dowing some Paper Work at my House. Rode to Chelsea. A man out of Oxford Road came to me about my House.

Saturday, the 25th Treated Mrs Watson with Cucumbers at Covent Garden. Br at Hungerford Cofe. Had some Locks taken off. A man came to me about my House while I was in York Building Walk. Maclean hung the Shop Ceiling with Paper. A lost Horse had like to have been kill'd by the Cofe & another Accident to a Cart by Northumberland House.[18] Tea at Cofe. N. & then went to York Building Walk. M.P. St Martin's & there was a Sermon.

Sunday, the 26th M. & N.P. Harrow. Gave an old Woman 6d. whom I convers'd with in [f.28^{r}] the Porch & she walk'd along way for her Age but she took a delight in attending the Public Service of the Church, & may I do so as long as I live. How comfortable must it be to us in old Age to reflect on our past good Transactions? What a mighty Consolation must it infuse into our Souls to take a Retrospect of our youthfull Days if they have been devoted to our Maker's Service when we come[19] to be full of Years, & are about to leave this World? When we have almost perform[ed] this long & tedious Pilgrimage of Life,[20] what Joy & delectation must it create in our Minds if we can say we have spent our past spent Days to the Honour [f.28^{v}] & Glory of God & serv'd him with Truth & Sincereity.

Old Brown was for going out of the Road several times & broke the Girth. Several of the Company retir'd after Din to be by themselves. Spoke to Dr Sanders. Met with a Lad whose Uncle went into Germany with eight Hundred men about a Year past & they are now reduc'd to about 135. A Melancholy Consideration, & what makes it more dreadfull is that only about 10 of them were kill'd, but the rest perish'd through the Hardships of the Campaign. Whereas we enjoy the Advantages of Peace in the times of War, let us in the first Place be thankfull, truly thankfull to Providence for His [f.29^{r}] Goodness to Us. Secondly Reform our Manners & repent of all our Iniquities & Thirdly Commiserate the Wants & Calamities of other Countries & Kingdoms & pray to God to bring about an honourable & lasting Peace to this Kingdom.

After Tea, set out for London & got Home in good Time, & met with no Misfortune & I am thankfull to Providence for it. Found Dame Pickering at Mortimer Street.

Monday, the 27th Br at Islington Wells. Went to the Strand House & spoke to Collet as he went by & saw Major Bates but did not speak to Him. Din'd in Swan Court.[21] An old man there seemn'd very cheerfull & of a contented Mind & her [*sic*] Husband had been in Greenwich [f.29^{v}]

Hospital, but left to enter into the Sea Service & now declines going in again on his Wife's Account & they seem to be a happy Couple. A pleasing Sight. Went by water to London Bridge[22] & return'd again to Westminster Bridge[23] in another Boat – a little Girl was mightily afraid of the Water, may She learn to fear & dread Sin in the same Degree & then it will be well for Her. As She grows in Years may she grow in Grace & always keep at an awfull Distance from wicked Actions. May she early learn to Love God & to hate the Devil & not to lisson to any of his criminal Temptations.

Tuesday, the 28th Went to Islington Wells. Br [f.30^{r}] at the Hutt. The Keys[24] not done & it was with some Difficulty Self found out the House. The Stair Case Paper taken down & put up again. Dr Ryan not at the Dispensatory. Din'd at Home & the roast Beef was too Salt. N.P. St George's. Rode about Hyde Park.

Wednesday, the 29th Islington Wells & Br at the Hutt. Got the two Keys from the Lockmaker's. Went to the Strand House.

Thursday, the 30th Islington Wells Br at the Hutt. Went to the Strand House. N.P. St George's. Drank Tea at the Admiral's & Mrs Pedigrew was there & Self overtook her & went with her as far as Red Lyon Street & then went [f.30^{v}] to Mr Robertson about the Houses.

Friday, the 31st Islington Wells & Br at the Hutt. Rode after Mrs Harris's Chariot. M.P. Gray's Inn. Abingdon Cofe.[25] Bought Tea Dust at Twinings. N.P. St George's & Mrs Summer came after me. Rode to Chelsea & there spoke to Mrs Aires & her Son. Call'd on the Admiral at Night.

Notes

1 The service was at St Martin-in-the-Fields. This church began as a medieval chapel and was rebuilt in 1543–4. It was rebuilt again in 1722–4 by James Gibbs. For full details see *London Encycl.*, p. 733–4.

2 A scourer was a person sent out to make enquiries.

3 This was Vauxhall Gardens, known as the New Spring Gardens until 1751, opened in about 1660. Admission was free. The garden manager from 1728 to 1767 was Jonathan Tyers. It was a great centre of various entertainments including fireworks, concerts, fancy dress balls and public suppers. On 21 April 1749 a rehearsal of Handel's *Music for the Royal Fireworks* was held there

by 100 musicians in front of an audience of over 12,000. For full details see *London Encycl.*, p. 910–2.

4 This is Morden College, St Germain's Place. The college was built in 1695 by Sir John Morden, a Turkey merchant, and was designed by Wren. It was erected to help 'decayed Turkey merchants' who had fallen on hard times through no fault of their own. The chapel on the west side contains some fine carving which may be attributed to Grinling Gibbons. Sir John died in 1708 and was buried there. For full details see *ibid.*, p. 527.

5 This was Ambrose Godfrey the chemist of Southampton Street, Covent Garden, 'Chemist to her Royal Highness the Princess Dowager of Wales.' See Mortimer, *Universal Director*, Part II, pp. 18–19.

6 By 'event' JN meant the outcome.

7 This was the wife of Charles Louis, Duke of Mecklenburg-Strelitz.

8 'to me' is crossed out in the text.

9 Lock's Hospital was in Southwark. It was a leper hospital built in the twelfth century. By the eighteenth century, leprosy had been eradicated in England and patients with venereal disease were treated there instead. For full details see *London Encycl.*, p. 465.

10 Queen Elizabeth was born at Greenwich Palace, the favourite residence of Henry VIII. For full details see *ibid.*, pp. 336–7. She was born to Anne Boleyn between three and four o'clock, on the afternoon of Sunday 7 September 1533. It was a quick and easy delivery. See C. Hibbert, *The Virgin Queen* (1990), p. 13.

11 Lord Northampton's Hospital was the Norfolk College Almshouses. It was founded in 1613 by Henry Howard, Earl of Northampton. It accommodated twenty residents, twelve from Greenwich and eight from Shottesham, Norfolk, Lord Northampton's birthplace. See *London Encycl.*, p. 335.

12 The Seven Years' War was still raging. The French station of Pondicherry in India surrendered to the British in January 1761. See J.S. Watson, *The Reign of George III* (Oxford, 1960), p. 73.

13 It is hard to see what JN means here, unless he is grieving over the cost of victory in terms of loss of life. There were no disasters at sea in this year. Indeed, in June 1761 the British had captured Belle Isle off the French coast, noteworthy because it involved the conquest of part of France. See *ibid.*

14 'at' is crossed out in the text.

15 On the site of the York Building Waterworks, begun in 1675 and destroyed by fire in 1690. The waterworks were rebuilt in the early eighteenth century, with a broad terrace and walk along the banks of the Thames. For full details, see *London Encycl.*, pp. 974–5.

16 On 15 July, Ferdinand of Brunswick defeated Broglie and Soubise who were attempting to invade Westphalia and Hanover at Villingshausen. See White, *Origins of Modern Europe*, p. 237.

17 '24' is crossed out in the text.

18 Northumberland House was in the Strand. It was built at the beginning of the seventeenth century for Henry Howard, the Earl of Northampton, and designed by Bernard Jansen and Gerard Christmas. The building was demolished in 1874 to make way for Northumberland Avenue. See *London Encycl.*, p. 554.
19 'arrive' is crossed out in the text.
20 'journey' is crossed out in the text.
21 Swan Court was at Narrow Wall.
22 The first London Bridge was built between AD 100 and 400 during the Roman occupation. The earliest stone bridge was begun in 1176 and houses appeared on the structure from the early thirteenth century. It became the custom to display the heads of traitors on the bridge until the practice ceased during the reign of Charles II. In 1758–62, the houses were removed under the supervision of Sir Robert Taylor and George Dance, who replaced the two central arches with a single large span. For full details, see *London Encycl.*, pp. 468–9.
23 Westminster Bridge was begun in 1738. It was designed by Charles Labelye and opened in 1750, with a grand procession of gentlemen and workmen preceded by trumpets and kettledrums. The present bridge was erected in 1854–62 by Thomas Page with Sir Charles Barry as architectural consultant. See *ibid.*, p. 949.
24 'Lock' is crossed out in the text.
25 This was Abington's near Grays Inn. See Lillywhite, *Coffee Houses*, pp. 69–70.

August 1761

Saturday, the 1st Islington Wells & Br at the Hutt. The D^r not at Home. Went on the Water with a Widow who had liv'd at Bath. Bought a dry'd Trout. Return'd by Water to [f.31^r] Hungerford & had some small Contest with the Waterman. Din'd at the three Tunns. Went to the Strand Ho. Came Home to Tea & found Mrs Rock here. Admiral Long set out on his Bristol Journey & so did Lord Harcourt for Harwich.[1]

Sunday, the 2nd Intended to have went to Richmond but did [not?] go. M.P. $Sacr^t$ Queen's Sq. Call'd on Allen. Recoinitur'd Mr Robertsons House & have Reason to think it was rob'd by someone belonging to it or who went there. N.P. St Mary le Bonne & heard Boote preach an excellent Sermon on our late Victories.[2] Lady Harcourt din'd with her Sister but did not call on my Sister.

[f.31^v]

Monday, the 3rd Br at the Hut after I had been at the Wells. Went to the Strand House. Spoke to a Plumber near Westminster Abby to put a new Cock to the Pipe & Self was to have met him but instead of that went by Water from Westminster to the Swan.[3] Din'd near the Royal Exchange & then went to the Punch House. Rode in the Park in the Evening.

Tuesday, the 4th Islington Wells. Br at Home. Paid for Horse Keeping. M.P. St Martins. Went by Water to the Swan & bought some dry'd Salmon Trout. Mrs Rock & Mrs Harcourt drank Tea here. [f.32^r] Self bought two fine Mirtle Trees for my Sister Rock. A very hot Day.

Wednesday, the 5th Islington Wells & Br at the Hutt. Bath'd at Peerless Poole[4] & one of the old Waiters knew me. I knew this Place in its infancy & have bath'd often & often here in my more younger days. Mr Kemp who made this Place is Dead & others have taken Possession of his Labours & this is no more than what's Common. The grand Affair in all our worldly Transactions is to demean Ourselves in such a manner as to secure to Title to our heavenly Inheritance & then we may dye with Peace & leave our Possession for the Enjoyment of other without [f.32ᵛ] any Reluctancy.

Saw at Haberdashers Chapple[5] in the Morning One I lik'd for a Wife, but could not find out what She Was. Rode Home by Highgate. Din'd at Home. Went not to the Strand House. N.P. St George's. William came for me with Surtut Coat, but mist of me.

Thursday, the 6th Islington Wells & Br at the Hutt. Saw Mrs Ann Collier of Hoxton Sq[6] at Haberdasher's Chapple Morning Service, the Lady Self saw there Yesterady & She proves to be a married Woman. Went to the Strand House. Went by Water to the Swan & din'd at Billingsgate & had a Gill of Wine by the Fish Mongers [f.33ʳ] Hall.[7] Return'd by Water to Hungerford. Rode in the Park in the Evening.

Friday, the 7th Islington Wells. Paid King the Carpenter. Went to the Strand House.

Saturday, the 8th Islington Wells & went with the Widow as far as Moorefields. Din'd at Home. Call'd at Mrs Rock's several times but not at Home. Paid for Horse keeping.

Sunday, the 9th Intended to have set out Early but prevented by the Rain. M.P. the Foundling Hospital. Waited on Mrs Harcourt[8] & Mrs Rock. About four N. Self & Giles set out for Newnham & laid at the Castle at Slow & got there safe & well & am truly thankfull for the Same.

[f.33ᵛ]

Monday, the 10th Had a Button put to the Saddle. Br at Nettlebed on my own Tea. Din'd at Newnham on Beans & Beacon in good Health & am thankfull to Providence for it. Waited on Lady Harcourt with Mrs Harcourts Compliments. Begun Harvest.

Tuesday, the 11th Lediard & Ball did not enter on their Harvest till to Day. A Fowl was kill'd. Beans & Beacon for Din.

Wednesday, the 12th Br at Oxford. Desir'd one of Corpus to acquaint Mr Skinner of my Arrival.[9] Din'd at Mr Lawrence's & he talk'd of sleeping after Din. Sent Parcels to the New Inn at Newnham.

[f.34^{r}]

Thursday, the 13th Sent John to the New Inn for the Things from Oxford & Giles for Barns. A Roast Fowl for Dinner. Bullock bought an old one Ey'd Horse of Palmer for £4 0 0.

Friday, the 14th Mow'd Barly. Begun brewing. Giles slear'd into the Kitchen with some sweet Worth.[10]

Saturday, the 15th Br at Cofe Oxford. M.P. Carfax. Took a turn in Christ Church Meadow with Giles. Bought 100 of Sellery Plants & Howse planted them. Gave the old man of Stoke 2d. Oh! that he was as full of Virtue as He is of Years, & then he might truly be said to have arriv'd to an honourable good old Age. [f.34^{V}] Return'd Home to Dinner. I beg of God not to give me a long Life but a good Life & to bless me with a good Conscience & the Hopes of a joyfull Resurrection at my last Hours. Call'd on Monday[11] & the Watch Maker. Went to Lord Harcourts with Mr Parson's Lectures & her Ladyship was not at Home but gone to the Bishop of Oxford.

Sunday, the 16th Forgot to have my Prayers with me before Sermon & made use of a Common Prayer Book. Read a Proclamation. A Duck for Din. Lady Harcourt etc at N.P. The first time of John Taylor's wearing Livery.

[f.35^{r}]

Monday, the 17th Took in a Wheat Rick & begun a New One. Went to Bowly about the Fire Dame Barns had made & the Way to the lower Field. Palmer's Horse very untowardly. Bath'd. John water'd the Sellery.

Tuesday, the 18th Carried Wheat. Beacon & Carrots & a Pudding for Dinner. A Fellow enquir'd after me & would not leave his Name. Set in order some Papers. Howse din'd here. Paid John Taylor Wages & agree'd with him for a whole Year. Wrote to Sister Rock & the Cheesemonger. Edmond Baker deliver'd in a Bill.

Wednesday, the 19th Compos'd part of a Sermon. Giles Smith carried the Housekeeper behind him to Oxford Races.[12] Gave [f.35^{V}] Molly

Basset good Advice but I fear not to much Purpose. Had the Dog kill'd fearing he was Mad.

Thursday, the 20th Br at Cofe & Din'd at the New Inn. Had a Peach & some Plumbs at Giles's. M.P St John's College. Went to the Race. Gave Giles a Chiscake & another Fellow One opposite the late Mr Sweet's House. Saw Mr Trollope on the Course but did not speak to Him. Got Home in good Time. Giles took his Brother up behind Him but Self made him descend again.

Friday, the 21st Begun the great Barly Rick. Had Giles measur'd at Balden for a new Livery. Spoke to Mr Anderson about Christian Barns. A roast Fowl & part of a Ham for Din. Bath in the River. The Fellow went off too soon.

[f.36^{r}]

Saturday, the 22nd Br at Oxford. M.P. Carfax. Had my Wig rectified at Parson's. Got Home the remainder of the Wheat. Drank Coffee at my Lady's. Spoke to Ward about doing Business for me. Tom Chapman throw'd a Carriage & had like to have greatly damag'd One of the Horses as he gave himself no trouble about the Affair.

Sunday, the 23rd Christian Barns very abusive. Read a Brief for several Fires. A Leg of Mutton for Din. After N.P. waited on Lady Harcourt & acquainted her about the dangerous Situation I was in from Fire from Barns. Dame Cissel shew'd me a Guinea Hen's Nest.

Monday, the 24th Self took a Peck of Camomile Tea. Rode about Nineveh & went to the lower Farm. Howse hang'd the Puppy. The Butcher brought at last a good 10s. 6d.

[f.36^{v}]

Tuesday, the 25th Took Giles & his Brother with me to Nineveh for Mushrooms. Spoke to Cummins about Christian Barns. Molly Basset return'd again & wanted to be paid off but was not.

Wednesday, the 26th Set out for Bampton & Br at Longworth. M.P. Bampton[13] & spoke to Dr Sipthorpe there. Saw Mr Trollope at the Fair. Saw a most wonderfull Bitch. Laid at Witney.

Thursday, the 27th Got to Oxford about 12 M. & bought some odd Things. Call'd for John's Br[other]. Came home by the lower Farm. Bath'd after Din.

Friday, the 28th Molly Basset intended to have been married to Day but was not. Had Dick Barns measur'd at the Balden Taylor's. Bought some Beef of the Butcher & paid Him for the Leg of Mutton. [f.37^{r}] Christian Barns got her Apron again from Molly Basset. Paid her Wages & stopt 3s. for an Apron she stold from the Housekeeper. Bath'd. The Watch Maker rectified the Clock & Edmond Baker the Case of it.

Saturday, the 29th Got down the Remainder of the Barly in the Croft & Ball caught a Rabbit there. Married Mary Basset my Dairy Maid & John Hall.[14] Drawn from Casey's Kiln Lime & Bricks. Went to White Lyons after Mushrooms & came Home without any. Paid Christian Barns in full 2s. 6d. Paid the Collar Maker. The Garden Turnips how'd & the Asparagrass Bed weeded. Bathed in the [river] [f.37^{v}] after Dinner. Displeas'd with Bullock for selling a Sow & Pigs without Orders.

Sunday, the 30th After M.P. spoke to Molder to dine at my House but he declin'd, but Dame Macksey came. Giles went Home with his Father & Brother.

Monday, the 31st A roast Rabbit for Din & Dame Andrews brought Beacon Money & din'd here. Met Thomas Anderson at Christian Barns Quarters & went with Him to Bowley's.

Notes

1 Lord Harcourt travelled abroad to fetch Princess Charlotte Sophia, second daughter of the Duke of Mecklenburg-Strelitz. George III married her in the Chapel Royal, St James's, on 8 September 1761. See Watson, *George III*, p. 7.

2 For examples of these victories, see July 1761, notes 12 and 13.

3 This was probably Old Swan Stairs, on the river just west of London Bridge.

4 Peerless Poole was a swimming pool opened in 1743 by a London jeweller called William Kemp. It was closed *c.* 1850. For full details see *London Encycl.*, p. 589.

5 The chapel was at the Haberdashers' Hall, rebuilt by Christopher Wren and opened in 1668. See *ibid.*, p. 349.

6 Hoxton Square was laid out during the 1680s. Many livery companies, including the haberdashers, acquired land there for their Alms Houses. See *ibid.*, pp. 398–9.

7 The Fishmongers' Hall, off Thames Street and near to the Old Swan, was a favourite haunt of JN's. The medieval hall was destroyed in the Great Fire and replaced in 1671. This in turn was demolished to make way for the new London Bridge in 1827. See *ibid.*, p. 281.

8 Mrs Harcourt was Lord Harcourt's mother.

9 The Reverend Mr Skinner, a Fellow of Corpus Christi College, had been standing in for JN at Nuneham during the London visit.

10 By 'sweet worth' JN meant flavoured herbs, or possibly vegetables or cabbages.

11 Monday was a firm of printers and stationers in St Aldate's.

12 These races were horse races held on Port Meadow on 19–21 August 1761. They were annual events and were a popular pastime. See *Encycl. Oxford*, p. 332; *Jackson's*, Wednesday 19 August 1761.

13 The service was at St Mary's church, one of the largest churches in Oxfordshire. See Sherwood and Pevsner, *Oxfordshire*, pp. 429–31.

14 This marriage is confirmed by the Nuneham Marriage *Registers*, p. 24.

September 1761

Tuesday, the 1st The Bricklayer pav'd[1] part of the Kitchen Court. The Pump Maker went away before he had compleated the Pump. Met Bowly at Barn's Quarters & upon his speaking to Her She remov'd to Dame Pearce's. Bath'd [f.38^{r}] in the River. Self went to Windmill Field. Employ'd Barnes.

Wednesday, the 2nd[2] Went with the Bricklayer to the Church Yard for an old Grave Stone to lay by the Pump & with much Difficulty he got it here, & was busy about the Court & the Drain.[3] A roast Duck for Din.

Thursday, the 3rd Br at Oxford. M.P. Carfax. Lediard went off his Wife being Ill. Boil Beef & Udder for Din. Breeches not ready. Left a Pattern at Mr Austin's. Old Brown had a deal of his Main gnaw'd off.

Friday, the 4th Call'd on Dame Lediard & gave her good Advice. Sent her some Pudding & Wine by her Daughter & one of Field's Wenches, & caught them afterwards at my Apple Tree. late at Cart.

Saturday, the 5th The Bricklayer finish'd the Drains. Moll not at Work. Went for Barns & [f.38^{V}] Field. Howse made Places for two Cows. Bullock begun plowing the Crofts. Rung'd the Hogs. John wash'd the Bottles. Edmond Baker hung'd the Glass.[4] The Millar brought Home 3 Bushel of Wheat.

Sunday, the 6th Spoke to Moulder to dine at my House after M. Ser. Self & John view'd my Turnips on the Hill. Spoke to Edmond not to disappoint me to morrow. Boil Beef for Din. N.P.

Monday, the 7th Edmond Baker excus'd Himself for not entering on Work. Wrote three Letters to three different Persons who applied to me for my Strand House. Two Teams at Plow. The Upholsterer's Apprentice came here.

Tuesday, the 8th Edmond Baker enter'd on Work. Hung the Bow Room & put up some [f.39r] Pictures. Busy at Harvest Cart. Sanders set up the Marble Chimney Peice. John got some prodigious fine Damsens.

Wednesday, the 9th More Paper put up. The Gilt Leather laid in Order & some strips had been cut away as I suppose, by the Rogue the late John Pearce. Examin'd one of the Ceiling Peices. John much displeas'd at Leicester's putting Dung in his Pocket. A Duck for Din. Gave the Ringers 2s 6d to drink for the safe Arrival of the King's intended Consort. God grant they may [live] long together in Love & Unity & by their pious & good Example work a thorough Reformation of Manners through the whole Nation.[5]

[f.39v]

Thursday, the 10th Br at Oxford. M.P. Carfax. Paid Mr Skinner £8 8s.[6] Bought Nails etc. Call'd at Mr Woods for a Pound of Glew. Had Giles about to buy him a Cap but did not. Call'd on my Neice.

Friday, the 11th With much Difficulty the great Ceiling Picture in the Bow Room was put up. Howse & John got the Doctors. A Chumb[7] out of one of the Trees had like to have fell on my Head, but Prais'd be God it did not & I am truly thankfull to him for preserving me safe & unhurt. Dame Sparrow came to me about a Debt of Lediard's.

Saturday, the 12th Got up the great Ceiling Picture in the first Room. Leicester did Jobbs. [f.40r] Went to Edmond's for Glew. Bullock mov'd Household Goods into the House in the Backside. Gave Mr Braine orders about the Harvest Home Supper to Night.

Sunday, the 13th Paid several of the Labourers & was puzled about Ball's Wages. Giles came Home & his Father, Mother & Br din'd at my House, & went to Morning Prayers. Self & John to Christian Barns & paid her her Wages. Spoke to Nickols about Beck Clarke's taking Penance.[8] Not many People at N. Prayers.

Monday, the 14th John Taylor drove me to Oxford for the first time. Br at Tom's Cofe.[9] M.P. St John's. Went to New College but no Prayers & took a Round in the Cloysters, I knew not off before.[10] [f.40v] Bought several things at my Neices. Mr Austin was chosen Mayor. Return'd

Home to Dinner. Draw'd Home the remainder of the Hain. Sent Polly a Letter.

Tuesday, the 15th John got the Balden Shoemaker to mend the Harness wch the Collarmaker had mended with old Leather not many days before. Sent Giles with my little———[11] to Vulcan's to be clean'd. Edmond Baker was to have done something to my Landau but did not. Boil neck of Mutton for Din. Howse return'd a thirty six Shilling Peice. Wantage & Lyon shoe'd up.

Wednesday, the 16th After Br Self set out in the Landau for London & din'd at Nettlebed, & laid at the lone House short of Maiden Head, & had Marlborough [f.41^{r}] Beer & Br[ead] & Cheese for Supper. The Harness was broke in coming out at the Inn at Nettlebed & my foreign Strap was us'd on that Account.

Thursday, the 17th Set out at 6 o'Clock & Br at the Hart on Hounslow. Walk'd ab[out] the Garden & waited long for the little Horse. Got to Din at Mortimer Street & had the Pleasure of finding all Friends tollerable Well, for wch Blessing I am thankfull to Providence as well as for bringing me safe & in good Health to this Place. Admiral Long return'd Home to Day.[12]

Friday, the 18th Sister Rock went with me to Westminster about taken[13] Places for the Coronation, & we return'd Home to Din. Spoke to Mr Lloyd near Westminster Hall. Met with the Mayor, [f.41^{v}] Ives & young Leake. N.P. St Anne's. Call'd at two Peoples Houses about my Strand House. Went to King's House & had the Pleasure of finding Him alive.

Saturday, the 19th Order'd the Coachmaker to make a New Frame for the Landau Window. Took John with me to the Strand for Cheese. Went to Hungerford Cofe on account of the Rain. Bought a pair of Buckskin Gloves. Din'd at Chairing Cross. Took four Places & a bed Chamber for the Coronation for £7 7s. Lorum the man about my Strand House spoke to me in Bridge St.

Sunday, the 20th M.P. St George's Queen's Square. Sacr^{t}. Went to the Foundling Hospital before Din. Went to Westminster after Din & mist going [f.42^{r}] to Church. Return'd Home to Tea. Mrs Pickering din'd here.

Monday, the 21st Took Provision to the Place where Self had taken Seats for the Coronation & secur'd the Key of the Chamber. After Din went for Miss Bush. Conducted Her & two Sister to Bridge Street against the Coronation. Self set up all Night. A poor woman had like to have been greatly damag'd by a———— [14] of deal Board falling on her Head. And another more dreadfull accident might have happen'd if not prevent by me by a Link being beat against the Platform & falling under it.

Tuesday, the 22nd The Procession of the Coronation went by about One o'Clock [f.42^{v}] at Noon & the Number of Spectators was very numerous, but I did not see it to advantage on the return from the Abby because it was too dark & the Company stood up. All of [us] footed it Home.

Wednesday, the 23rd After Br Self Conducted Miss Bush Home in my Landau. Went to Westminister for my Baggage. Spoke to Mr Dingly. Turn'd out of Westminister because I would not pay One Shilling. Din'd at the Widow Gould's & saw Her Daughter.

Thursday, the 24th Br at Hungerford Cofe. Lett my Strand House to Mr Lorum for £50 a Year. Drank Tea with [f.43^{r}] Mrs Rock. two Sister pay'd Mrs Maw a Visit in my Landau. N.P. Conduit St Chapple. Went about the House in Holles Street where the Auction is to be.

Friday, the 25th Went to see the young Widow Self got acquainted with at Islington Wells & She lives with her Brother a hedge Schoolmaster[15] near More Fields, & she seem'd to be pleas'd with my Company & invited me to come & drink Tea with Her. Call'd on Mrs Pickering & threaten'd to seize Challiners Goods, if he did not pay One Guinea by next Saturday se'nnight. Got Home before Din & view'd my Lord Foley's Garden.[16] Sisters went to Chelsea in my Landau & Self went with Hetty [f.43^{v}] over the Stones. Went to St George's Church but did not stay till Prayers begun having an Occasion to make Water often with some small sort of Pain & also a tendency to go to stool.

Saturday, the 26th Paid for the Raperation of my Landau. Left my Advertisement of the Herbal at the Printing House. Spoke to a Salesman at Newgate Market about sending Calves to [be] sold by Him, but he advis'd me to sell them at Home. Bought at Bromigh a large Quantity of Hanging Paper.[17] Bought Tea & Coffee at Twining's. Br at George's.

Went to Chelsea by Water not intending so to do when I first went into the Boat. [f.44^{r}] Din'd at Pinchbecks & saw the Dwarf.[18] Got Home by Tea time. Spoke to One of Lord Harcourt's Maid Servants as she was viewing the Figures by Hyde Park Corner through Mistake.

Sunday, the 27th Sent John & Giles to early Prayers. Went with Landau to St Georges. M.P. & staid [for] the Sacr^{t} & a few Communicants indeed. Went into the Park before Dinner. Late at N.P. St Georges Queen's Square.

Monday, the 28th Borrow'd five Guineas of Sister Rock. Compos'd part of a Sermon. Sister & Polly went to see Mr Arnold at Turnham Green. Drank Tea with the young Widow.

[f.44^{v}]

Tuesday, the 29th Went to Bromigh to forbid the Sending of the Paper thinking Self may buy it cheaper. Call'd on Dunning about the Window Lights. After Br set out for the Widow, & conducted her in my Landau to Don Saltero's Cofe at Chelsea.[19] Show'd Her the Moravian's House & the Physick Garden & then went to Din at Pinchback's & saw the little Man & the King of Prussia & several other Figures in Waxwork, & all exstreamly strong, bold, & natural. Conducted Her home & drank Tea with Her.

Wednesday, the 30th Bought John Taylor a Velvet Cap & Cloath for Giles's Coat. Bought twenty one Peices of Paper for hanging. Waited [f.45^{r}] on Mrs Maw with a Print of the Coronation. Admiral Long stay'd till about 9 o'Clock at Night & Self went Home with Him.

Notes

1 Altered from 'begun paving.'

2 JN has again made a slip in his numbering of the days. '2' was '3' here and '3' was '4' in the following entry.

3 JN's apparent desecration of this grave appears in marked contrast to his vehement protest at Lord Harcourt's later removal of the entire churchyard to make way for his park.

4 By 'Glass' JN meant mirror.

5 JN is misinformed here. George III married Charlotte on the previous day. See August 1761, note 1.

6 The Reverend Mr Skinner took care of JN's church during his previous London visit.

7 By 'Chumb' JN meant a chump, or thick piece of wood.

8 This should have been performed on 11 March 1761, but JN was then away in Witney. See earlier entry. Presumably JN was now making arrangements with Nichols, the parish clerk, for the penance to take place. Rebecca was the daughter of Edward and Elizabeth Clarke. She was baptized on 24 June 1742 and buried on 17 October 1792. She married William Carr on 1 December 1779. In March 1761, Rebecca, 'a Single Woman', was found guilty in the Archdeacon's Court at Oxford of 'the foul Crime of Fornication'. She was due to perform her penance at Nuneham church a few days later. The record describes how she was to enter the vestry of the church between 10 a.m. and noon and, without a sheet (i.e. not to wear the white sheet or carry the white rod which was customary on such occasions), to repeat the following words after JN:

> Good People, Whereas to the great Displeasure of Almighty God and the Offence of this Neighbourhood, I have committed the foul Crime of Fornication and stand Convict thereof by my own Confession, I am therefore according to Order of Court wither to make this my Acknowledgment. I confess my Fault and am Sorry for the Same, moreover asking Forgiveness of Almighty God and promising by his Assistance not to commit the like offence any more and that he may give me Grace so to do, I desire you all to join with me in Prayers to him for the Help of his holy Spirit . . . .

See *Oxfordshire Archives*, MS. Oxf. Archd. Papers C. 130, fo. 52.

9 Tom's Coffee House was at 115 High Street. Between 1759 and 1764 it was run by Thomas Hobson. It was the haunt of the 'most gay and expensive', with a back room nicknamed the 'House of Lords', complete with comfort able Chippendale armchairs reserved for senior members of the University. See Aubertin-Potter and Bennett, *Oxford Coffee Houses*, pp. 21, 41.

10 For full details see Sherwood and Pevsner, *Oxfordshire*, p. 172.

11 Another omission in the text.

12 Long returned from Bristol, where he had been since 1 August. See earlier entry.

13 By 'taken' JN meant reserved.

14 Another omission in the text.

15 A 'hedge Schoolmaster' was used as a term of contempt, implying that the brother was not very good at teaching. The widow was Mrs Dellafey.

16 Lord Foley had a large mansion with a fine garden close to what was to become Foley Street. JN with his gardening interests was a natural visitor. See *London Encycl.*, p. 288.

17 Bromwich and Leigh were wallpaper sellers in Ludgate Hill. See Mortimer, *Universal Director*, Part II, p. 54.

18 As early as 1734, Edward Pinchbeck (born in 1713) had a booth called the 'Great Theatrical Booth'. This was on the bowling green behind the Marshalsea down Mermaid Court next to the Queen's Arms Tavern. There he showed 'the so much famed piece of machinery, consisting of large artificial wax figures five foot high, which have all the just motions and gestures of human life'. Edward was the son of Charles Pinchbeck, the inventor and clockmaker. See Lillywhite, *Coffee Houses*, pp. 473, 572; *Dictionary of National Biography* (Oxford, 1917), XV, p. 1193.

19 Don Saltero's Coffee House in Chelsea was opened on the corner of Lawrence Street in 1675. By JN's time it was on the site of what is now Cheyne Walk. Don Saltero was the nickname of James Salter, a barber and former servant of Sir Hans Sloane. In 1728 the premises were advertised as a 'Museum Coffee House', with a growing collection of curiosities, some of which JN describes here. See *London Encycl.*, p. 233; Lillywhite, *Coffee Houses*, pp. 194–5.

October 1761

Thursday, the 1st E.M.P. St James's. Bought Brass Handles for the Locks. Saw the learned Canary Bird[1] & heard two men play several Tunes on Glasses about half full of Water. At this Performance Self convers'd with a Lady in Mourning with two Children & could take her to be my Wife if she was willing to have me for her Husband. Mrs Ridly drank Tea here. Waited on Admiral Long & he expected me in the Morning at his House to write a Letter for Him.

[f.45^{v}]

Friday, the 2nd E.M.P. St James's. After Br went to Moorefields for Mrs Dellafey & treated her with the Sight of the learned Canary Bird & then waited on her Home. Took Polly in my Landau to Dinner at the Admiral's & my Sister Rock was to have went but declin'd it not being well. After Dinner went to N.P. St Georges & return'd to the Admiral's again for Tea & gave his Man 1s.

Saturday, the 3rd E.M.P. Covent Garden. Treated Sister Rock & Polly with the Sight of the Canary Bird. Self din'd at the Widow Gould's. N.P. St George's.

A Fire had very like to have broke out in a[2] Room over the Coach House had it not been timely & [f.46^{r}] providentially discover'd by Dame Pratt; for it had burnt through a Board under the Bricks & under it was the Rack with Hay in it.[3]

Had it continu'd burning a few Minutes longer it might have got an head & then the Consequence might have been very dreadfull. The Hurry, Confusion, Fright & Terror it would have caus'd to me as well as Loss is happily prevented, & I am truly thankfull to Providence for this instance of his Goodness to Me, & should I hereafter grow unmindfull of his Favour & neglect to give him the Tribute of Praise for them, may I suffer for my Ingratitude. To be silent for Mercies receiv'd from God & soon [f.46^{v}] to forget, argues an ungenerous & vicious turn of Mind & often proceeds from down right Pride. As we can merit nothing from

God, surely we should be sincerely thankfull for the least as well as the greatest Demonstrations of his Goodness to us, when he bestows on us the Blessings of Life or keeps off an independent Evil, & then we may hope to enjoy his Favour, & that he will not afflict us out of Measure. When we have escap'd any impendent Danger & are quite safe & secure, how agreeable is the reflection of it to the Mind, if our Hearts overflow with the Jubilee of Praise & Gratitude to God. God expects [f.47^{r}] we should be truly thankfull to Him for his past & present Favours & the prevention of any threatening Misfortune, & if we neglect our Duty in this instance we deprive ourselves of a great Pleasure & act in a Manner very offensive to Him.

Sunday, the 4th M.P. St Georges Queen's Square & Sac^{rt}. Sent the Landau for Sisters. Wantage dropt a Shoe. N.P. Oxford Chapple. Drank Punch at the Admiral's with Mrs Aires.

Monday, the 5th E.M.P. St Anne's. Call'd for the Buttons for Giles' Livery. Bought a Pair of Pumps. Bought some China in Swallow St. Took Polly with me in the Park. One Taylor refus'd to repair my Cloath & another Taylor's House stunk [f.47^{v}] most Abominable. Poor Tetty went to bed pretty much out of Order. Self & two Sisters drank Tea at Mrs Ridley's & there were two Ladies more.

Tuesday, the 6th Call'd on Ludgate Hill about the Paper.[4] Bought a Velvet Cap for Giles & a Silver Tassell. Bought three Bottles of Olives & a Quart of Oyl. Took Mrs Rock in my Landau to Spring Garden to see the Canary Bird & the Poll broke.[5] Had the Harness mended. Twice at the Admiral's. N.P. St George's. Sent Challiner two Rent Receipts. Saw a man with his Knee turn'd outwards. I am thankfull to Providence that he has form'd all my Limbs uniform & regular.

[f.48^{r}]

Wednesday, the 7th Not up till about 9 o'Clock M. & shamefull thing. The Paper was sent Home. Self & the Widow walk't about Kensington Garden[6] & then din'd at the Tavern on a very nice Chick. Saw at the same Place an apple Tree with Blossoms on it.

Thursday, the 8th Went to the Fire Office about the Damage done in the Room over the Coach House. Call'd at Stark's for a dozn of Boarders he sent me short. Br at Hungerford Cofe. Call'd at my Strand House about the Pavement. Self was to have given Mrs Rock an Airing but she declin'd going when I went with my Carriage because Mrs Harcourt's Maid was gone to Market. Admiral Long was to [f.48^{v}] have drank Tea here, but he forgot the Engagement. E.M.P. St James's. Call'd on Mrs Dellafey. Polly din'd at the Admiral's. N.P. St Georges. I find I have got an ugly Cold.

Friday, the 9th Self Br with Mrs Dellafey & then waited on Her to Kew Gardens where we were much entertained, tho' it remained doubtfull for some time whether the Gardiner would let us see them, till I talk'd about giving him a Shilling.[7] The Chinese Pagoda ten story hight & the two heathen Temples on each Side of it, are striking Things. The Temple of the Sun & the Temple of Fame are very well worth seeing. The Ruins also are very natural. The [f.49^{r}] Chinese Temple by the Water is very delightfull. The Flower Garden & the Avery as well as the Gold & Silver Fishes are very entertaining. The Chinese Parteridges are vastly Beautifull. Call'd on Mr Arnold. Din'd at the Pack horse at Turnham Green. Drank Tea Evening at Mrs Dellafeys & then return'd Home.

Saturday, the 10th [Old Michaelmas Day] E.M.P. Covent Garden. Strol'd about the Market & bought some Flowers. Chang'd Dust Tea at Twinings. Br at George's Cofe.[8] Brought the Coachmaker to alter the Landau just as my two Sisters were agoing [f.49^{v}] into it but they were providentially stopt till it was made safe for them, & then they paid a Visit in it to Miss Bush. All Praise to God for this instance of his Providential Care towards [them?]. Admiral Long with Mrs Ayres & her Son spent the Evening here.

Sunday, the 11th M.P. at the Foundling Hospital & from thence Self sent the Landau to take two of my Sisters to St James's Church. Went to St Mary le bonne Church N.P. with two of my Sisters in the Landau. After Tea N. went to the Admiral's.

Monday, the 12th E.M.P. St James's. Took two of my Sisters to Kew & as they could not be admitted into the Garden till about [f.50^{r}] two o'Clock & went with them [to] Richmond Gardens & in our return call'd on Mr Arnold. Self & Polly din'd at Admiral Long's. Bought some Pellitory of Spain[9] for my tooth Ache.

Tuesday, the 13th Remov'd some Pictures out of the Garret. Boil Beef for Din but did not relish it. Call'd at King's. Took Mrs Rock some Pellitory of Spain & drank Tea with Her. Oysters for Supper, but did not eat many of them. Drank about a Pint of Way[10] before Bed Time.

Wednesday, the 14th M.P. Berwick Street Chapple. Call'd at King's. Took Giles & John with me to bring Board[ers] from the Strand House. Read News at Slaughter's Cofe. N.P. St Georges. Paid the Coachmaker & the Sadler. Call'd on Admiral Long's.

[f.50^{V}]

Thursday, the 15th Self John & Giles busy before Br in getting the Pictures out of the Garret, & taking them into the Coach House & King & his Brother pack'd them up. N.P. St George's. Took my Leave of Admiral Long at his House. Administer'd the Whip to William & Giles.

Friday, the 16th With some Difficulty the Picture Case was got to the Hog in the Pound. Fifteen Gallons & some Pints of Porter put in the Vessel & the Tap Hole fail'd. Set out about 10 o'Clock M. & Din'd on Hounslow Heath, & got to my old Quarters beyond Maiden Head by Tea time. Toasted Cheese for Sup.

Saturday, the 17th Got to Henly to Br. Din'd at Benson. Got Home by Tea Time [f.51^{r}] Safe & in good Health & am thankfull to God for this his Goodness & Care towards [me]. Br[ead] & Olives for Supper.

Sunday, the 18th Pray'd by Dame Andrews & Turner before Br. & sent the former some Wine. Master Field officiated for Nickols. Lord Harcourt spoke to me after Church was over. A Duck for Din. A thine Congregation at N.P. Took the Gun out of the Housekeepers Room.

Monday, the 19th Br at my Lord's. Pray'd by Andrews & Turner. John shot 3 Pidgeons. Went to the Balden Taylor. Boil Pidgeon & Beacon for Dinner. Winnow'd seven Quarter of Barly.

Tuesday, the 20th Lord Harcourt sent me a Letter about Exchanging my Living for one of £400 a Year in Herefordshire.[11] [f.51^{V}] Went out with my Gun, but shot Nothing. Read the News at the Golden Ball. Part of a Duck hash'd for Dinner. Bullock paid the Corn Money. Gave Dame Field of the New Town One Shilling, her Husband being very Ill.

Wednesday, the 21st Cut my Beard off before I set out for Oxford. Left my Leather Breeches with the Maker to alter them. Br at Cofe at Oxford. M.P. St Thomas Parish Church.[12] Call'd at Giles's & Mrs Treacher went through the Garden with me for the Church. Bought some things at Mr Lawrence's & took a Parcel to me Neice from her Mother. Bought some things of Mr Austin. Return'd Home to Dinner. Met Miss Weston near my Lord's & found he set off for [f.52r] London in the Morning.

Thursday, the 22nd Part of a Neck of Mutton for Din. Ten Bushel of Malt sent in. My Lord begun selling off Brains Goods.[13] Went to the Balden Taylor with Cloath for Williams Surtut Coat & met Him as he was returning Home from the Sale.

Friday, the 23rd Begun brewing. Part of a cold Fowl hash'd up for Din. Cut Toe Nails. Draw'd to Howse's a Load of Bean Stubs.

Saturday, the 24th Call'd for my Leather Breeches. Br at Cofe Oxford. Bought of Mr Lawrance two Hundred 1/4 of Smyrna Plumbs, two Gallons of Rum etc. Bullock went to Oxford with a Cart & brought three Parcels from the New Inn at Newnham [f.52v] but the Paper is missing. Wet very much in coming Home. Bought a Calves Head & some Beef.

Sunday, the 25th My Lady Harcourt was not at Church this Day. After M.P. Self went to the New Town – found Lediard had been at Rome. Sent Turner some Wine & Field some Ale. Part of the Calves Head hash'd. Not many People at P.N. Gave the Paper Boy a Penny & Cummins Boy a halfpenny. Dame Lediard came for a Bottle of Ale according to Orders.

Monday, the 26th Begun brewing Strong Beer. After Br Self & Giles went to the Balden Taylor's with several things. Read the News at the Golden Ball. Browns Shoes were remov'd.[14] Bullock displeas'd because I would not [f.53r] let him fetch Water from the River.

Tuesday, the 27th Br at Cofe Oxford. Had the Saddle & Kettle mended. M.P. St Johns.[15] Din'd with my Neice. Paid Parsons £3 3 0 in part of

£6 6 0. Paid for the Carriage of things from London.

Brought Home a new Pair of Hussar Boots. Met Lady Betty Harcourt near the Mile Stone Oxford.

Wednesday, the 28th Call'd at the New Inn. Took some things to the Balden Taylor. A Duck for Dinner. Bullock sold at Shillingford Market Wheat & Barly.

Thursday, the 29th Set out about 7 o'Clock M. & Br at the Crown at Wantage. Went to the Auction at the Bear[16] & Miss Frogly told me She was [f.53^{V}] agoing to be married & invited me to come & see Her. See the ups & downs in Life, her Father is dead, her Mother keeps out of the Way & is likely reduc'd to very low Circumstances, & She herself is about entering into the holy State of Matrymony. God grant it may be for her spiritual & temporal Good. Took a View of Mr Price's Premises & find he has made several Improvements since I was there last, May he likewise have improv'd Himself in Virtue & Goodness. Din'd at Church Hackburn [East Hagbourne] on the Carcase of a Duck Self took with me, & found the old Landlord Hearty & in good Health. [f.54^{r}] Enquir'd after the old Cyderman & found he was dead, & its to be fear'd made a very bad End, as he had for some time neglected his Church & lead a very sloathfull & inconsiderate Life. May I take Care I don't fall into the same & make no better exit out of the World, than he did.

This Day my dearest Mother was delivered of Me,[17] & when I come to dye may I have no Reason may I have no reason [*sic*] to lament the day of my Birth & my coming into this World. Give me Grace O my God, I beseech so to pass the Days of my Pilgrimage here, that when I find I have just finish'd it & am about to take my final of all Sub [*sic*] [f.54^{V}] Sublunary[18] Enjoyment, I may do it with Cheerfullness & Resignation.

Its my desire to please my God & to do the whole of my Duty, & through his Assistance & my own best Endeavours, I trust, I shall ever be in readiness for my final Departure out of this World. It matters not much how long or how short my time may be here, but only how well I spent my time of abode on[19] this Side of Eternity. To live altogether free from Troubles & Disappointments is not my Ambition, its not what I expect or look for, but its my desire to be resign'd to the Will of God in all things, & to wait with Patience the removal of any pressing Evils.

[f.55^{r}]

I see Misfortunes befall other & why should I look for better Treatment. No Station of Life is out of the reach of Adversity, & when

Adversity overtakes us let us indeavour to make a proper use of it, & render it productive of much good to us, if Possible. The Utility of Affliction is very conspicuous from the Reformation it often works in our bad Morals, & by stopping us in an evil Course, & when it has that happy affect on us, we ought to be thankfull to Providence for it.

I hope I am in readiness for my latter End & that when I come to dye, that then I shall dye with Peace & Comfort. I am thankfull for the long [enjoyment?] [f.55^{v}] of Life & for the many Comforts & Blessings I have rec'd from the Hands of God & when it shall be his Will to take me hence, may I be all resignation & Subjection, & give up without any Reluctancy.

May my greatest Sollicitude consist in preparing myself for my departure hence, that a sudden Death may do me no harm. A conscientious Discharge of my Duty & a daily perseverance in the Paths of Virtue & Holiness is the best Preparation for Death, & may I demean & regulate myself accordingly. May I not be amorous of a long Life, but a good One & so spend the remainder of my days here in such a manner that through the Merits of my Saviour I may rationally hope for everlasting Happiness.

[f.56^{r}]

Friday, the 30th Cut my Beard off before Br. Treated the Two Labourers with a Quart of Ale. After Br prol'd about & view'd the Ricks near the Church. Mistoke a little Girl for a Boy at the Ferry, & gave him ½d. Got Home to Dinner.

Saturday, the 31st Br at my Lord's & he was gone to Blenheim.[20] Brought Williams Surtut Coat from the Balden Taylor & left an old Waistcoat for Raperation. A roast Fowl for Din. Talk'd to Mr Edmond about the Portico. Barly Straw put in the Cow House.

Notes

1 This was at Spring Gardens, a pleasure-ground first laid out at the beginning of the eighteenth century. See *London Encycl.*, pp. 809–10.

2 'The' is crossed out in the text.

3 This gives JN a perfect excuse for one of his pieces of moral reflection.

4 JN called at the firm of Bromwich and Leigh. See September 1761, note 17.

5 'Was' is crossed out in the text.

6 The gardens of Kensington Palace were a fashionable place to stroll. There was a Broad Walk with temples, ponds and a revolving summer house built in 1733. For full details see *London Encycl.*, pp. 424–5.

7 Kew Gardens combine a scientific centre with an eighteenth-century pleasure-ground. The area was developed by Frederick the Prince of Wales, and later by his widow Augusta, Dowager Princess of Wales, who created a botanic garden of nine acres in 1759. George III continued the royal patronage after 1760. Between 1759 and 1761, Sir William Chambers designed many of the buildings that JN describes here. The great pagoda stands ten stories and 163 feet high. The 'Chinese Parteridges' are, of course, pheasants. Plates of 'The Aviary', 'The Great Pagoda', 'The Mosque', 'The Gothic Cathedral' and various general views that JN must have known are to be found in Sir William Chambers, *Plans, Elevations of the Gardens and Buildings at Kew in Surrey* (1763), *passim*. See also *London Encycl.*, pp. 664–6.

8 There were several coffee houses of this name, but JN may have eaten at George's in Piccadilly 'Opposite the Church,' as he was in the vicinity. See Lillywhite, *Coffee Houses*, pp. 226–7.

9 Pellitory of Spain came from a composite plant, *Anacyclus Pyrethrum*. The root was used frequently as a remedy for toothache. See *OED*.

10 Whey is the watery part of milk remaining after the separation of the curd. See *OED*.

11 There is no indication where this is, but it gives some idea of the value of Nuneham and suggests that JN was not entirely happy with the changes in the parish. He did not move, however, remaining at Nuneham until 1786.

12 This was St Thomas's church in Becket Street. It took its name from the recently murdered Thomas Becket and began as a chapel towards the end of the twelfth century. It was built by the canons of Oseney Abbey. Church attendance declined during the eighteenth century, so that the number of communicants had fallen to ten by 1802. There was a recovery during the nineteenth century and some extensive restoration took place after 1846. See Sherwood and Pevsner, *Oxfordshire*, pp. 298–9; *Encycl. Oxford*, pp. 425–6.

13 William Braine was the innkeeper at Nuneham. He was in debt and his goods were being sold off. Mr Bowley handled the affair for Lord Harcourt.

14 Old Brown was one of JN's horses.

15 The service was at St John's College chapel where JN was a frequent visitor. For full details see Sherwood and Pevsner, *Oxfordshire*, pp. 196–7.

16 Both The Crown and The Bear were in the Market Place. See Pevsner, *Berkshire*, p. 255.

17 JN is inconsistent over the date of his birthday. In 1759 he claims it was on 28 October. See earlier entry.

18 'Sublunary' means of, or belonging to, this world.

19 'Here' is crossed out in the text.

20 Presumably JN went to Blenheim to visit George, 4th Duke of Marlborough who had inherited the title in 1758. See D. Green, *The Churchills of Blenheim* (1984), Chapter 4.

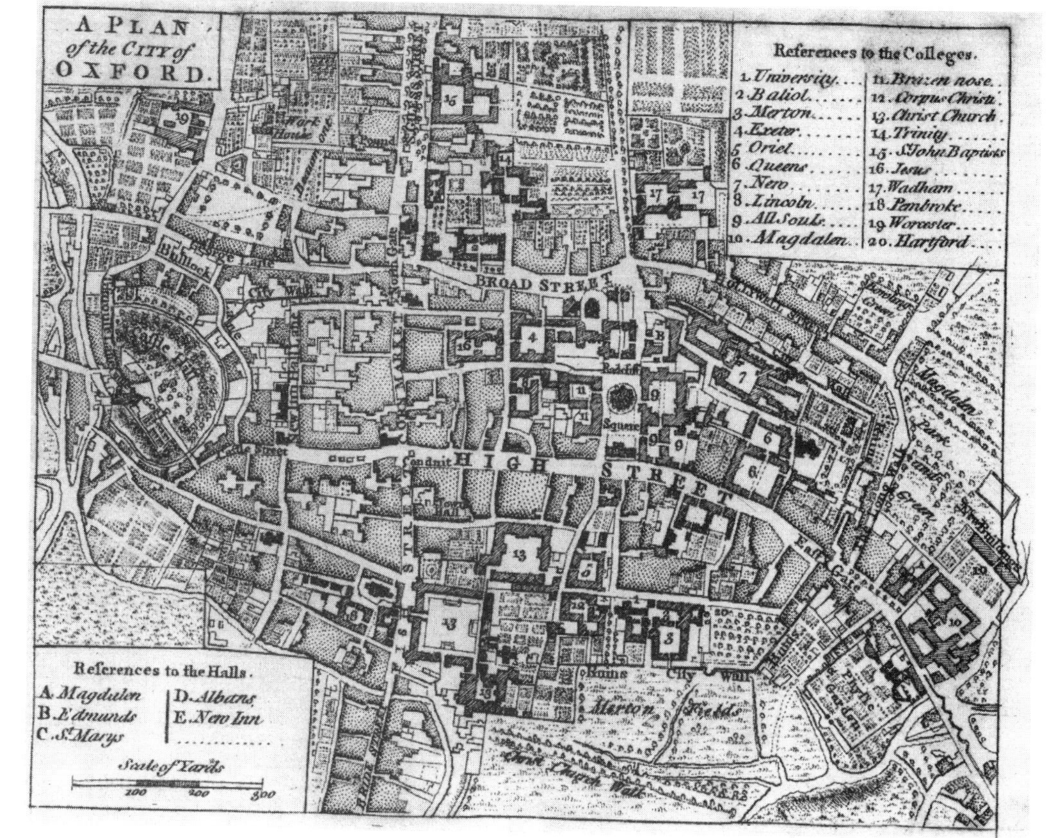

Plate 15 A plan of Oxford, from A. Drury, *A Collection of Plans of the Principle Cities of Great Britain c. 1764*; by kind permission of the Bodleian Library (Gough Maps, 143, fo. 6)

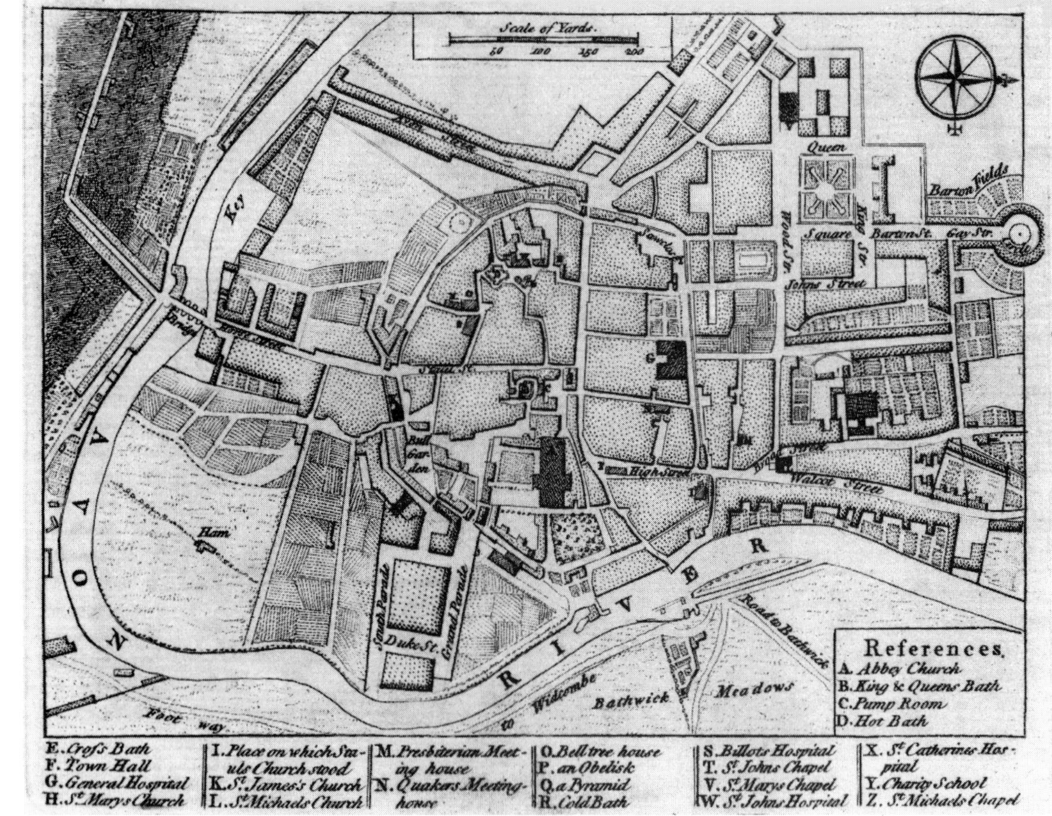

Plate 16 A plan of Bath, from A. Drury, *A Collection of Plans of the Principle Cities of Great Britain c. 1764;* by kind permission of the Bodleian Library (Gough Maps, 143, fo. 12)

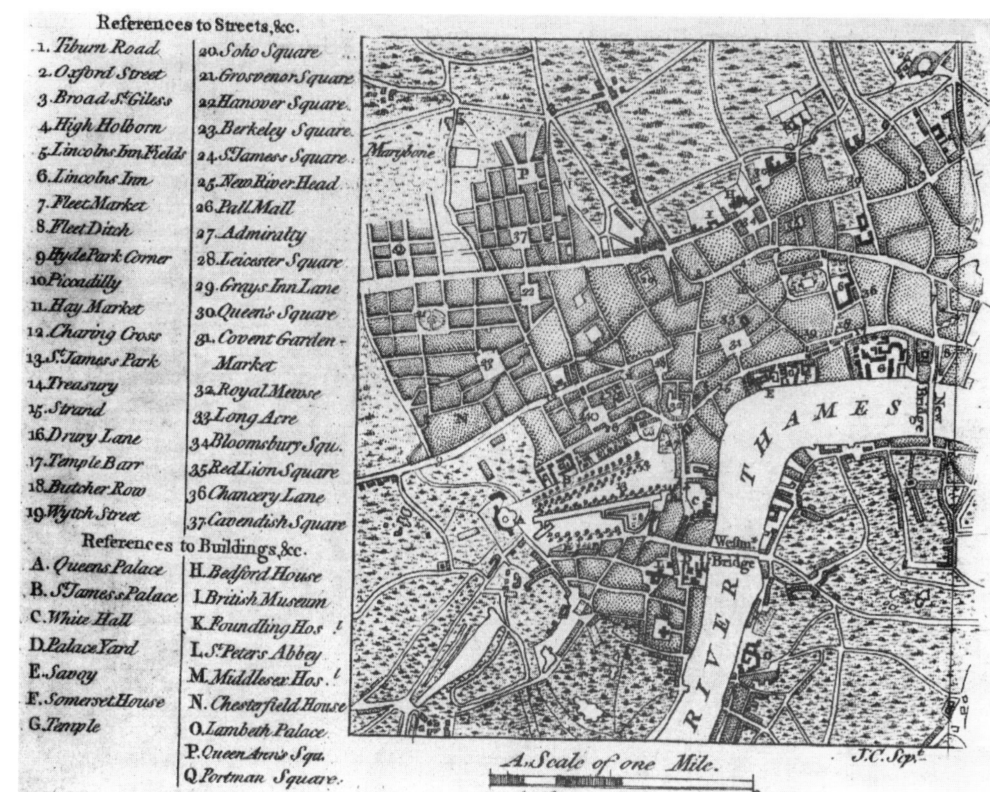

Plate 17 A plan of London, from A. Drury, *A Collection of Plans of the Principal Cities of Britain c. 1764*; by kind permission of the Bodleian Library (Gough Maps, 143, fo. 3)

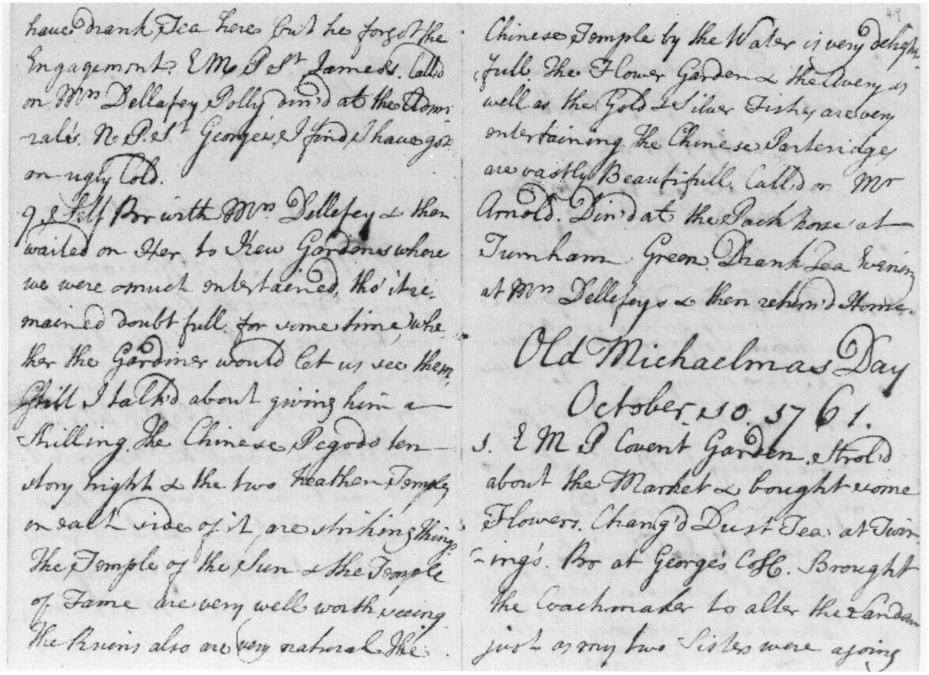

have drank Tea here but he forgot the
Engagement. E M P St James's. Call'd
on Mrs Dellafey Polly din'd at the Admiral's. N P St George's & I find I have got
an ugly Cold.
I & Self Br with Mrs Dellefey & then
waited on Her to Kew Gardens where
we were much entertained, tho' it remained doubtfull for some time whether the Gardiner would let us see them
till I talk'd about giving him a
Shilling. The Chinese Pegoda ten
story hight & the two Heathen Temples
on each side of it are striking things.
The Temple of the Sun & the Temple
of Fame are very well worth seeing
The Ruins also are very natural. The

Chinese Temple by the Water is very delightfull. The Flower Garden & the Avery as
well as the Gold & Silver Fishes are very
entertaining the Chinese Partridges
are vastly Beautifull. Call'd on Mr
Arnold. Din'd at the Pack horse at
Turnham Green. Drank Tea Evening
at Mrs Dellefey's & then return'd Home.

Old Michaelmas Day
October 10. 1761.

1. E M P Covent Garden. Strol'd
about the Market & bought some
Flowers. Chang'd Dust Tea at Twinings. Br at George's CoH. Brought
the Coachmaker to alter the Landau
just as my two Sisters were agoing

Plate 18 An extract from James Newton's diary recounting his visit to Kew; by kind permission of the Bodleian Library (MS. Eng. Misc. e. 251, fos 48v and 48r)

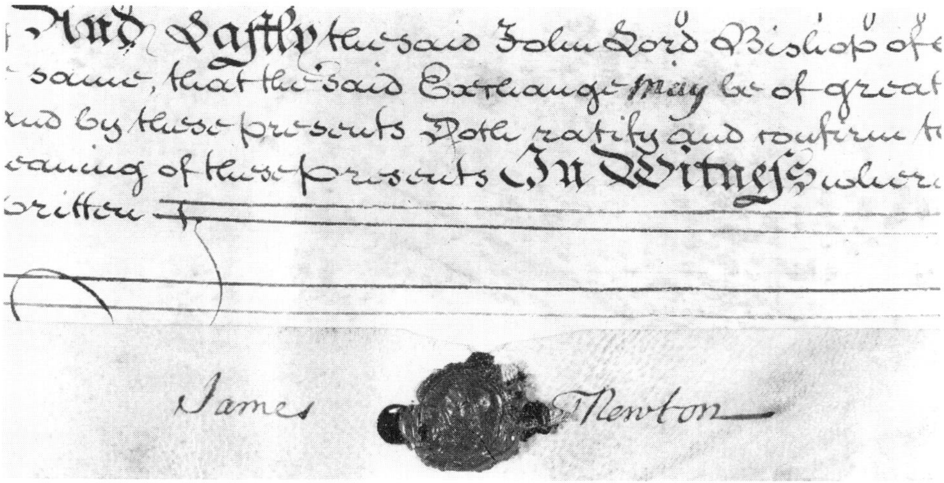

And Lastly the said John Lord Bishop of
same, that the said Exchange may be of great
and by these presents Doth ratify and confirm
meaning of these presents In Witness where
written

James Newton

Plate 19 James Newton's signature on the Tripartite Deed for the exchange of Glebe, 27 April 1759 (*Oxfordshire Archives*, MS. Oxf. dioc. Pprs. c. 2197, no. 8)

[f.56^{v}]

November 1761

Sunday, the 1st After Br Self went to my Lord's to return him Thanks for his Letter. After M.P. Self John & Giles walk'd about. Din'd at my Lord's. Not many people at N.P. Sent Giles to let the Housekeeper know the Beef was not to be drest for Dinner, but Beacon & Pudding. Lediard told the Gamekeeper I ow'd him Money after I had paid Him.

Monday, the 2nd Lord Harcourt & Family set out for London. Lediard enter'd not on Work, & Joe is to go off, as he dont Care to thresh by the Quarter. Winnow'd Barly. Read the News at the Ball. Part of a Fowl hash'd for [f.57^{r}] Dinner. Slept by the Fire after Tea at Night & that was not right. Ball did a Job belonging to the Jack.

Tuesday, the 3rd Howse & Joe laid out the Ground for the Plantation towards the House. Laid the Boards under the Hovel. Bullock draw'd out ten Quarter of Barly & brought Home a Sack of Wheat Grist. Boil Beef & Udder for Din & very tough. John dug up the Garden Carrots. Sent Dame Andrews some Wine. Slept after Tea wch is a very bad Custom.

Wednesday, the 4th Begun putting down the new Sheeting. Lime & Bricks from Casey's Kiln. Took John's Breeches to the Balden Taylor. Sent Dame Andrews part of a Fowl & a Bottle [f.57^{v}] of Ale. A little sort of an Hurricane blow'd some of the thatch of the great Barly Rick. Draw'd away the Ashes out of the Brew House Court. Begun sinking a Place of the little House.

Thursday, the 5th Joe put some Thatch on the great Barly Rick. John waited on the Bricklayer. Bullock draw'd to the House a large Load of Stones. Went about the Glebe before Din. Begun the second Volume of Tillotson's Sermons.[1] Sent two Fowls with William Surtut Coat to the New Town to go by the Stage to morrow.

Friday, the 6th Laid up a Waggon Load of Firing out of the Cart Hovel. Finish'd Wheat sowing. Draw'd Dung to the Garden. Employ'd a Carpenter & Bricklayer [f.58^{r}] about the House. Remov'd two great Tubs into the Barn.

Saturday, the 7th Br at Cofe Oxon. Bought some Meat of Collier & he put me off with a sorry Udder. Bought Drabb[2] etc of Austin for a Lapell Coat. Had a Bundle of Laths out of St Giles's. Return'd Home by Dinner & had[3] Beef Stakes for Din. Joe put Fuel under the New Hovel. Saw two of the the Miss Mathers at Colliers.

Sunday, the 8th Part of a Calves Head hash'd for Din. John not read[y] to go with me to Church in the Morning. Church'd a Woman. Read Prayers by Candle Light at N[igh]t.

Monday, the 9th Self & Giles rode to Abingdon & bought Tongue & Udder etc. Treated Dame Shephard with a Cake. Discompos'd with the toothache. A fine [f.58^{V}] roast Fowl for Din but did not eat one Leg of it.

Tuesday, the 10th Out of Order with the Toothache. Us'd some Pellitory of Spain. Read the News at the Golden Ball. Eat a very little Dinner. John suddenly taken Ill. Could not eat without Pain from the swelling of my Gums or the roof of my Mouth.

Wednesday, the 11th Not well. Bullock went to Shillingford Market but sold nothing. Eat but little at Din.

Thursday, the 12th John took the Housekeeper behind to Oxford on old Brown. Ornamented my Bed Chamber with Guns, Pistols etc. Bullock went out late to Plow.

Friday, the 13th The Beacon remov'd out of the Lumber to the Rack. Self remov'd several [f.59^{r}] Pictures into the Closet by my Study. Roast Tongue & Udder for Din. Bullock rusty[4] because I found fault with his manner of going on.

Saturday, the 14th Br at Oxford Cofe. Sent a Gun to the Gunsmith. Left the Brass Nails at Mr Woods. Bought some Russia Drab. Bought some things at my Nephew Lawrence's. Met with no good Pellitory of Spain at Oxford. Bullock sold Corn. Found myself pretty hody[5] to day &

am thankfull to Providence for this instance of his Goodness to me, & I hope I shall make a proper use of it & become more willing & ready to leave this World & above all, take the greatest circumspection of all my Actions, that they [be?] [f.59^{v}] according to God's[6] Will & Pleasure, & then I shall be in an happy Situation & a fit Condition to leave this World.

What is this World, not a Place for any long Continuance, but only as a Passage to a better Place, & if we would arrive at that Place we must spend our days well, lead holy, devout & religious Lives & then we may depart hence without Reluctance being assur'd that we shall become great Gainers by it.

Sunday, the 15th This being Newnham Feast, Self preach'd on this Text, All is Vanity.[7] After M.P. Self & John went about the Glebe before Din. Old Moulder din'd here. Boil Beef & Udder [f.60^{r}] for Din. A thine Congregation at N.P.

Monday, the 16th Self & Giles went to the Balden Tayler with things. Went to the Golden Ball but did not see the News. Fry'd Cabbage & Beef for Din. The Housekeeper went to see Dame Andrews.

Tuesday, the 17th Took the Pictures out of the Case. Spoke to the Gamekeeper about the Wood. Read the News at the Golden Ball & there saw Shakespear. A roast Fowl for Din. Edmond Baker came after his Man. Tom wanted more Pay but Self did not agree to it.

Wednesday, the 18th Clean'd abundance of Pictures. Tommy Lawrence[8] Br[eakfasted] here. Spoke to Dame Gillet to keep the Water Tub at the End of ye House. Spoke [f.60^{v}] to the Housekeep[er] about Christians not being Willing to turn Fan with Tom.

Thursday, the 19th Begun winnowing Wheat & Christian refus'd turning the Fan with Tom but at last comply'd rather than quit her Place. William Field departed this Life this day & Self did not so much as hear of his being Ill, & I hope he was prepair'd for his latter End & that I may be so when mine shall Come.

Friday, the 20th Finish'd winnowing Wheat. A Duck for Dinner. Put up one of the Sows for piging.[9] Bullock fastened a Board on the Bull's Horns. John dug up the Carrots in the Farm Garden & they were not good.

[f.61^{r}]

Saturday, the 21st Br at Cofe Oxon. Bought Materials for a new Surtut Coat. Bought things at Nephew Lawrence's. Bought a Calves Head & Plucks of Collier[10] & the greatest Part of the Liver was convey'd away. Bought a Hock of Brawn. Joe shot 3 Sparrows. Joe, John & the Bricklayer got one of the Guinea Hens.

Sunday, the 22nd Self & John after M.P. went about my old Garden & Orchard. Dame Macksey din'd here. Buried William Field & omitted the Evening Service. The Sow pig'd 7 Pigs & four were found dead. The Clarke gave Notice of young Ball & Mary Chandler[11] being to be ask'd. Giles Smith wore his new Livery for ye first Time.

[f.61^{V}]

Monday, the 23rd The Bricklayer shot a Hare in my Premises & Self sent Him with a Cock & Carrots to my Sister Rock. Charles Scissel begun working for Me. The Bricklayer wanted to be paid for his Bricklayer's Work, but Self declin'd it. Got the Bottle Rack into the Brewhouse Court. Self & Giles went with the Materials of my Surtut Coat to the Balden Taylor. Read the News at the Golden Ball. Saw a Hare near the Wood & spoke to Nickols in it. A roasted Calves Heart for Din. The Carpenter fixt the two Scrapers in the Kitchen Court etc.

[f.62^{r}]

Tuesday, the 24th The Housekeeper bak'd Br[ead]. Order'd Ball to make two fastings for the Shutters. Advis'd several of my Parishioners to prepare themselves for the Reception of the holy Sacrament, but I fear with no great Success, therefore it will be their Fault & not Mine. John went after a Covey of Parteridges, but to no Purpose. Begun digging Holes towards[12] ye upper End of the Garden.

Wednesday, the 25th Br at the Cofe Oxon. Saw a Boy going with my Screen to Woods. Chang'd a pair of Stockings at Austin's. Bought a Jack Line.[13] Examin'd threes [*sic*] with Mr Tegg for Planting. The Gun not ready as the Gunsmith is very Ill. May God Almighty sanctifie his Illness to his spiritual Good & Profit. Return'd Home to Din. [f.62^{V}] & sent Mrs

Pinnel a Letter Self brought from Oxford. The Oxford Bucks at the Cofe talk'd of young Stuart's bad behaviour.[14]

Thursday, the 26th Self & Giles went to Blackwood & I took to the three Quarters of an Acre wch the Gamekeeper laid out for me & gave Nickolls orders to fell it. Went to the Clifton Cooper's House, but not at Home. Return'd through Forewood.

Friday, the 27th The Cooper did some odd Jobbs. Ball made a turn Screw for me & sho'd old Brown all round. Try'd my Lapell Coat at the Taylor's. Bought a Bit of Beef of the Balden Taylor. Gave Brierly a Bottle of Ale. Draw'd Mole[15] towards the House for the Trees & [f.63^r^] return'd with Stones into the Timber Yard.

Saturday, the 28th Draw'd Wood into the Crofts for hedging. Brick'd up the Doorway out of the Ale Cellar in the Court. Went to Sutton[16] after the Gardiner & ingag'd him to come next Wednesday se'nnight. Stew'd Beef for Din.

Sunday, the 29th Self ask'd[17] Ball & my Housekeeper. Beacon & Carrots for Din. Ball drank Tea at my House with the Housekeeper. Few People at N.P.

Monday, the 30th Draw'd four Load of Wood into the Crofts for Mounding. Self & Giles went to the Wood – from thence to the Golden Ball. A leg of Mutton for Din & Dame Andrews din'd on it. Paid for the Leaden Pump.

Notes

1 John Tillotson was Archbishop of Canterbury from May 1691 until his death on 22 November 1694. He married a niece of Oliver Cromwell in 1664. According to Burnet, 'he was not only the best preacher of the age, but seemed to have brought preaching to perfection'. For full details see *Chambers Biographical Dictionary*, J.O. Thorne and T.C. Collocot (eds.) (1984), p. 1328. There are numerous editions of his sermons published between 1707 and 1886. If JN had the latest version, it would be that edited by John Birch in three volumes, published in 1752. See Bodleian Library Catalogue.

2 Drab was a kind of woollen cloth. See OED.

3 'a' is crossed out in the text.

4 By 'rusty' JN meant angry.

5 Hoddy or hoddie means well and in good spirits.
6 'his' is crossed out in the text.
7 This comes from Ecclesiastes, Ch. 12, v. 8. Nuneham church was dedicated to All Saints, but there had been no special celebrations a fortnight earlier on 1 November. See earlier entry.
8 Thomas Lawrence was the second son of Issac Lawrence who had married JN's niece. 'Tommy' died on 26 February 1765. See *Jackson's*.
9 By 'piging' JN meant farrowing.
10 The plucks are the heart, liver and lungs of an animal.
11 Mary Chandler was JN's housekeeper.
12 'at' is crossed out in the text.
13 By 'Jack Line' JN meant a fishing line.
14 Charles Edward Stuart (1720–88) was the Young Pretender. In an attempt to regain the Scottish and English thrones, Charles landed in Scotland in July 1745 and raised his standard at Glenfinnan. With an army of Highlanders and other Jacobites he took Edinburgh, won the Battle of Prestonpans (September 1745), and reached Derby. His army was destroyed at Culloden (April 1746). Sheltered by faithful followers including Flora MacDonald, he escaped to France and ended his days as a drunkard in Italy.
15 Mould is loose, broken earth used in the planting of trees.
16 Sutton Courtenay was a village nearby. For full details see Pevsner, *Berkshire*, pp. 235–7.
17 i.e. read the Banns of Marriage.

[f.63^{v}]

December 1761

Tuesday, the 1st Self hung several Pictures up in the Bow Room. Took in part of a Bean Rick. Stew'd Beef for Din. Discharg'd two Brace of Pistols & Loaded them again. The Ducks wings were Cut. Some Fowls put up for fatting.

Wednesday, the 2nd[1] Roast Duck for Din. Bullock went to Shillingford Market, but sold Nothing. Lent Christian Barns a Bead[2] & gave her Straw to lay under. Self, John & Giles went to the Wood.

Thursday, the 3rd[3] Hash'd Mutton for Din. Employ'd Dick Barns to keep the Cows & the Sheep from the Turneps & took him with [me] to the Balden Taylor.

Friday, the 4th[4] The Carpenter return'd to his Work [f.64^{r}] after being away many Days. Walkt to Abingdon with Giles to buy a Foulweather Coat for Dick Barns but did not meet with One to my Mind. Return'd Home to Din & had hash'd Duck.

Saturday, the 5th Went to the Balden Taylor's but not at Home & forbid the Foulweather Coat. Gave Goodman Brierly a Bottle of Ale & Dame Pearce & Nan Stevens Liver & Muggerum.[5] Dock'd Charles Scissel 2s. 6d. for Shoes his Wife cheated Giles out off.

Sunday, the 6th Lord Harcourt invited me to Din but Self declin'd as I did intend to begin Evening Prayers between two & three o'Clock. Invited young Ball to drink Tea. Beat Dick Barns for not keeping the Cows.

[f.64^{v}]

Monday, the 7th Bullock brought Home a Load of Bushes from the hanging Lands & Polls & Rods from the Wood. Br at the Cofe, Oxon. Bought Butter etc at my [Nephew?] Lawrence's. Left an Order with Mr Stagg for 148 Trees. Brought Home my Gun & left another to be repair'd. Sent John to the Schoolmaster of Balden to let him know I did not yet awhile care to sell the Hogs.

Tuesday, the 8th Winnow'd Beans. Rode to Sutton through Abingdon. Met with Prowse who had caught an Hare but did not care to sell Her. Gave Howse a Dram of Gin.

Wednesday, the 9th Bullock brought from Oxford[6] [f.65r] One hundred and fifty Trees for Planting & the three Screens. The Gardiner was to have come,[7] but the Rain prevented Him. A roast Pig for Din. Press'd off the Wine. The Housekeeper wanted more Sugar but went without it.

Thursday, the 10th Begun my great Plantation in the Crofts. Met Lord Harcourt & two more Gentlemen. Went to the Wood. Gave good Advice to some of my Parishioners. Gave Dame Bennet 6d. Pease Soop & Sparib for Din.

Friday, the 11th Found several Trees were wanted to compleat my Plantation & I rode to Oxford with an Order for forty more. [f.65v] Lord Harcourt & two more took a View of what was going forwards in the Crofts. Joe brought Home from the Turnips a Carriage of Furze Faggots. Nickolls & Newman begun staking the Trees.

Saturday, the 12th Bullock sold Barly at Oxford & brought Home forty Fruit Trees. Employ'd Joe about setting up Hurdles about the Backsides. Draw'd Mole to lay about the Trees. Draw'd a Post from Edmond's for a Gate Post. Had the Trivet[8] to Ball to mend. Spoke to Andrews about working for Me.

Sunday, the 13th The last time of Asking Ball & my Housekeeper.[9] The Dairy Maid's Sister & her Father's Apprentice din'd here. Went to Christian Barns & Dick who had let the Cows get to the Turnips by not shutting an Hurdle.

[f.66r]

Monday, the 14th Kingston finish'd planting the remainder of the Trees & those brought last from Oxford & planted some of them in the New Orchard. John shot three Pidgeons. Gave Turner some Turnips & had a tythe Pig from him. The new Gate & pailing finish'd at the Farm. Entertain'd a Man who came to see John Taylor.

Tuesday, the 15th John set off to see his Father. Went to Abingdon after Winterbourn the Chimney Doctor. Bought more tar Rope & half a Peck of the finest Flower. Retun'd Home to Din through Forewood. Mr Peede not at Home.

Wednesday, the 16th Draw'd another Load of Bushes for the Trees. The Qicksetters begun their Jobb. Hung Pictures up in the Picture Closet. The Carpenter hung [f.66^{v}] the Door at the bottom of the Stairs the wrong Way. A Hog's Ear for Din.

Thursday, the 17th Br at Oxford Coffee Ho. Went to Paradise[10] about Quicksetts etc. Paid for three Bands. Din'd with my Neice Lawrence on the House Lambs her Mother sent Her. Bought Hinges for the Bow Room window Shutters.

Friday, the 18th Paid the Gamekeeper, the Land Tax & Window Bill.[11] The Stair Case Door was hang'd. Saw at the Balden Butcher's the Bull design'd for the Poor of the Parish. Bullock draw'd out Barly. Advis'd the Dairy Maid to receive the Sacrament at Christmas. Left with Dame Andrews Sixpence for her aged Father.

[f.67^{r}]

Saturday, the 19th John Taylor return'd Home from seeing his Father. Giles came with the Quicksetts. I sent him to Oxford yesterday, staying there all Night as they were not brought to his Quarters in Time. Self married Edward Ball & Hannah Chandless.[12] Took an Account of Linnen etc. Gave Christian & John leave to go to Ball's Entertainment. A very rainy Day.

Sunday, the 20th Spoke to my Lady Betty after M.P. Boil Pidgeons & Hocks for Din. Lady Betty at N.P. with a little Lad. Spoke to John about receiving the holy Sac^{rt} & he thinks himself too young & flighty. Slept before the Fire & that was not right.

[f.67^{v}]

Giles Smith talk'd about going Home because I snub'd Him but he did not.

Monday, the 21st The Chimney D^{r} was to have come but did not. Sent to the New Town a Pig, two Fowls, a Chine to go by the Coach to morrow for Mortimer St & a Peice of Beacon for Dame Pickering. The Pig's Pettitoes[13] for Din. Prick'd my Finger in packing up the Basket. Howse brought the Pig to the House.

Tuesday, the 22nd Charles Scissel kill'd a Ram for the Poor of the Parish. John Taylor being ill with a soar throat, Self sent Him some warm wine sweeten'd with rob of Eldar.[14] Christian boil'd a Fowl for my Din. Gave several of my Parishioners good Advice, but I fear not much to their Profit.

[f.68^{r}]

Wednesday, the 23rd Br at Oxford Cofe. M.P. St Mary's.[15] Sold to Mr Lawrence twelve Pound of Mutton Suet. Enquir'd after an Housekeeper. Return'd Home to Din. Call'd for the Ketch belonging to the Latch. Gave an old Man at Oxford 2d & a poor———[16] with Children 1d. Bullock sold at Shillingford Market Barly & Oates. Drank a Dram of Rum at Mr Austin's.

Thursday, the 24th Paid Hannah Chandless her Wages.[17] Distributed among the Poor of the Parish a whole Sheep within a Triffle. Charles, Giles & Self went after Holly & Ivy. Saw my Asses in White Lyons. Paid one of the Quicksetters 5s in Part of Payment.

[f.68^{v}]

Friday, the 25th [Christmas Day] Administer'd the Sacrament to the lame Woman at the New Town & others, but waited a pretty while for the Clarke. Pretty much puzzl'd in adjusting my Sermon before I went to Church. Invited Moulder to dine at my House. Lady Harcourt & Lady Betty rec'^{d} the Sacr^{t}. Slept before the Fire & that was not right.

Saturday, the 26th Gave 2s 6d for the Ringers of the Midnight Peel. Treated the Clarke with a Breakfast After M.P. Self etc went after the

Asses but [f.69^{r}] found them not. Gave Dick Barns a Dinner & found Bett had taken to the Shoes I had sent Him. 1 turn of Firing drawn up to the House. Tapt a Vessel of Ale & of Perkin.[18]

Sunday, the 27th Call'd Giles etc. Christian stay'd at Home at Noon but went to Church Morning. Brought Dick Barns home with Me & gave him his Din. A Letter from Polly & Skill about my House in the Strand. Gave Bullock & his Boy a Supper.

Monday, the 28th Sent my Lord his Bill. Took in part of the great Barly Rick. Rode to Mr Peede's but not at Home. Gave the Letter to Skill to a boy I met with to put in in the Post at Abingdon. Old Brown stumbl'd, if not fell with me, but I kept on Him & am truly [f.69^{v}] Thankfull for not being exstreamly damag'd by Him. Teach [me], O my God, to enjoy a gratefull & thankfull Heart and ever to make the best Returns I can for any Favour receiv'd at thy Hands. The Dairy Maid was pretty much out of Order.

Tuesday, the 29th Draw'd out Oats & Barly. Scissel carried Furze Faggots into the Cow House. A Quarter of a Chaldron of Coals.[19] Self & Giles went to Mr Peede's & he paid his Tythe. Met with the Asses, but did not drive them Home. Gave Bullock a pair of Breeches. John took the Plumbs out of the Tub.

Wednesday, the 30th Br at the great House. Draw'd to the Home Close for Hedging two load of Wood & one of the young Lime Trees was broke in twain. Went to the Balden Taylor & Shoemaker with Things. [f.70^{r}] Read the News at the Golden Ball & met with Dr Beacon & he invited me to Dinner, but Self did not go. Took to Dame Macksey a Bottle of Ale & some Plumb Pudding. Miss'd some of the Pudding at Home & Christian was much displeas'd at my talking to Her about it. Paid Edward Ball the Remainder of three Bills.

Thursday, the 31st Winnow'd Oats & Beans & took a Barly Rick in. Took to Ball two thimbles to sharpen. Call'd on Dame Macksey. Pray'd by the Lame Woman & sent her & Nickols of Balden, two Bottles of Ale. Snub'd Dame Andrews for her Husband not coming to work for me after he had done sawying.

Notes

1 Again JN has changed the date. '3' is crossed out and '2' superscribed.
2 By 'Bead' JN means bed.
3 Again JN has changed the date. '4' is crossed out and '3' superscribed.
4 Again JN has changed the date. '5' is crossed out and '4' is superscribed.
5 Muggerum was the leaf fat from the pig JN had killed.
6 'Abingdon' is crossed out in the text.
7 This arrangement was made on Saturday 28 November. See earlier entry.
8 A 'Trivet' is a three-legged stand to hang a pot over a fire. See *OED*.
9 The third time of publishing these banns of marriage.
10 This was Mr Tagg's market garden where JN was a regular customer.
11 The Window Tax was a charge on windows levied at a variable rate. It was introduced in 1696 and was often paid in half-yearly instalments.
12 The marriage is shown in the Nuneham Marriage *Registers*.
13 Pettitoes are pig's trotters.
14 The 'rob' is the juice of a fruit reduced by boiling to the consistency of syrup and then preserved with sugar. This is yet another instance of JN's kind nature.
15 This was either St Mary The Virgin, the University Church in the High Street, or St Mary Magdalen in Magdalen Street. See Sherwood and Pevsner, *Oxfordshire*, pp. 283–5, 293–4.
16 There is a gap in the text here.
17 Hannah was by now Hannah Ball, but JN used her maiden name.
18 Perkin is a liquor made from the washings after the best cider has been produced.
19 This is equivalent to nine bushels, since a chaldron is thirty-six bushels. See *OED*.

[f.70[v]]

January 1762

Friday, the 1st Self distributed One hundred of Furze Faggots among the Poor of the Parish. Brown shod up against the Froast. Found Scissel very ill in Bed, God grant, his Illness may bring about his Amendment of Life.

Saturday, the 2nd Br at James's Cofe Oxon.[1] Call'd on my Neice. Made Enquiry after an Housekeeper. Bought a Cinder Sieve. Paid for the Raperation of the Gun. Got a Tything Table. Two Fellows riding briskly by Lyon put him on his Mettle. Got Home to Dinner. Tom turn'd a strange Horse out of the Backside.

Sunday, the 3rd Call'd all the Servants up. The Shoe maker brought Home my Boots & Shoes & he was treated with two [f.71[r]] Pints of Ale etc. John & Giles went to Church in the Surtut Coats. After M.P. Self, Dick & John went to Church Hill, & Dick came in for his Din. None of my Lord's Family at N.P.

Monday, the 4th A New Tasker from Balden.[2] A late Servant of Miss Deene of Chalgrove offer'd her Service for a Housekeeper, but was not accepted. From the Wood one load of Wood & two of Rods. Read the News at the Golden Ball & there gave Bennets Boys & another Girl some Ale. Call'd at the Collar Maker.

Tuesday, the 5th The Horses were bleeded, the Sheep mark'd, ruddl'd[3] & Handl'd, & the little Pigs Cut. A Turkey kill'd for the Use of the Family. Self tap't a Vessel of small Beer. Employ'd Joe & John about the Quicksetts.[4]

[f.71[v]]

Wednesday, the 6th Br at the great House. A roast Turkey for Din. Bullock attempted to catch some Hares but did not.

Thursday, the 7th Lord Harcourt sent Word that Bowly would come to me in the Evening to settle Accounts, but they were not settled for my Lord Demanded £61 for rent due at Ladyday 1759 wch Self had paid already & very luckily I found my Lord's Receipt. John Taylor complain'd of Giles being impudent to Him. Discharg'd two Brace of Pistols & loaded them again.

Friday, the 8th Br at the great House & acquainted my Lord of his great Mistake about Rent but now he demands two thousand Furze faggots out [of] [f.72^{r}] those I cut in Forewood wch seems to be a very unjust Demand. Went to the Balden Taylor. Bought some Beef at the New Town. John & Joe finish'd the Quick. The Upton man return'd to his Work.

Saturday, the 9th Br at Oxford & expected to have seen War Proclaim'd against Spain but that was done Yesterday.[5] Bought things at my Nephew Lawrence's. Bullock sold Barly at Oxford. One of the young Heifers slipt her Calf. Joe & John began trenching the Nursery.

Sunday, the 10th After M.P. Self went to see Dame Gillet who lately broke her Arm. Call'd at the Dames Macksey & Quarterman & left a Bottle of Ale of each of them.

[f.72^{v}]

Monday, the 11th Bullock went to Abingdon for a Boar & to sell Barly. After Br Self set out for Church Hackburn [East Hagbourne] & got there by Dinner time but found the Road exstreamly bad, & very windy besides.

Tuesday, the 12th After Br set out for Wallingford & din'd at the Lamb,[6] but found it mighty windy. The Landlord has dy'd since I was there last & great part of the House hath been rebuilt. Set[7] in a comfortable little Room by the Kitchen.

Wednesday, the 13th Set out after Br. Enquir'd the Price of Coals & spoke to the Blacksmith at Dorchester about Iron Bars. Bullock draw'd

One hundred Furze faggots to Balden. Employ'd the Upton Man about cutting Bushes in Comb Bottom. John put the [f.73^{r}] Harness in the Lumber Room because it had been damag'd in the Coach Ho[use] by Vermin. Joe hung the Flitches in the Beacon Loft.[8]

Thursday, the 14th Christian Bak'd Bread & a Pidgeon Pye, & Self eat of it for Dinner.

Friday, the 15th Drawn Bushes for the Vineyard & the Trousing in Comb Bottom.[9] Busy in setting the small Beer Cellar in order.

Saturday, the 16th Br at Oxford. Paid Giles's Father for his Son's Wages. Went to Paradise. Sent Polly a Letter. Spoke to young Mrs Hill of Sandford at Parsons but did not know her at first Sight.

Sunday, the 17th After M.P. Self & Giles went to the New Town with Ale & Pidgeon Pye for Mackey & Quarterman. Invited Moulder to Dinner.

[f.73^{v}]

Monday, the 18th Took in part of a Bean Rick. Bullock went to Wotton after a Boar, but did not buy Him. Went to Nickolls in the Wood & it was very windy. God grant, it has not done much Damage by Sea & Land. Lent Christian old Brown to go Home. Casey paid for 2 Years Tythe & Self paid Him his Bill. John Taylor got rusty[10] & was for going, but thought better of it. Giles went to Bed not well.

Tuesday, the 19th Bullock draw'd Mole towards the Flower Garden. Went to old Ball about Furze Faggots but it was his Son that was to have had them. Read the News at the Golden Ball [f.74^{r}] & gave Dame Brown's boy 1d. Joe begun thatching the Wheat Rick, that was yesterday Damag'd by the High Wind. Treated Dr Beacon's Clarke & his Boy with Ale & Plumb Pudding & Self engag'd to bury a Child to morrow at Balden.[11] John & the Carpenter got the great Vessel of small Beer out of the Brewhouse into the Cellar. Gave Charles Scissel a Parcel of Shavings.

Wednesday, the 20th Buried a Child at Balden for Dr Beacon & stay'd with Mrs Beacon till the Corpse was brought. Giles & Scissel brought Home the Asses. Agree'd with the Stadham [Stadhampton] [man] about grubbing the Trees in Broadmore Close. The Upton Man has [f.74^{V}] done the trousing very bad. Din'd in the Kitchen. Many Mice[12] were caught among the Wheat in the Barn. Bullock draw'd 1 Quarter of Barly to Dorchester. Nickols & Newman begun faggoting the loose Stuff in the Crofts.

Thursday, the 21st Draw'd a Load of Soap Ashes[13] Home from Oxford. Nickolls & Newman busy in the Crofts.

Friday, the 22nd Draw'd Home another Load of Soap Ashes. Took in a Barly Rick. Gave Scissel leave to take Home a Burthen [a load] of Furze. Agreed with the Stadham man to trench the Vineyard.

Saturday, the 23rd Took in a Cut of the great Barly Rick. Br at Oxford. Lead [f.75^{r}] my Horse as far as the Turnpike Road. A Balden man begun threshing Barly. Nickolls & Newman planted in Combe Bottom Willers.[14]

Sunday, the 24th Made it late before I begun M.P. Leg of Beef for Din. James Hoare & Dick Barns din'd here. Read part of a Homely at E.P. & not many People there according to Custom.[15]

Monday, the 25th Bullock draw'd to the House Fuel & then I found some Faggots had been stole, & afterwards he bought at Abingdon a Boar. Sent Dick Barns & Bett to School but their Dame did not care to have them come because they were so lowsey. Read the News at the [f.75^{V}] Golden Ball. Howse went Home Ill.

Tuesday, the 26th Bullock draw'd out Barly & the Carriage stuck in the late Common. Joe mark'd the trees in Broadmore Close & went with me to the lower Farm.

Wednesday, the 27th Gave Nickolls & Newman a Br & paid their Bill. Bullock draw'd from Oxford[16] one Load more of Soap Ashes. The Stadham man finish'd the Vineyard. The Carpenter was suddenly taken Ill.

Thursday, the 28th Rode to Sutton after Kingston by the Way of Abingdon. A Letter from Polly. Bought two Balls of Tar Rope. A Turkey & Ham for Din.

[f.76r]

Friday, the 29th Br at the Cofe Oxon & there met with Sir John. Din'd with my Neice. A Woman at Noah's Arke offer'd her Service for an Housekeeper but was not accepted. Bullock draw'd Home another Load of Soap Ashes.

Saturday, the 30th Bullock draw'd the Faggots from the Home Close & set them up in the Timber Yard, & draw'd Furze Faggots to the House. Went to the Lock but could not find the Master. Mr Yeateman came for a certificate of my dearest Brother Rock's Death.[17]

Sunday, the 31st Christen'd Scissel's Child[18] & after M.P. Walk'd about the Glebe before Din. Boil Pidgeons etc for Din. [f.76v] Spoke to Anderson about signing a Certificate to morrow. Lent Christian Barns a peice of Tapestry & gave her a Dish of Tea. Not many People at N.P. the more the pity.

Notes

1 This was James's Coffee House at 104–5, High Street. It was run by James Horseman between 1753 and 1760 and thus was also known as Horseman's. It was popular with members of All Souls, Corpus Christi, Merton and Oriel. See Aubertin-Potter and Bennett, *Oxford Coffee Houses*, pp. 19, 41.

2 A tasker was a worker paid by the task or piece as distinct from a day labourer.

3 Ruddled meant marked with ruddle, a red variety of ochre.

4 Quicksets are hedges formed from live plants. See *OED*.

5 This was Recorded in *Jackson's Oxford Journal*. In fact, war on Spain had been declared on 4 January and the issue had led to the resignation of William Pitt during the previous October. He had advocated an extension of the Seven Years' War, but was faced by an increasingly pacifist government. Only when it was rumoured that Spain was making an alliance with France was war declared and Pitt's attitude vindicated. See Watson, *George III*, pp. 73–7.

6 For full details see Pevsner, *Berkshire*, p. 250.

7 By 'Set' JN meant Sat.

8 'Up' is crossed out in the text. A flitch is a side of bacon. See *OED*.

9 To trouse means to cut brushwood. Trousing refers to brushwood cuttings from hedges.

10 By 'rusty' JN meant angry.

11 The burial took place at St Peter's church, Marsh Baldon, where Dr Beacon was rector. For full details see Pevsner and Sherwood, *Oxfordshire*, pp. 698–9.

12 'Rat' is crossed out in the text.

13 These ashes were obtained from the harder woods, from which the lye was extracted and in which household fat was boiled to make soap. Often the ashes from bakers' ovens were used in this process.

14 By 'Willers' JN meant willows.

15 The main part of the village was now over a mile away and church attendance was falling.

16 'Home' is crossed out in the text.

17 Samuel Rock died on Christmas Day 1758 and was buried on 1 January 1759, as described in the opening entry of the *Diary*.

18 The child was a girl, Elizabeth, according to the Nuneham *Registers*.

February 1762

Monday, the 1st Sent Nickolls with the Register to Braine in Oxford Goal for him to sign a Certificate of my dearest Brother Rock's Death, & he went thence with [it] to Mr Yeateman's. The Stadham man begun grubbing the Job [*sic*] at the Nursery. Joe shot a wild Duck. Self settl'd Accounts with the Balden Taylor. Read [f.77^{r}] the News at the Ball. John took some of the Harvest to the Balden Taylor & lost a Strap by the Way.

Tuesday, the 2nd Bowly came to me about Accounts but they were not settl'd. Joe & Self went about the Glebe but shot nothing, though we started an Hare. Bullock went to Oxford for a Load of Manure for the Home Close. Christian Barns wash'd here.

Wednesday, the 3rd Br at Oxford. Din'd with my Neice. Paid for Soap Ashes. Order'd at Paradise several Sorts of Trees & Flowering Shrubs etc. M.P. St Tebbs. Bullock sold no Corn at Shillingford.

[?] Wednesday/Thursday, the 3rd/4th[1] Br at Oxford. Din'd with my Neice. Went to paradise & bespoke several things.

[f.77^{v}]

Thursday, the 4th Bullock draw'd from Oxford a Load of Soap Ashes & the Trees etc from Paradise. Joe wash'd the Trees with Lime Water. Took things to the Taylor's & call'd at the Collar Maker's. Buried Dame Baker.

Friday, the 5th Kingston begun planting the Orchard & Vineyard. Bullock draw'd Hurdles from the Turnips. Saw an Hare in the Hanging Lands.

Saturday, the 6th Kingston planted Trees & Vines about the House & the Flowering Shrubs in the flower Garden, & several things in the Nursery. Bullock sold Thirty Quarter of Barly at Oxford, but came Home without a Goose. Took in part of a Bean Rick. Gave a Bur-[f.78^{r}]-coat [Burcot] man 1s. famous for a multitude of Children.

Sunday, the 7th Found it very cold after M.P. so made for Home. John gave Tommy Smith a stroke with a Stick in the Church for being saucy. A wild Duck for Din. Sent John to acquainted [*sic*] the Balden Butcher that one of the Sheep was not well. Hewlett came about the Boar Stags. Not many People at N.P.

Monday, the 8th Sent Charles Scissel to the Balden Butcher about the Bad Sheep & he came & was very noisy. Bullock draw'd Barly out. Self read the News at the Golden Ball. Bullock came home very Ill.

Tuesday, the 9th Joe draw'd out Barly. Went to [f.78^{v}] see Bullock. Charles Scissel kill'd a very fat Sheep.

Wednesday, the 10th Charles cut the Sheep out. The old Cock Turkey was kill'd. Gave part of the Sheep away & some of it to Nickolls of Balden & also some Ale & an old Wig. Sent Giles for Malt & Hops.

Thursday, the 11th Christian begun brewing two Bushel of Malt, & Giles help't her. Sent the Basket with Mutton & the Turkey for Mortimer St by the Stage. Took in a greet Part of the old Barly Rick. The Balden Butcher took away the Sheep & paid for them.

Friday, the 12th Made Fires in three of the Rooms above Stairs. The Carpenter came [f.79^{r}] here about 3 o'Clock N. & Self did not care to employ Him. Bullock was to have went out with Barly but the Weat[h]er prevented Him. Tom said he saw John with a Gun & it was false.

Saturday, the 13th Paid Edmond Baker One Bill. Br at Oxford Cofe. Bought things of my Nephew Lawrence & of Mr Tegg. Had Scissars grounded. The Balden Butcher stole a College Crust out of Giles' Basket. Din'd in the Kitchen. Bullock bought a Gander at Warborough[2] & brought Home some Coals.

Sunday, the 14th A Letter from Polly & the Fellow who brought it from Abingdon wanted Money, but had None. Jenny Hoare [f.79^{v}] din'd here. The Clarke smote some boys at Church for being rude.

Monday, the 15th After Br Self set out for Church Hackburn & it was pretty windy, & by Mistake went to Wallingford before I got to Brightwell. Enquir'd the Way of two Quakers. Found my old Landlord in good Health, but he had like to have been kill'd by a Fall in his Cellar. Din'd on the cold Mutton I took with me. Spoke to Higler's Wife in the Kitchen & she was acquainted with Bett Beasely.

Tuesday, the 16th Cut my Beard off before Br. Went about my Landlord's great Orchard. Got the Blacksmith to clinch Browns Shoes. Went to the great Farm. Got to Shillingford before Din & walk'd about the outside of the Town. Quarter'd myself [f.80^{r}] in the little Room by the Kitchen.

Wednesday, the 17th Self Br with one of the Landerdess's[3] Daughters. Gave the old Clarke of St Leaonards 6d.[4] M.P. at Wallingford & then Self set out for Home. Rode about the old Castle & the Trenchments.[5] A Millers man of the Town had his Arm torn to Peices by the Mill, a melancholly Affair & I am thankfull to Providence for keeping me from any such Misfortune. Met Bullock agoing to Market on the little Mare without her Shoes. The Cock & Beacon for Din.

Thursday, the 18th Charles Scissel kill'd a Sheep, & part of it was drest for Din, & Dick Barns had some of the Lights for his Din. Bullock at Plow on the Hanging Lands.

Friday, the 19th Charles cut the Sheep out. Bullock [f.80^{v}] at Plow. Nickolls & Newman about the Trowsing. Gave some Mutton away to the Poor. The Hogs had like to have devour'd Turners Cabbage Plants in his Garden. Met Dame Ball at Dame Andrew's. Joe & Jack took a Basket to the New Town to go by the Coach to Morrow for Mortimer St.

Saturday, the 20th Howse & Charles grub'd Bushes. The Barly was winnow'd. The Hounds devour'd an Hare on my Premises. The Coachman said he would not take the Basket if it did belong to my Lord Harcourt.

Sunday, the 21st A Leg of Mutton for Din & Jenny Hoare din'd here. After M.P. went to Dame Barns & she was roasting a Shoulder of Mutton but Dick did not choose to Dine at my House. Bowly at N.P., not a common thing. The Snow drove into the House it being very windy.

[f.81^{r}]

Monday, the 22nd Bullock draw'd out Barly & the Wheat was win-now'd.[6] It being a bad Day Charles was not at work.[7] Jenny went off in the Morning.

Tuesday, the 23rd [Shrove Tuesday] Joe shot an Hare & some small Birds. Paid the Game Keeper, some Tax Bills & the Poundage for 1/4 Acre of Wood. Dame Allain din'd with me & paid half Tythe for her Lambs & Self paid her 10s. on my Sister Rock's. Bullock paid a largish Sum for Corn.

Wednesday, the 24th [Ash Wednesday] Br at Oxford. M.P. St Mary's. Paid Mr Skinner,[8] the Barber & Mr Lawrence, forgot to be paid for the Mutton fat. Return'd Home to Din.

Thursday, the 25th Set off for London with the Landau through Widmill Field but did not get into it, till I had got to the [f.81^{V}] Turnpike Road & had with me two Hams, one old Cock Turkey & an Hare. Din'd at Nettlebed. Got to my old Quarters near Maidenhead at Night & had Br[ead] & Cheese for Supper.

Friday, the 26th Set out about 7 o'Clock M.[9] & Br at the White Hart on Hounslow Heath. Got to Mortimer St to Din, & in good Health & found my Sisters tollerable well, for both wch Blessings I am truly thank-full to Providence. Went to Admiral Long with an Ham.

Saturday, the 27th Hunted about after a Coach House but did not accommodate myself with One. After Din went to the Strand House & put up the old Bill. Bought a Watch String of Mr Clarke. Miss Bush came here in a Chair.[10]

Sunday, the 28th Went to the Foundling Hospital in my Carriage. M.P. & took a Turn [f.82^{r}] in it in Hyde Park before Dinner. N.P. St Georges. Dame Pickering came here. Waited on Admiral Long wch is not right well.

Notes

1 Again, JN slips up with the dates. He repeats '3', but the entry clearly relates to a fresh day, presumably Thursday 4 February. The confusion is impossible to unravel for certain, but the 7 February is a Sunday as it should be, as suggested by the nature of the entry.

2 Warborough is a village just beyond Dorchester. See Pevsner and Sherwood, *Oxfordshire*, pp. 821–2.

3 'Landerdess' is a term JN uses for the wife of a Landlord.

4 This is St Leonard's church, Wallingford, a Norman church badly restored in the nineteenth century. See Pevsner, *Berkshire*, p. 248.

5 For details of the castle remains see *ibid*., pp. 248–9.

6 'Threshed' is crossed out in the text.

7 It was 'a bad day' indeed. JN's comments on the weather are confirmed by *Jackson's Oxford Journal*. Sunday 21 February saw a blizzard in Oxford and the surrounding countryside, causing several deaths. On Monday 22 February, Charles Scissel did well to stay at home. The newspaper records the finding of the body of David Knapp in the snow between Little Wittenham and Dorchester.

8 The Reverend Richard Skinner was again going to stand in at Nuneham during JN's forthcoming visit to London.

9 '6' is crossed out in the text.

10 By 'Chair' JN meant a sedan chair.

March 1762

Monday, the 1st Paid the Upholsterer & the Glasier. Went to two People about my Strand House. Bespoke Brandy & Rum at the London Punch House. Din'd in Swan Court. Met Skill at the Strand House. M.P. Berwick St. Mrs Rock drank Tea here & Self went Home with Her.

Tuesday, the 2nd Bought Hay & Straw at the Hay Market. Went to the Strand House. Din'd in Swan Court & there was a new Recruit much damag'd [f.82^{v}] with the fowl Disease. Sent my Landau to Admiral Long's Coach Ho[use].

Wednesday, the 3rd M.P. Berwick St. John & Giles brought Wood from the Strand H[ouse] to Mortimer St. Din'd near the Roy[al] Exchange. A Pint of good Wine at the Half Moon in Cheapside & one of the Servants offer'd to another Servant Vinegar by the way of Wine. Call'd on Miss Bush about conducting Her Home. Paid my Tenths, & for the Licence of my Landau. Rec'^{d} £2 6 8d. at the Bank for one Year's Interest of 13 Blank Ticket making £78 Stock. Lett my Str[and] House to Mr Skill for £50 for one Year certain.

[f.83^{r}]

Thursday, the 4th Self & Polly din'd at Admiral Longs with Mrs Aires, her Son & Ray. Admiral Griffin came in before Din, & told the Admiral that he had propos'd Him for a Member of the Society of Arts.[1] Sent for my intended Housekeeper.[2]

Friday, the 5th Kept at Home. Br by Self in the Dining Room. John rode his Horses about.

Saturday, the 6th Self found I had got a Cold before he arose. Paid a Quarters Land Tax for my Strand House due last Christmas. Call'd on the Glasier. Din'd near the Royal Exchange & the Landlord had lately rec'^{d} an Incendiary Letter,[3] but was in hopes of finding out the Author of it.

Punch at the Punch [f.83^{v}] House. Made Enquiry after a great Cheshire Cheese. Paid for the Use of Horace. Met with Billy playing by himself. Sent from the Half Moon out of Cheapside three Gallons of Port Wine for the Use of my Friends in Mortimer St.

Sunday, the 7th Queen's Square M. Sac^{rt} & came home in the Landau & brought Mrs Rock with me from Mrs Harcourt to Din. N.P. Mary Bone. Spoke to Mr Jones about the bad Wine from the Half Moon Tavern & he understood[4] to have it chang'd. Bought a 2s. 6d. Cake at Mary Bonne.

Monday, the 8th Brought Miss Bush here & the old Cock Turkey was drest for Dinner. Took alone an Airing in Hyde Park. Call'd on the Admiral. Hunted after my [f.84^{r}] Silver Shoe Buckle but could not find it. Poor Tetty fatigu'd herself too much about Din. Intended to have given Mrs Rock an airing but She declin'd going as Mrs Harcourt had been lately troubled with a Fit.

Tuesday, the 9th Polly & Miss Bush went in my Landau to see Mrs Maw. Shoes repaird. M.P. Berwick Chapple. Amus'd myself in Westminister Abby. Saw my old Friend Lloyd in Westminister Hall.[5] Din'd at the Widow Gould's, & a young woman came after One Brown.

Wednesday, the 10th Bought a Cheshire Cheese in Thame St for £2 5 0. The Weight 109,[6] & it was put in the Basket Jack brought [f.84^{v}] With Him. Din'd near the Royal Exchange & then went to the Punch House. Call'd at the half Moon & the Landlord said the Wine he sent was very Good. Stopt at Middle Row, & had some Chat with the Bookseller's Neice. Cheapen'd[7] four Guinea Hens. Return Home to Tea.

Thursday, the 11th Giles Shovels the S[n]ow away from before the House, for their was a very great Fall of Snow indeed. Sent Will for my intended Housekeeper. N.P. St Georges.

Friday, the 12th Saw a pretty Young Woman come out of the British Museum.[8] M.P. Queen's Square. John pretty much out of Order. N.P. The Chapple. Fasted till Tea Time at Night.[9]

[f.85^{r}]

Saturday, the 13th Self & Giles at Covent Garden. E.M.P. Bought some things at Covent Garden & proll'd about there. Bought Tea & Coffee at Twinings. Met Dr Sanders in the Strand. Call'd for Jack's Coat. Compos'd part of a Sermon. Went to Hart the Banker in Pall Mall for £15 for Miss Bush. N.P. St George's. Waited on the Admiral & the Dean's Lady had got many Visiters.

Sunday, the 14th M.P. Queen's Sq & Sac^{t}. Return'd Home in the Landau & dropt in at the Foundling Hospital towards the end of the Sermon & saw there Mr Strode. N.P. St George's. Jack got rusty.

Monday, the 15th E.M.P. St James's. Miss Bush [f.85^{V}] receiv'd a Letter from Burcoat [Burcot] intimating the return of the Gout on her Father. Jack wanted Money but none was advanc'd. Compos'd part of a Sermon.[10]

Tuesday, the 16th E.M.P. St James's. Compos'd part of a new Sermon on Covetousness. Polly & Miss Bush rode out in my Landau. Br by Self. Paid Mrs Ridly a Visit. Acquainted my intended Housekeeper's Sister that I was not to leave London till next Week.

Wednesday, the 17th E.M.P. St James's. Went to see Mrs Dellafey but she was gone out to Dinner. Call'd on Dame Pickering & gave Challiner Notice what he might Expect, if he did not advance some Rent against Lady Day. [f.86^{r}] The Carpenter Challiner employ'd wanted me to pay[11] Him but I did not. Gave Mrs Rock an Airing in Hyde Park.

Thursday, the 18th E.M.P. St James's. Mrs Rock drank Tea here & we were much entertained with the little Girl Mrs Ridly sent here.

Friday, the 19th E.M.P. St James's. Got the Handle of the Landau mended & Self put it on. Got my Shoes from the Cobler. Paid Mrs Maw a Visit. Bought some Chelsea Bunns.

Saturday, the 20th E.M.P. St Anne's. A Fire early this Morning happen'd in Cravens Buildings.[12] Sent Giles Home with Coffee. Br at George's. Din'd near the Royal Exchange. Half a Pint of Wine near London Bridge. [f.86^{V}] Came Home over Westminister Bridge. Spoke to Mr Shewell about Mrs Rock's Navy Bills. Jack brought two Trusses of Hay from the Market.

Sunday, the 21st M.P. St Georges Queen's Sq & Sacr^{t} & a very few Communicants indeed, a very Melancholy Sight. Gave Mrs Rock an Airing. N.P. St Georges Hanover Square. Waited on Admiral Long.

Monday, the 22nd Lord Harcourt not at Home. Self & Giles walk'd to Mrs Dellafey's as Jack did not overtake us with the Landau but he got to Moorefield at last and then I gave the Widow an Airing. Din'd near the Royal Exchange. Bought 2 Dozn of Lemons for 6d.

[f.87^{r}]

Tuesday, the 23rd E.M.P. St Anne's. Took a View of the late Fire in Craven St. Bought some Cheese at my new Tenant's.[13] Bought a pair of Boots & Gloves for Jack Taylor. Wash'd my feet & cut my Toe Nails. Lord Harcourt not at Home. Call'd on Admiral Long. Took a Turn in the Mall.[14] Tetty & Mrs Whiteman went out in my Landau. The Yard Door look'd as if it had been forc'd. Mrs Rock not at Home. N.P. St George's.

Wednesday, the 24th Waited on Lord Harcourt about the Tythe & excus'd myself from letting Him all my Tythe, & return'd Home to Br.[15] Walk'd out before Din towards Paddington, [f.87^{v}] & saw a Carriage belonging to the Royal Family. A Lady mounted on a little Palfrey semn'd mighty timorous. Drank Tea with Mrs Rock at Mrs Harcourt.

Thursday, the 25th E.M.P. St Annes. Bought four Guinea Hens & four Powters.[16] Busy part of the Day in packing up Things. Took my Leave of Admiral Long.

Friday, the 26th Walk'd to my Housekeeper's Lodging & took Her up in my Landau. Din'd at the White Hart on Hounslow Heath. Laid at the Ram beyond Maidenhead & got there time enough for Tea.[17]

Saturday, the 27th Br at Nettlebed. Reach'd Newnham to Dinner. Walk't over the Common. Found the Landau was [f.88^{r}] Damag'd when I was come Home. Thanks be to God for bringing me safe to this Place once more. Could not readily find the Way to my Chamber being in the Dark.

Sunday, the 28th After M.P. Self went to the New Town & gave Dame Mascsey a bottle of Ale & Whyat one too. Fowl & Beacon for Din.

Went a new Way to Church. Found some Ale in the Brew House & Christian, Giles & John were concern'd in the Theft.

Monday, the 29th Howse kill'd a Porker. Self administer'd the Sacrament to John Whyat who is in a very bad Way as to his Body, but not so as to his Soul, I hope. A Haistlet[18] for Din. The Pidgeons & Guinea Hens were let out. Sent Giles [f.88V] to the Clifton Cooper.

Tuesday, the 30th Howse cut the Porker out. Self pray'd by John Whyatt, & gave Him & others some Pig Meat. Pork Stakes for Din. Bullock deliver'd in his Acts.[19] The Cooper did some Jobbs.

Wednesday, the 31st Br at Oxford. Din'd at my Nephew Lawrence & bought several things of Him & Joe brought them Home with my famous Cheshire Cheese, the Housekeeper's Boxes & ten Bushel of Malt from Sandford.

Notes

1 Admiral Long was elected a Fellow of the Society of Arts on 26 January 1761. He was indeed proposed by Admiral Griffin, himself elected a Fellow on the same day. I owe this information to the kindness of Mrs S. Bennett, Acting Library Administrator at the Royal Society of Arts. It is strange that JN gives different election dates.

2 Since Hannah Chandler's marriage, the appointment of a new housekeeper was one of JN's prime concerns.

3 By 'Incendiary Letter' JN meant a letter tending to stir up trouble.

4 By 'understood' JN meant undertook.

5 This is only surviving part of the original Palace of Westminster, built by William Rufus in 1097. During the eighteenth century the building housed the Law Courts, as well as shops selling Law books, prints, toys and material. JN would have had much to amuse him. For full details see *London Encycl.*, pp. 950–1.

6 If this refers to weight in pounds, it was a large cheese indeed!

7 By 'Cheapen'd' JN meant bartered for a lower price.

8 The British Museum was a new venture in JN's time. It was set up only in 1753. For full details see *London Encycl.*, pp. 89–91.

9 JN probably attended prayers at the Oxford chapel close to his house. It was a Friday in Lent which may have occasioned his fast.

10 The sermon was presumably for use at Nuneham. There is no record in the *Diary* of JN's preaching in London.

11 'Employ' is crossed out in the text.

12 Craven's Buildings were in Craven Street. The area was being developed throughout the eighteenth century. See *London Encycl.*, p. 207.

13 One of the properties that JN owned was a shop. It was perhaps what JN referred to as the 'Strand House'. Mr Skill was indeed a new tenant, the arrangement having been concluded only on 3 March. See previous entry.

14 Pall Mall was first laid out in 1661. By JN's time it was renowned for expensive shops and grand houses. For full details, see *London Encycl.*, pp. 578–9.

15 'Hetty and Mrs Whiteman went out in my Landau' is crossed out in the text.

16 A pouter is a breed of domestic pigeon characterized by a great power of inflating its crop which may well cause astonishment. See *OED*.

17 JN was indeed as good as his word, given on 16 March, about leaving London 'next week'. See earlier entry.

18 Haslet is a dish prepared from the roasted liver and heart of a pig. See *OED*.

19 By 'Acts' JN means axe.

April 1762

Thursday, the 1st Brew'd ten Bushel of Malt. Pease Soop & roast Pork for Din. Draw'd off 5 Gallons of Wine [f.89^{r}] for Mortimer St & Joe took that & the Pork with him at Night to the New Town to go by the Coach to morrow.

Friday, the 2nd Saw Mr Lawrence at the New Town & brought Him home with me to Din. Went to the Balden Taylor. Bought a New Loaf.

Saturday, the 3rd Br at Oxford. Went to Giles's Father & he din'd with Him. Din'd at Langfords[1] & was well accommodated. The Butter fell out of Giles's Basket.

Sunday, the 4th [Palm Sunday] Went to Church over Alder Hill gate & shew'd my Housekeeper Christians Habitation, my Lord's House & my late Gardens & Orchard. Self forgot to give Notice of the [f.89^{v}] Communion next Sunday, but did at Evening Service. Advis'd Jack to receive the holy Sacrament. Perceiv'd at Church my Sight was not so good as usual & should it quite fail for me God's will be done.

Note

1 It has not proved possible to locate this place precisely.

Biographical Index of James Newton's Acquaintances

This is a list of some of the people mentioned in the *Diary*. Every effort has been made to produce as complete a record as possible but, to some extent, it must be selective. Occasionally it has been impossible to find out anything about a person occurring as an isolated name with no other means of positive identification. Such souls must be consigned eternally to the secrets of time.

Many details of Nuneham villagers and other local people have been revealed by close analysis of the parish registers and *Jackson's Oxford Journal*. These individual references have not been given, but the following works may be consulted: *Transcript and Index of Nuneham Parish Registers, 1715–1840*, F.R.L. Goadby (ed.) (1980), Bodl. MS. Top. Oxon. d. 838; *Transcript of Marsh Baldon Parish Registers, 1662–1840*, F.R.L. Goadby (ed.) (1980), Bodl. MS. Top. Oxon. d. 836.

The Nuneham Parish *Registers* are deposited in the Oxfordshire County Record Office, reference *Oxfordshire Archives*, MSS. D.D. Par. Nuneham Courtenay, a.1; c.5; c.6.

Dame Allain: Nuneham villager. She was a friend of JN's who paid tithes to him. She had a daughter but there is no record of a husband.

Thomas Anderson: Nuneham villager and labourer. He was baptized on 9 October 1715, the son of George and Ann.

Dame Andrews: Nuneham villager. She was married to one of JN's labourers. JN christened her child at home on 14 May 1761. Her 'aged father' also lived in the village.

Mr Austin: John Austin. He was mercer at 3 Northgate Street, Oxford. He was Mayor of Oxford in 1742–3 and again in 1761–2. He became Master of the Mercers' Company in 1765.

Phanuel Bacon or **Beacon**: Educated at St John's College, Oxford: BA 1719; MA 1722; BD 1731; DD 1735. See *Alumni Oxonienses 1715–1886*, J. Foster (ed.) (Parker, Oxford, 1888). I, p. 45. Rector of St Peter's church, Marsh Baldon from 1735 until his death on 10 January 1783, aged 83. He was buried at Baldon a week later. Throughout his life he was a close friend and neighbour of JN. After the death of his first wife, Margaret, Dr Beacon was married on 24 January 1769 to Catherine Sanderson, a spinster living at Baldon. She was the daughter of the late Wrigglesworth Sanderson, surgeon, of Oxford. The service was conducted by JN in Marsh Baldon. Beacon was a reasonable and moderate man with progressive views, keen to hasten the enclosure of his village. He was one of the six commissioners appointed to oversee the exchange of glebe between Lord Harcourt and JN in 1759. His memorial is on west wall of Marsh Baldon church.

Mrs Bacon or **Beacon**: Born Margaret Pollard. She was the first wife of Dr Bacon, the Rector of Marsh Baldon. She died in September 1767, aged 71. There is a wall monument to her in St Peter's church at Marsh Baldon.

William Baites or **Bates**: Nettlebed villager. He was a servant to JN from March 1760.

Edmond Baker: Nuneham villager. He was buried on 16 April 1788. He married Christian, who was herself buried on 26 December 1793. Their son, Edmond, was baptized by JN on 9 May 1759. It appears from the *Diary* that Baker was a carpenter whom JN employed frequently.

Dame Baker: Nuneham villager. JN buried her on 4 February 1762, a fact confirmed by the Nuneham *Registers*.

Edward Ball: Nuneham villager. He was born in 1708 and buried on 27 March 1793. He married Hannah Chandler, JN's housekeeper, on 19 December 1761. Ball was employed by JN as handyman, general labourer and blacksmith.

Barnes: Christiana or Dame Barnes. She was a Nuneham villager with several children. In 1759 she was a friend of JN who showed her considerable kindness. But by 1761 she had offended him by making dangerous fires on the estate.

Elizabeth 'Bett' Barnes: Nuneham villager and servant to JN.

Dick Barnes: Richard Barnes. He was a Nuneham villager and farm hand for JN, often looking after the cows.

Dame Bennet: Nuneham villager. She married Thomas on 17 July 1742 and had sons, the 'Bennet's Boys'.

Mr Bowly: William Bowly. He was buried on 16 December 1781, aged 82. He was described as a 'gentleman of Nuneham' and was the agent involved in many land and property deals in the Oxford area. He also acted as Lord Harcourt's land agent. According to a memorial plaque placed on the east wall of the 1764 church by George Simon, 2nd Earl, Bowly was, 'A Faithful Friend and Servant to the Harcourt Family . . . who in Abilities and Integrity in his Station, has seldom been equalled, never surpassed.'

William Braine: Innkeeper at Nuneham Courtenay at The Harcourt Arms, referred to in the *Diary* as the 'New Inn'. He was a bad manager and ran up debts to a certain William Baker. He organized the Harvest Home supper for JN in September 1761. By the following month the inn was to let and his furniture was being sold off to meet some of his debts. Mr Bowly handled the business. Braine was imprisoned in Oxford castle by 1762. He was married to Anne and had a son, Edward, baptized on 16 September 1750.

Henry Bricknal: Servant to JN from October 1759. He came from Oxford.

William Brierly: Nuneham villager. He was buried on 22 August 1764. He was married to Bridget who was buried on 27 March 1761.

George Brookes: Nuneham villager and labourer for JN.

Robert Bullock: JN's farm manager in 1761. He came from the neighbouring village of Marsh Baldon. He married Mary Gillet on 17 November 1760 and had three children; Robert, baptized on 19 July 1761; Sarah, baptized on 6 March 1763; and James, baptized on 5 July 1767. He was buried at Nuneham on 22 March 1784.

Mr Bush: Jonathan Bush Esq. He was JN's neighbour at Burcot. He was married with a son and a daughter, Miss Bush. In 1759 he acted as one of the Commissioners overseeing the enclosure and Lord Harcourt's exchange of glebe with JN.

Tom Chapman: Nuneham villager and farm worker on the estate.

John Clarke: Nuneham villager and shepherd for JN. Son of Edward and Mary. He was born on 14 March 1721 and baptized four days later. He married Mary Wiggington on 18 April 1745 and died on 25 September 1794.

William Clarke: Nuneham villager and farm labourer. He was baptized on 9 November 1738, son of Edward and Mary Clarke. He was buried on 18 February 1786. He had daughters.

Mrs Costard: JN referred to her as 'the late Mrs Costard' on 20 June 1759. This is Mary Costard, wife of Robert, a servant of Edmond Baker. She was buried on 26 May 1743.

John Cummins: Nuneham villager. He married Elizabeth on 14 June 1756. She was buried on 24 October 1813, aged 88. They had a son, John, and two daughters.

Dame Field: Elizabeth Field. She was a Nuneham villager, wife of William Field and mother of 'Master Field' and 'daughters.' By October 1761 she had moved with her family to the 'New Town'.

Master Field: Nuneham villager. He was the son of William and Elizabeth Field. He occasionally deputized as parish clerk in place of William Nicholls.

William Field: Nuneham villager and labourer for JN. The son of John and Elizabeth Field, he was baptized on 26 December 1736, very ill by October 1761 and died on 19 November 1761. JN buried him three days later. He married Elizabeth, 'Dame Field', and was father to 'Master' Field and 'daughters'.

Robert Gillet: A butcher who served JN. He was buried on 25 February 1789. On 27 September 1730 he married Ann Blainch and they had three children: Mary, baptized on 22 September 1734; Sarah, baptized on 16 July 1737 and Thomas, baptized on 17 August 1743.

Mr Glass: Samuel Glass. He was a surgeon in High Street, Oxford. He died in February 1773 after suffering a stroke.

Admiral Griffin: Thomas Griffin of Holles Street, London. He was a friend of JN and of Admiral Long. He was Captain of the Shoreham Frigate in April 1731, after which he held various commands with service in the West and East Indies as well as India. He became a rear-admiral on 5 July 1747 and vice-admiral 12 May 1748. In 1750 he was court-martialled at Chatham for failure against the French at Pondicherry, found guilty and suspended from his rank and employment. Although later restored, he was allowed to proceed no further up the promotion ladder. He became a Fellow of the Society of Arts on 26 January 1761, declining his membership for no apparent reason in 1767. After a brief political adventure as MP for Arundel, Griffin retired from public life and died in Wales in 1771. See J. Charnock, *Biographia Navalis*, 6 vols. (1794–8), IV, pp. 224–330; B. Williams, *The Whig Supremacy* (Oxford, 1962), pp. 261–2.

Richard Haisly: Nuneham villager. He was born in 1716 and buried on 7 October 1792, aged 76. He married Elizabeth, buried on 13 May 1792, aged 72. Haisly had seven children: Robert, baptized on 4 September 1743; Elizabeth, baptized on 22 December 1745; Mary, baptized on 25 March 1747, who married Thomas Jennings on 3 October 1770; Elizabeth, baptized on 20 December 1749; Anne, baptized on 21 March 1753; Sarah, baptized on 29 February 1756, who married Thomas Tutty on 9 April 1776 and was buried on 6 January 1819; Martha, baptized on 1 February 1761, who married John Gunter on 22 February 1784.

Mary Hall: Housekeeper, dairymaid and servant to JN from 30 June 1759, when she was known as Mary or Molly Bassett. She took over from Elizabeth Overton and gave her notice to quit on 11 February 1760. She married John Hall on 29 August 1761. Mary was constantly receiving 'advice' from JN which, he hinted, she never took.

Mrs Harcourt: Lord Harcourt's mother who lived in the family house in Cavendish Square. She often socialized with JN, his sisters and Mrs Rock.

Simon, 1st Earl Harcourt: Born in 1714, died in 1777. Educated at Westminster School. He acted as Lord of the Bedchamber in 1735–51 and was present with the King, George II, at the Battle of Dettingen in 1743. In 1749 he was created 1st Earl Harcourt & Viscount Nuneham. He built Nuneham Park in the Palladian style during the years after 1756, sweeping away the old village when planning his classical landscape for the new house. He created the 'New Town' on the Oxford–Henley road, with its matching pairs of cottages each side of the highway, its inn, still used as such, and its forge, now a garage. Lord Harcourt was Ambassador to Mecklenburg-Strelitz on the occasion of George III's marriage to Princess Charlotte in 1761. According to Horace Walpole, 'Lord Harcourt is to be at the Court of the Princess of Mecklenberg, if he can find it'. See *Harcourt Papers*, E.W. Harcourt (ed) (1876–1905), III, p. 92. He was Master of Horse to the Queen Consort in 1761–63, Lord Chamberlain to the Queen in 1763–68, Ambassador to Paris in 1768–72 and Viceroy of Ireland in 1772–77. He married Rebecca, daughter of Charles le Bas of Northamptonshire, on 16 October 1735. He died by accidental drowning in a well. 'It appears that his dog had fallen in, and that the earl, endeavouring to recover him, had lost his poise & fallen in himself.' See Horace Walpole, *Journals*, 16 September 1777. Lord Harcourt was also a noted huntsman and had considerable East India Company investments. There is even a record of a Harcourt East Indiaman.

Lady Rebecca Harcourt: Daughter of Charles Le Bas of Pipewell Abbey, Northamptonshire. She married Simon Harcourt on 16 October 1735 and died suddenly when at tea at the Hon. Colonel Houghton's on 16 January 1765. She was buried at Stanton Harcourt.

Lady Elizabeth Harcourt: 'Lady Betty'. She was born on 18 January 1738, the second of the 1st Earl's four children. She married Sir William Lee Bt., of Hartwell, Buckinghamshire, on 20 June 1763. Lady Harcourt was one of ten young ladies to support the train of Queen Charlotte at her wedding to George III on 8 September 1761.

James Hoare: Son of John and Anne who were Nuneham villagers. James was baptized on 19 January 1747.

Reverend Joseph Hoare: Principal of Jesus College, Oxford, from 1768 until his death in 1802. He matriculated at Jesus College on 14 March 1726, aged 18; BA 1730; MA 1733; BD 1741; DD 1768. See *Alumni*, II,

p. 668. Hoare deputized for JN at Nuneham, probably as a result of the influence of Lord Harcourt.

Thomas Hopkins: Villager of Nuneham and servant to JN.

William Howse: Nuneham villager, JN's servant, farm labourer and gamekeeper. He married Elizabeth Auger on 3 July 1748. Howse had five children: William, baptized in July 1749; John, baptized in August 1750; William, baptized in March 1753; Sarah, baptized on 30 December 1759 and buried on 5 December 1768; Anne, baptized on 11 July 1762.

Lord Hyde: Thomas Villiers. He was the second son of William, 2nd Earl of Jersey. He was born in 1709 and educated at St John's College, Cambridge. He was emissary to the king of Poland and to the Elector of Saxony in 1740–7, to Vienna in 1742–3 and to Berlin in 1746–8. Thomas Villiers was MP for Tamworth in 1747–56 and Lord of the Admiralty in 1748–56. He was created Baron Hyde on 3 June 1756 and Earl of Clarendon on 14 June 1776. He died at Watford, Hertfordshire on 11 December 1786, aged 77. On March 30 1752, he married Charlotte, daughter of William Capel, 3rd Earl of Essex. Horace Walpole considered him 'So dull a man' and 'a very silly fellow'.

William Ives: Mayor of Oxford in 1738–9, 1749–50 and 1763–4. He died in office in January 1764, being the first Oxford mayor to do so for over 160 years according to *Jackson's Oxford Journal*. He owned a house in Littlegate, St Ebbe's. In September 1761, JN met Ives in London where he was in attendance on Sir Thomas Munday, the Mayor of Oxford, who was exercising his civic privilege of acting as Butler during the coronation feast for George III.

William Jackson: Farm labourer for JN. He married Mary Gibbons on 16 May 1757. He had three sons: William, baptized on 24 August 1760, buried on 2 June 1761; William, baptized on 3 January 1762; James, baptized on 24 June 1764.

Thomas King: Born in 1744 and buried on 13 October 1799, aged 55. He was a labourer and servant to JN.

Isaac Lawrence: Referred to in the *Diary* as 'my nephew'. He was Mayor of Oxford in 1759, 1768, and 1784 until his death in July of that year. Lawrence was a prominent Oxford citizen with a grocer's shop and warehouse in Cornmarket Street. He also owned a house in St Giles which he rented out. He had three sons and a daughter. His wife was JN's niece, Zenobia.

James Lawrence: Nuneham villager. His wife was called Jane. Lawrence had three daughters: Mary, baptized on 12 February 1758, buried on 27 June 1758; Elizabeth, baptized on 23 December 1759; Mary, baptized on 1 February 1761, buried on 8 July 1761, while JN was away in London. This funeral was conducted by the Reverend J. Wells.

Samuel Lawrence: Son of Isaac Lawrence and 'my Neice'. He married a Miss Andrews of Burford in January 1780.

Zenobia Lawrence: JN's niece. She died in September 1762. She is not named in the *Diary*, but we can identify her as Zenobia Lawrence. She was the wife of Mr Isaac Lawrence of Oxford. She had three sons and a daughter. See Newton Family Tree.

James Leicester or **Lester**: Nuneham villager and servant to JN in 1761. James married Dinah Dean, aged 21, on 5 January 1758, with her parents' consent as she was pregnant. A large family then followed: James, baptized on 8 January 1758, buried on 22 July 1764; John, baptized on 6 May 1759, buried on 16 March 1767; Richard, baptized on 7 December 1760, buried on 13 January 1768; Sarah, baptized on 6 May 1764; Richard, baptized on 4 March 1770; Mary, baptized on 17 May 1772; Catherine Frances, baptized on 20 August 1775. A series of Nuneham village children were baptized 'Catherine Frances' from 1775 because of Harcourt influence.

William Liddiar or **Lediard** or **Lidyard**: Nuneham villager. He was born in 1730 and buried on 1 June 1803, aged 73. He married Anna Mary who was buried on 6 June 1798, aged 67. He had three children: Mary, baptized on 16 January 1756; William, baptized on 27 March 1763, buried on 27 March 1794; Ruth, baptized on 7 September 1766.

Admiral Long: Robert Long. He was one of JN's best friends. He lived in Holles Street, London, after his retirement from the navy. He had a varied career firstly as Captain of the Shoreham Frigate from 21 March 1726, then as commander of the *Russel*, an 80-gun vessel, in 1741. He served in the Mediterranean during the war with Spain and was present in naval action off Toulon. He returned to England as a rear-admiral on 21 June 1747. On 26 January 1761 he was elected a Fellow of the Society of Arts. The admiral died on 6 July 1771.

Dame Macksey: Nuneham villager. She was the wife of Edward, buried on 25 October 1767. She dined at home with JN twice during 1761.

Moulder: John Moulder. He was the son of John and Elizabeth, baptized on 26 January 1717. On Christmas Day 1761 he was invited to join JN for Christmas dinner.

John Newman: Labourer for JN. He was engaged during 1761 when the rector's new plantations were being laid out. He helped Kingston, the gardener, and was chiefly employed in staking the new trees in the Crofts. He was the son of John and Ruth and was baptized on 26 December 1724.

Nicholls: William Nicholls. He was baptized on 17 July 1726, the son of William and Elizabeth. He was a servant to JN and also acted as Parish Clerk. In this capacity he witnessed several marriages performed by JN at Nuneham.

Lord Nuneham: Eldest son of Lord Harcourt. He was born on 1 August 1736 at Cockthorpe and educated at Westminster School. He was styled Lord Nuneham in 1749–77, becoming 2nd Earl Harcourt on his father's death. Lord Nuneham was MP (Whig) for St Albans in 1761–8. He was elected F.S.A. on 27 February 1766 and became a D.C.L. Oxon., on 31 August 1786. He acted as a page at the coronation of George III on 22 September 1761. He was Master of the Horse to the Queen Consort in 1790–1809. On 26 September 1765 he married his cousin, Elizabeth, at Nuneham. The service was conducted by Joseph Hoare. He died on 20 April 1809 in Cavendish Square and was buried at Stanton Harcourt.

Elizabeth Overton: Housekeeper and servant to JN. She was paid off at the end of June 1759. On a visit to Bath in 1761, JN sought her out, possibly to re-engage her. He eventually met her in Bristol. See *Diary*, 18 and 31 May 1761.

Palmer: Giles Palmer. He was buried at Marsh Baldon on 25 February 1788. He was a tenant farmer on the Nuneham estate. JN bought a horse from him.

Dame Pearce: Nuneham villager. She was ill in May 1761 and received a gift of food from JN in December of that year.

Reverend Pinnel or **Pinnell**: John Pinnell. He was rector of Ducklington, Oxfordshire in 1747–98. He was born in 1710 and educated at Magdalen College, Oxford: BA 1728; MA 1731; BD 1739. See *Alumni*, III, p. 1119. He acted as a locum for JN at Nuneham and was one of the six commissioners appointed by the Bishop to oversee the exchange of glebe in 1759. He was married with one daughter.

Henry Pitson: Nuneham villager and farm labourer. He married Elizabeth, 'Dame Pitson', who was buried on 27 January 1779. They had five children: Elizabeth, baptized on 22 May 1744; John, baptized on 12 October 1746; Mary, baptized on 4 June 1749, buried on 31 March 1784; Thomas, baptized on 2 February 1751; Diana, baptized on 23 March 1755.

Dr Evans Pitt: Born in 1703. He was educated at Christ Church, Oxford, BA 1723; MA 1726; BMed 1729; DMed 1733. See *Alumni*, III, p. 1120. When he died he had just been appointed Regius Professor of Medicine on the death of William Woodford. See *Jackson's*, 30 January 1759.

'Polly': JN's sister, Mary. She was born in 1713 and died in 1788. She lived in London at the Mortimer Street house, where she was visited regularly by JN. Zenobia Rock had moved in with her by 1761. Mary was buried on 15 September 1788, aged 75, in the old ground of St James's, Clerkenwell Green.

Parson Portal's Wife: Frances Portal. She was buried at St Helen's, Abingdon, on 7 May 1772. She was the wife of the Reverend Andrew Portal, vicar of St Helen's ('great Church'), Abingdon in 1757–75 and *ex officio* vicar of St Nicholas ('little church'). He was born in 1725 in Derbyshire and educated at Exeter College, Oxford. BA 1761; MA 1765. See *Alumni*, III, p. 1132. He had a son, Thomas. Portal was Lecturer at St Helen's in 1753–7; Usher of Roysse's Grammar School in 1751–8 and Headmaster in 1774–5. He died in 1775 and was buried at St Helen's on 16 July.

Dame Quartermain: Elizabeth Quartermain. She was a Nuneham villager. She was buried on 24 July 1764.

Lady Reed: Harriet Reade. She died on 23 December 1811, aged 85. She was the wife of Sir John Reade of Golden Square, London, who died on 9 November 1773, aged 52. There is a monument to the Reades in the church of St Mary, Shipton-under-Wychwood, Oxfordshire.

Mrs Rock of Oxford: Ann Rock. She was the mother of Samuel Rock, widow of Mr Rock and mother-in-law of JN's sister, Zenobia. Mr Rock was secretary to the 1st Viscount Harcourt (1661–1727) who appointed him one of his executors and guardian of his grandson, the 1st Earl. By 1761–2, Mrs Rock had moved from Oxford to live in London with Mrs Harcourt.

Samuel Rock: Husband of JN's sister, Zenobia. He died on Christmas Day 1758. He was buried at Nuneham on 1 January 1759, on his wedding anniversary. Samuel married Zenobia Newton on 1 January 1728 in St James's church, Clerkenwell. See Clerkenwell *Registers*, P76/JS/9. In the Nuneham *Burial Register*, JN wrote: 'Samuel Rock my dearest Brother in law, and Husband of Zenobia Rock, my own dearest Sister.' The Clerk's entry in the rough copy of the *Register* reads: 'Mr Rock Esq, was Bur^{d} the first Day of Jan. 1759.'

Zenobia Rock: 'Sister' Rock'. She moved to the family house in Mortimer Street, Cavendish Square, London, to live with her mother and sister 'Polly' (Mary) in 1759, after the death of her husband, Samuel, on Christmas Day 1758. JN's *Diary* opens with Samuel's funeral, on New Year's Day 1759. Samuel and Zenobia were married in St James's church, Clerkenwell on 1 January 1728. See Clerkenwell *Registers*, P76/JS/9.

Charles Scissell or **Cissel**: Nuneham villager and labourer for JN in 1761. He married Anne on 5 October 1756. Elizabeth, his daughter, was christened on 31 January 1762. 'Dame' Cissel on one occasion cheated Giles Smith out of a pair of shoes.

Thomas Silvester: Nuneham villager and servant to JN until the end of August 1759.

Humphrey Sipthorpe or **Sibthorpe**: Sheridan Professor of Botany at Oxford in 1747–84. He was born in 1712 and died on 17 August 1797. He was educated at St Edmund Hall and Magdalen College: BA 1734; MA 1737; BMed 1743; DMed 1745. He was a Fellow of Magdalen

College in 1734–41. As professor, he gave only one lecture and that was not very successful. He became a great friend of JN. Perhaps they shared a common interest in plants and trees. We do not know the name of his wife.

Reverend Richard Skinner: Born in 1728 and died on 27 November 1795. He was a Fellow of Corpus Christi College and stood in for JN at Nuneham during his absence at Bath in 1761. Richard matriculated at Corpus on 13 March 1745: BA 1749; MA and Fellow 1753; BD 1761. He later became the rector of Bassingham, Lincolnshire.

Giles Smith: Servant of JN accompanying him to London and Bath in 1761. He is recorded as having parents and a brother who resided in Oxford.

Dr Smith: Neighbour and friend of JN. He lived in Marsh Baldon close to the rector, Dr Bacon.

Sparrow: George Sparrow. He was a Nuneham villager and labourer for JN. He dug out the foundations for the second wing of the new parsonage in 1759. George was married to Martha who was buried on 20 May 1771.

Nancy Stevens: Nuneham villager.

Stewart: James Stuart. He was born in 1713 and died in 1788. He was an architect, known as 'Athenian' Stuart owing to his fondness for the Greek style. He was employed by Lord Harcourt to undertake some of the interior decoration of the new house at Nuneham. Stuart had dealings with JN during the course of the rebuilding of the village, the parsonage and the new classical church, begun in 1764 to replace the medieval structure.

Mr Tagg or **Tegg**: Market gardener in Paradise Square, Oxford. Hearne wrote in 1726: 'Mr Tagg who rents Paradise Garden and many other Places about Oxford, told me today that he pays the workmen £700 per. an. He succeeded one Wrench the best Kitchen Gardener in England to whom he had been Servant and whose widow he married.' The business was still thriving in 1771. JN was a frequent customer, especially throughout 1761 while he was creating his new garden.

Mrs Tegg: Mrs Tegg or Tagg. She was the wife of Mr Tagg, the market gardner and nurseryman at Paradise Garden, Oxford.

John Taylor: Servant of JN, hired in June 1761. He had a father living 'away.'

Mrs Treacher: Wife of Alderman Treacher of St Thomas's Parish, Oxford. John Treacher had a malthouse in Paradise Yard, St Ebbe's. He bacame Mayor of Oxford in 1764 after William Ives had died in office.

William Turner: Nuneham villager. He married Mary Chadwell on 7 October 1756. She was buried on 3 July 1769. William had two children: Elizabeth, baptized on 1 January 1758, buried on 3 November 1759; Edward, baptized on 26 December 1759.

John Ward: Upholsterer and furniture-maker in Oxford. He also auctioned furniture and household goods, as he did for JN at Caldecott in 1759.

Francis Wastie: Gentleman from Cowley. He served on the commission arranging the exchange of the glebe and the enclosure of 1759.

William Wells: Nuneham villager. He was married to Dame Wells, whose mother was 'likely to die' by May 1761.

John Whyat or **Whyatt**: Nuneham villager. Ill by 1759, very ill by March 1762. He was buried on 23 April 1762. On 16 October 1723 he married Barbara Goswell, the 'Bab Whyatt' who remained in her old cottage long after the village was moved to its new site.

Bab Whyatt: Barbara Whyatt a Nuneham villager. She married John on 16 October 1723. She was the old lady allowed to live on in her cottage when the rest of the village was removed. See M.L. Batey, *Nuneham Courtenay, Oxfordshire* (3rd edn, 1984), p. 18.

Mr Weston: William Weston. He was a neighbour of JN's. He married Mary Newman at Nuneham on Christmas Day 1749.

Thomas Williams: Labourer who worked for JN. He was married with a son-in-law.

Index

Only main references to people most mentioned are given, as a full listing would be impracticable. The letters 'BI' after a name indicate an entry in the Biographical Index. A figure in parenthesis after a page number indicates the number of references to the subject on that page. Place names are listed as in the text with the modern spelling in parenthesis.